As we walked away from the bloodied trail I looked back over my shoulder at the lifeless bodies we had left behind. They were now stretched out alongside one another like ten sacks of fertilizer in the damp grass. A ray of sunshine broke through the thinning fog and illuminated the scene of death. A thought out of nowhere came to me, a paraphrase of a famous poem: Men once living now were dead. Shortly before, they had lived, felt dawn, seen sunset glow. They had loved and were loved. Now they were lifeless bundles laid in a row. In this rude excuse for their own Flanders Field they presented their souls to God and their corpses to the buzzards. I walked away in silence. For the next several minutes, and not for the first time either, I wondered exactly what it was I was doing here in this foreign place. I asked myself what it was I found so valuable that I was willing to risk death for it, what it was I found so valuable I was ready to kill for it.

ONCE A WARRIOR KING

ONCE A WARRIOR KING

Memoirs of an Officer in Vietnam

David Donovan

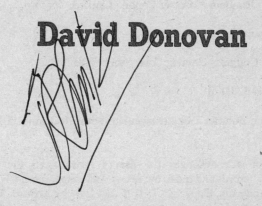

BALLANTINE BOOKS • NEW YORK

For Master Sergeant John N. Testor,
who came home again,
and for First Lieutenant Richard H. Davis,
who did not.

Copyright © 1985 by McGraw-Hill

All rights reserved under International and Pan-American Copyright Conventions. Except as permitted under the Copyright Act of 1976, no part of this publication may be reproduced or distributed in any form or by any means or stored in a database or retrieval system, without the prior written permission of the publisher. Published in the United States by Ballantine Books, a division of Random House, Inc., New York, and simultaneously in Canada by Random House of Canada Limited, Toronto.

http://www.randomhouse.com

Library of Congress Catalog Card Number: 85-102

ISBN 0-345-33316-0

This edition published by arrangement with McGraw-Hill Book Company

The author acknowledges the use of lyrics from the song "Fernando," words and music by: Benny Andersson, Bjorn Ulvaeus, and Stig Anderson. Copyright © 1975 and 1984 by Artwork Music Co., Inc. for the USA and Canada. Sole selling agent: Ivan Mogull Music Corporation. Used by permission. All rights reserved.

Printed in Canada

First Ballantine Books Edition: August 1986

20 19 18 17 16 15

Contents

Preface

THIS is a story of Vietnam. It is important for the reader to understand that the story is mine alone. I do not pretend to speak for anyone else; I am not the Vietnam Everyman. The events and opinions are related from my point of view without apology. The book is written as a recollection of war, necessarily emerging from the storehouses of my own memory. Other men have their own tales and their own opinions.

Because my assignment in Vietnam was not the usual GI troop duty, my viewpoint is often not that of the many veterans who served with the large American units in Vietnam. Those units had full quotas of brave young men, and nothing I say should be construed as a general criticism of all those American soldiers who were caught up in a vicious struggle and gave it everything they had. I was a *cô vấn*, an advisor who lived in a small, isolated village far out on the Plain of Reeds. I and four other Americans lived there alone and fought our own little war. This book portrays my memory of that experience.

I have given real persons fictitious names, save for the brief mention of Anthony Herbert and a reference to William Calley. To keep the story simple I have used the pretense that members of my team did not rotate, but were present with me through my tour. In fact, team members came and went as their tours of duty required. The stories involving Sergeant Fitz, the team medic, for example, are really stories of two different medics who served on my team. Quoted conversations are merely my attempt to present the essence of words spoken long ago, and are not meant to imply that I have total recall.

There will be many who will say that this book and my recollections are too simplistic for such a complicated issue as the Vietnam war. I would agree; my story is simplistic. It eschews the finer topics of international politics, military strategy, global economics, and who did what to whom first. These subjects are well worn and only lead to endless debate and disagreement, achieving nothing. Rather, this book tells the story of a very average American who was sent to war by his country, who saw strange things, who did strange deeds, and who is finally ready to tell the tale.

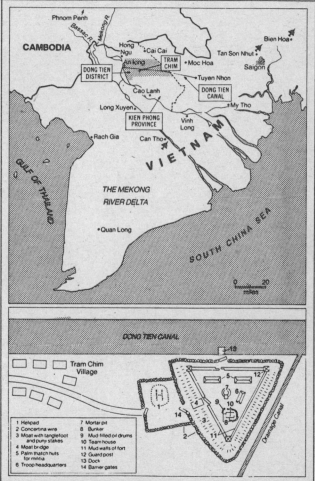

Prologue:
An Incident in Dong Tien, 1969

THE fog clung to the damp earth like a vaporous shroud. Leaves of the jungle underbrush collected the tropical moisture and dripped like a thousand slowly leaking faucets. The first gray light of morning filtered through the mist and revealed the hazy greenness of the world around me. The jungle was as thick as the fog and I could see no more than a few yards in any direction; even the open rice paddy out in front of me was still captive to the thick haze.

I was hiding in a small patch of jungle. I lay quietly and looked out over a narrow trail that remained disappointingly empty. The earthen path emerged from the mist to my left and passed immediately in front of me. I knew it came in from somewhere out across the paddy lands to the north and meandered on toward a village off to my right. Five men from my own village, my American teammate, Sergeant Abney, and I were lying in ambush, waiting for a squad of enemy guerrillas that should have come by sometime during the night.

We had set up our ambush early the previous evening, but the guerrillas had not appeared. Now I was ready to leave. I figured that if the Cong were not here yet, they weren't coming, and like the other six men with me, I was wet, cold, and sore all over. Even tropical nights can be chilling when you lie for hours in muck and mud puddles, and hours of wet immobility can turn muscles into cords of aching stiffness. I was miserable.

I was pleased with my men's performance despite the absence of our prey. We had been waiting quietly since we first moved into position. I had not heard anyone talking, I had not seen any cigarettes glowing in the black night; we just watched the darkness for our approaching enemy. The leeches had crawled up our legs and the insects had bitten and stung, but we had remained still and silent. Now daylight was returning, and it seemed we had waited for nothing. I was so sore that even my teeth hurt, and I was about ready to pass the word to break ambush and move out toward home.

"Trung úy!" I heard an urgent whisper off to my left. The grass rustled ever so slightly and I saw the face of one of my village militiamen through the thick brush. He jerked his head toward my left and whispered, *"Công lai!"* The communists were coming.

I nodded silently and peeked back through the tall, wet grass in front of me. Instantly my aches and pain were gone; my heart beat like a drum and my teeth clenched in nervous tension. I peered down the trail to my left, but at first I saw nothing through the morning haze. Staring more intently, I did see movement in the shadowy fog. What were at first merely specters in the morning grayness soon turned into men. One by one they emerged from the dense vapor, ten men walking silently in column along the trail. They were short, wiry men dressed in drab peasant attire, and in addition to their weapons nine of them carried large packs on their backs. I could tell by their gait and the slump of their frames that they were exhausted.

I guessed that they had come across the Cambodian border early the previous evening and had been on the march all night. Something had slowed them down, though; they should have come by our location hours earlier, and by first light they should have been safely in their sanctuary area deeper in the province. Whoever was waiting at their rendezvous was probably very worried by now. It was clear that these guys were some kind of resupply group bringing in quite a load of material.

The packs that the nine carried were large and tightly stuffed. Each man had to struggle under that burden as well as carry his AK-47 rifle and the ammo strapped to his chest. The second man in the column had no bundle on his back; instead he had some sort of cloth satchel suspended on a strap across his shoulder. As I watched, he muttered something in a sharp tone to the man in front of him. I guessed the satchel carrier was the group's leader, and for some reason I immediately disliked the little man. I decided that he must be at least part of the reason his squad was running behind schedule. I did not think that he was an experienced guerrilla fighter, else he would have known better than to bring his men so exhausted into this kind of daylight. I figured he was some sort of political officer who had been put in charge of this group for some reason of expedience. Now he had marched his squad to the point of virtual paralysis; they had lost their alertness and were no longer watching for the dangers around them.

I knew how they must feel, having experienced that sort of mind-numbing forced march myself. Each man had his eyes glued on the ground in front of him, concentrating on making the one step it took to cover just that distance. Each labored step required such effort that the men were no longer paying attention to anything else. They had bunched up together, too, another cardinal sin I blamed the leader for. He should have kept his men spread out so they would not all come into an ambush zone or a land-mine kill zone at the same time. Now he had blown it. He and the men he had marched to the point of numbness were falling perfectly into our trap. They were about to die.

I was the last man on the right of our ambush position; the enemy were approaching from the left. That meant I could wait until the first man of the enemy column was in front of me before I triggered the ambush. When I opened fire everyone would let loose at the two or three Viet Cong closest to him. With this group bunched up like they were, we should easily be able to get them all. It should all be over in less than a minute.

I pressed my cheek against the stock of my M-16 and slowly brought its black front sight blade around to the waist of the small man at the head of the enemy column. For a fleeting moment I felt sorry for the belabored Viet Cong guerrilla. I thought it was too bad for him that he had drawn such a dumb-assed squad leader. I felt a mixture of sadness and anger that this man was about to die because of his leader's incompetence. I hoped I would get a chance to turn and take care of the leader myself before someone else blasted him to oblivion.

In a strange sort of way I was angry at the leader for allowing what was about to become a slaughter of his men.

My target was now about ten yards away and directly in front of me. The moment before I pulled the trigger, as always, a curtain dropped over my emotions. I had learned the magic trick of making feelings and emotions vanish, of just becoming a cold and dispassionate automaton at the moment of execution. I began a careful trigger pull. Jerking the trigger would only pull my aim off; the squeeze had to be even and steady. I was ready for the slight kick against my shoulder when my first blast finally killed the morning calm. My target disappeared in the jumbled vision caused by vibrating sights and the distorted air around the muzzle blast.

I heard the others open up instantly and quickly made a mental note that we had gotten it right, we had started the ambush together. It is important that an ambush be sprung with full force. It's a powerful psychological factor that helps immobilize the victims. The shock and confusion can stun them momentarily, and the fleeting second when they pause in disbelief may be the only second you need to kill them.

I delivered my first short burst at the belly of my target. At the second burst I could no longer see him, so I quickly dropped my sights and fired toward the ground where he should have fallen. I didn't even take the time to really look for him—I was already swinging my barrel back toward the leader, the second man in the column. We were now at somewhere around three seconds into the ambush.

My gun sight found the Viet Cong leader. It had taken him that fateful second to believe what was happening, and he was only now dropping into a crouch. His face was pulled taut in an expression of mixed shock and protest. At T + 4 seconds I put a burst of approximately six rounds somewhere between the satchel man's belt and his shoulders. This time I clearly saw my target lurch backward, then drop like a stone. I moved my barrel back to where my first target had been and released another spray in that direction just for insurance.

At T + 6 seconds I looked down the line to see how things were going. One of the Cong had somehow gotten off the trail and out into the paddy beyond. He was lurching through the shin-deep water as if the heavy burden on his back was keeping him off balance. Suddenly he threw out his arms and dropped face down into the water. The roar of the other rifles and our one machine gun was a constant thunder in my ear. I fired another burst in the general direction of the men out on the trail.

At T + 8 seconds I changed magazines. M-16's came with only twenty-round magazines, and with a maximum firing rate of six hundred rounds per minute it didn't take long to empty one. At T + 12 seconds I put my rifle back up and fired at some movement I thought I saw out in front of me. Our firing was slowing down, but I didn't know if we had finished off all the Cong or not. I could see bodies scattered along the trail in front of us, but I didn't have time to count them. I was looking down the little path for anyone who had not been hit when the ambush was triggered. As impossible as it seemed, someone might have made it to a protected position behind a paddy dike or in some depression on the other side of the trail. I wanted to keep firing at anyone I even suspected of shooting back. One measure of a well laid and well sprung ambush is that your enemy doesn't even get a chance to fire back; I wanted to prevent any return fire if I could.

Except for the one man lying spread-eagle out in the rice paddy, the only Viet Cong I saw were lying motionless on the trail. At T + 16 seconds all firing had stopped. The jungle reclaimed its silence. We all lay in our positions and waited. It was as if we expected the ambush victims to rise up and begin fighting back. The fog seemed to intensify the quietness as we lay there in the wet brush, our fingers still taut against our triggers and our eyes darting quickly along the trail in front of us. I looked back to where the trail emerged from the fog and wondered if there were more Cong out there in the white darkness. I waited for what seemed to be forever, but it probably wasn't over ten seconds. Nothing moved in the gauzy mist. I glanced back at the bodies lying out on the trail, waited for another breath or two, and finally pushed myself up off the ground. Kneeling now, I gazed at the bodies lying like boulders strewn along the narrow path. They were inert, unmoving, and apparently without life. At T + 30 seconds I stood up and cautiously stepped out of the jungle onto the trail. I paused briefly to peer down the trail into the fog, then at T + 35 seconds I waved my men out of their positions. We had to search the dead. The ambush was over. The astringent smell of gunfire had my heart racing and my head was spinning with the rush of victory.

Now our drill was to rummage quickly through the pockets, packs, and equipment of each victim and collect anything of military or intelligence value. It was illegal to take personal effects from the dead, but I never saw a corpse left with a good watch, either. I found the lead man lying in the middle of the trail where he had disappeared from my gun sight. Two or three rounds had hit him in the chest and his shirt was soaked with blood. I cut open his pack and quickly sifted through the clothes, medicines, and other odds and ends. I kept only a few ampules of the drugs. They had labels which indicated their origin in Poland and East Germany.

I turned my attention to the man I presumed to be the Viet Cong leader. He had fallen back a yard or so from the trail and had rolled down into a slight depression. I took the satchel from his limp arm and looked inside. As I suspected, it was full of papers and record books. There were loose pages, notebooks, and packets of letters. I dropped the medicines I had already collected into the satchel and slung it over my shoulder. Two militiamen came by, gathering up the Cong weapons and ammo, while two others of my group went through the other packs. I walked swiftly down the trail, telling the men to hurry. They worked quietly and quickly. Within five minutes we were ready to go.

I called in Sergeant Abney and the one village militiaman who had been ordered to stay back in the jungle with him to act as our security watch. Abney, his crumpled bush hat pushed back on his head, came over to me with excitement dancing in his eyes. "Shee-it, *Trung úy,* we really kicked their ass didn't we?"

"You goddamned right we did," I replied, the excitement of triumph rising in my own voice. "This'll be worth a beer and a night's sleep when we get back to the compound!"

"Damned right." He chuckled. "The others are going to shit when they see all this stuff." He was right. In small-unit guerrilla wars you can spend hundreds of hours on night ambush operations and rarely come away with such a clean sweep as this one had been. The other three Americans on our team were going to be green with envy. Well, they were going to at least act like they were.

I made sure the burden of our booty was evenly distributed among our little group and we headed for home in a dispersed squad column formation. I told Abney to take second place in line and I went to bring up the rear. We had about a five-kilometer walk back to our village and I wanted to make sure that no one fell behind. We were all tired from the sleepless night and the adrenalin rush of combat. The trek home loaded with the weapons and gear of ten other men was not going to be easy.

As we walked away from the bloodied trail I looked back over my shoulder at the lifeless bodies we had left behind. They were now stretched out alongside one another like ten sacks of fertilizer in the damp grass. A ray of sunshine broke through the thinning fog and illuminated the scene of death. A thought out of nowhere came to me, a paraphrase of a famous poem: Men once living now were dead. Shortly before, they had lived, felt dawn, seen sunset glow. They had loved and were loved. Now they were lifeless bundles laid in a row. In this rude excuse for their own Flanders Field they presented their souls to God and their corpses to the buzzards. I walked away in silence. For the next several minutes, and not for the first time either, I wondered exactly what it was I was doing here in this foreign place. I asked myself what it was I found so valuable that I was willing to risk death for it, what it was I found so valuable I was willing to kill for it.

PART ONE

The Beginnings

Then out spake brave Horatius,
The captain of the gate:
"To every man upon this earth
Death comes soon or late.
And how may man die better
Than facing fearful odds,
For the ashes of his fathers,
And the temples of his Gods?"

"How Horatius Kept the Bridge"
Thomas B. Macauley (1800–1859)
A poem once taught to young boys.

Chapter 1

HEAT rushed up from the hot tarmac and pushed against me like the baked air from an oven. Nearby jeeps and crew equipment shimmered in the hot air. I could see buildings and planes in the distance as they danced in a haze made pungent by the familiar smell of diesel exhaust and the strange smells of a foreign dust. The cool comfort of a Braniff Airlines 707 was only three feet behind me, but there was no turning back. I had arrived in Vietnam. It was April, 1969.

I was an infantry lieutenant fresh from the Special Warfare School at Fort Bragg, North Carolina. I had been trained in counterinsurgency and counterguerrilla operations and in military assistance operations with foreign governments. I had been given courses in Vietnamese history, customs, and language. I was primed and prepared. I figured I was six feet, one inch of ready American soldier.

I knew when I stepped off the plane at Tan Son Nhut airbase that I would not be assigned to one of the big American army units in Vietnam. I was going to be posted to some Vietnamese village where I was to try and help the people with rural development projects and with the defense of their villages against the communists. I had butterflies in my stomach; I knew I wasn't in for a picnic, but I felt prepared for my job, and I was excited about the opportunity to do good for the Vietnamese people. As it turned out, I suppose, I was six feet, one inch of naive American soldier.

At the bottom of the flight stairs a sweating, harried-looking young private pointed the way to a line that was forming for a bus ride to our in-processing station. I walked over and stood in line in the suffocating heat. I felt my sweat soak through what had once been a starched khaki uniform, and I could see the guys around me start to wilt, too. The tarmac was hot enough to cook on, and by the time a growling, screeching old army bus finally pulled up beside us I thought my feet were going to be pan-fried right there in my shoes. I wasn't alone, either—all I had to do was look around me to tell that everybody was miserable.

The old bus, olive-drab green, with chicken wire over the open windows, chattered to a halt at the head of the line. The driver snapped the doors open with a bang and with a perverse grin on his face yelled out to us, "All aboard for Vee-et-nam! Just remember, boys, your taxes are paying for this!"

I WAS IN-PROCESSED AT CAMP ALPHA, A SPRAWLING ARMY complex just outside Tan Son Nhut airbase in Saigon. I spent three days there being briefed, drawing equipment, and finally receiving my assignment. My orders confirmed what I had been told back in the States: I was going to be sent out as an advisor. I was assigned to MACV Team 84, the province advisory group in Kien Phong province. I had never heard of that particular province, but the officer in charge of the assignment desk told me it was down in the Mekong Delta, out on the Plain of Reeds. He also pointed out that my orders assigned me to Team 84 without further specification. I would have to wait until I got to Kien Phong province to find what my specific assignment would be.

On the morning of our second day in-country a group of about ten of us who had been assigned to MACV—or Military Assistance Command Vietnam—were sent out to draw our TA-50 equipment (helmet, backpack, mosquito net, boots, jungle fatigues, all that sort of stuff) and our individual weapons. It turned out that officers could check out an automatic pistol or an M-16 rifle, whichever we wanted. That sounded like a ridiculous choice to me; I couldn't imagine anybody taking a .45 caliber service automatic over an M-16 assault rifle. Hell, we were talking about going to a war, not a parade! Apparently my view was shared by the others in the group—we all took the rifles. We were also issued a bandolier of ammunition

for each rifle and a cleaning kit. All of that added to the stack
of TA-50 gear had each of us staggering back to our billet
under a cumbersome heap of government-issue cloth and hardware. Once we got our gear stowed, there was nothing to do
but hang out at the personnel desk and wait for our orders for
movement.

I got my orders that same afternoon. These orders detailed
me to the Ninth Infantry Division for one week of temporary
duty. Some of my friends also received orders for a week with
the Ninth; others were sent to some of the other large infantry
outfits. I learned it was a general policy for everyone en route
to an assignment like mine to be sent to an American unit for
a short break-in period. We were to spend a week going out
on combat patrols with the units, and if we got through that
all right, we were sent on to our team assignments across the
country. I think MACV wanted to check us all out, and they
wanted us to get our feet wet in situations where we could
call on plenty of help. Once we got out on our teams we were
going to have to shift for ourselves.

The Ninth Infantry was stationed at Dong Tam down in the
Mekong Delta. All of us going in that direction had to report
to a terminal at the Tan Son Nhut airbase early the next morning so we could catch a ride down to Dong Tam on a C-130
cargo plane. There weren't any seats in the plane, so they tied
us to the floor with the big cargo straps. We sat on the cor-
rugated metal floor with our legs straight out in front of us
while the crew chief pulled a single strap across the legs of
one row of men at a time. When he snugged it down tight that
meant we couldn't move for the duration of the flight. It also
meant that if something happened we were going to have a
hard time getting out of the damned plane! I spent the entire
flight to Dong Tam with my heart in my throat, figuring we
were going to catch fire or be shot down at any minute. I was
never so grateful to get out of the air as I was when I felt the
wheels of that C-130 touch down on the airstrip that served
the Ninth Division's headquarters.

All I remember of the large American cantonment at Dong
Tam is that it was a sprawling jumble of prefabricated metal
buildings and sandbagged barracks, bunkers, and motor pools.
And it was a filthy damned place, too. Whenever I think of
Dong Tam I think of grime-covered buildings, mud-covered

floors, and dust-covered everything else. It was a depressing place to be—one hot, airless building giving way to the next— and at night there were constant mortar and rocket attacks that kept us shuffling back and forth to the bunkers. I hated the place after being there about one hour.

On the afternoon of my first day I was sent over to A Company, Third Battalion, Sixty-first Infantry Brigade, with orders for my first combat operation. I was to accompany a squad-size night ambush patrol that would be leaving the company area late in the afternoon. I sat on the edge of my temporary bunk and stared at the typewritten instructions I held in my hand. "Well, this is it," I said to myself. "Welcome to your war."

I found the squad in their barracks about thirty minutes before our scheduled departure time, so I introduced myself around and tried to let them know I wasn't there to pull rank or start giving orders. I was there simply as an infantryman trying to pick up some practical experience. Their squad leader, a nineteen-year-old buck sergeant, was the man in charge; I was along as just another grunt. Around four o'clock in the afternoon a truck picked us up, took us out of the Dong Tam base area, and dropped us in the countryside where we were to operate for the night. Our patrol was to take us down a road, through a small hamlet, and off into an area of jungle that was broken only by an occasional small field or rice paddy. That night we were to set up an ambush on the banks of a strategic canal junction.

I was nervous as hell. I was a new officer to the field and I figured everyone could tell it from the fresh green look of my fatigues and the sick green look on my face. I was scared, but I was also uptight simply because I wanted to do well on my first patrol. That is to say, I wanted to survive the operation without making a complete fool of myself.

It seemed to me that the patrol started off well enough. The squad maintained its combat formation and the men showed what I took to be an experienced alertness as we moved along the jungle-bordered road. I took a lot of comfort from the fact everyone seemed to know what he was doing. We made our way through a small hamlet, then moved on into the jungle and began working our way through the thick green vegetation toward our objective. After picking our way quietly through the dense tangle for some time, we came to our canal. It turned out to be over head deep and quite wide, and to my surprise there was a swift current. We had to get across to the other side with our radios, machine guns, ammo boxes, and other gear. We couldn't swim across with it all, so we made field expedient rafts from our ponchos and some tree branches.

One of the men swam across the canal, pulling a rope along with him. He secured the rope to a tree on the other side and moved off into the jungle on that side to have a look around. He soon returned and gave the all-clear sign. One by one we entered the water, grabbed the rope, and pulled ourselves and our individual rafts to the other side. I was a little uneasy at seeing the men, as they got out of the water on the opposite bank, just standing around drying off and talking to each other. They should have moved on into the jungle and established a protective perimeter for the men still crossing the canal. Nothing happened during the crossing, though, so I thought I was just being a bit too persnickety. After all, these guys were the veterans; I was the virgin.

We moved on, past the place where we wanted to set up the ambush for the night. It was still daytime and we had to presume that the Cong might be watching us. We did not want to set up the ambush in broad daylight and give away our position for the night. The standard practice was to keep on moving until sundown, then to stop, set up a perimeter, and break out the C-rations for chow. After dark, we would quietly regroup and backtrack to the assigned ambush position. The idea was to have the Viet Cong think we had set up for the night in a place different from where we actually were.

On this particular evening, we stopped on the edge of a rice paddy that bordered the jungle. We spread out in a defensive perimeter and used the paddy dike as our field fortification. Then we broke out our C's and dug away at the tin cans with our P-38 can openers. My main course was cold processed ham and eggs in a can. It hit my stomach like a lump of lead, and the dried crackers and small tin of peanut butter were just as bad. I poured some water into my canteen cup and dissolved my packet of cocoa powder in it. That wasn't very good either, but at least it left a sweet taste in my mouth. As usual, the best things in a C-ration box were the little pack of four cigarettes and the two pieces of chewing gum.

My partner, a Spec-4 rifleman, and I hunkered down under the rim of the paddy dike. We had taken off our web gear to ease the pain in our shoulders, but had kept on our helmets. Mine felt like it weighed a ton. I was finishing up my can of ham and eggs and considering whether or not to take off my helmet and just lie back for a few minutes when a shot cracked out from somewhere back in the jungle. A spurt of dust jumped up out in the middle of the dry paddy bed.

My neck and shoulders telescoped in so fast I almost squashed my face into my C-ration can. Another shot rang out and a bullet whined by overhead. The squad leader started shouting instructions. Everyone was to get behind the dike, lie low, and watch for the sniper somewhere out there in the trees. Men were scurrying low over the banks of the paddy, struggling to drag their gear and rifles with them. In a moment everything was still. We all watched for some movement out there in the trees. It was late in the afternoon and the sun was already sinking below the horizon. The humid magenta sky overlooked a dark green jungle that was turning even darker in the approaching twilight. The night animals and birds began their occasional calls and cries. We watched, we waited, we saw nothing.

Gradually the tension eased, and one by one we began to go back to our chow. All of us kept looking back over our shoulders toward the jungle, but we were intent on cleaning out our C-ration cans. I was scraping the bottom of my tin of peanut butter when another shot rang out from the dense woods. A bullet zipped overhead and smacked into the dike on the other side of the paddy. This time the reactions were more subdued. Except for a slight wince, I just stayed low and polished off the peanut butter. It seemed that all the other guys did likewise. The veterans on the squad were already joking that this sniper couldn't hit the side of a barn if he were inside it. None of his shots so far had even come close. The advice being passed around was to stay low, finish the meal, and let the Cong keep wasting his ammo. He would have to stop shooting when it got too dark to see. Then we could move back to our ambush position.

After the sixth or seventh round I no longer even flinched when one of the solitary shots was fired. I thought I was the picture of aplomb. Here I was, eating my C-rations and joking with my partner while some guy kept firing off rounds at us. Every time another bullet kicked up the dust on our dike we made another joke about our friend the incompetent sniper. Underneath my surface bravado, I kept praying for nightfall.

The purple-hued dusks of the tropics are as brief as they are beautiful. The darkness arrived almost suddenly, and our errant marksman stopped firing, as predicted. We reharnessed ourselves to our combat gear, arranged ourselves in a squad column, and moved back into the black tangle of jungle. Night movements are always difficult, not only because a man can't see where he is going, but also because silence in movement is both important and very difficult. Falls and stumbles have to be borne without the automatic soldier's curse; jokes and casual conversation have to cease; silent footsteps must become the focus of everyone's attention.

After what seemed like an endless trek in complete darkness, the line came to a halt. As all of us had been trained to do in many drills, everyone went down on one knee as soon as the column halted. Each man faced out in the direction opposite that of the man in front of him. It seemed to be a useless exercise in this case, since I could barely see the man a few feet in front of me and I could see nothing in the impenetrable forest on either side.

The squad leader came back down the line, softly explaining the situation to each man. We were at the canal again. We were going to set up an ambush on its bank. Anything that moved on the canal this time of night was presumed to be enemy. It was long after curfew and the local villagers were supposed to be home already. Only the Cong or other illegals were out moving around in the jungle this time of night, so anyone who passed our way was free game. The squad leader told us we were going to move on up to the bank, where he would place us into position.

As we moved on in closer to the canal, we passed a small deserted brick house that I had noticed when we passed by earlier in the day. The walls were pockmarked from the impact of many bullets. The house had the look of a small French villa and I figured the owners must have once been very prosperous. The white walls were set off by a red tile roof and floor, and the windows and doorways were bordered with blue glazed tile. The remnants of decorative wrought-iron gratings covered the windows and hung askew from the doorposts. The house was a far cry from the bamboo and grass thatch hooches of most villagers, and it was in what must have once been an idyllic setting. Now it was practically in ruin, the voracious jungle was already putting its twining clutches around the gates and balustrades. Across the canal the damp jungle stretched away to dark disorder.

The patrol leader positioned us along the canal bank, each man paired with another and all of us looking out over the canal. I was concerned about our leaving the house behind us with no one in it to cover our rear. If by chance the Cong had seen us move back into this position, they could approach the house without our being able to detect them. Once inside the house, they could command our position on the canal bank and would have the benefit of the protection of the house walls. If this worst-case type of situation actually developed, we would be in real trouble.

Despite my worry I didn't say anything. I figured I was too green and probably too scared to have things sorted out right in my mind. I tried to comfort myself with the thought that the patrol leader was surely experienced enough to know whether or not he should worry about the house.

We laid out our ponchos and pulled some grass and brush in front of our positions. We constructed our camouflage so as to be unnoticed by anyone coming upon us from the canal. The water level in the canal was three or four feet below the edge of the bank, so it was a simple thing to protect ourselves from that direction. From the house, though, we were wide open.

Later, the moon came out. It was a full-blown beauty, shining down in a silvery glow on the darkened jungle. I didn't like it. Now it seemed to me that we were really sitting ducks for anyone coming at us from our rear. With the moon out and shining like a bloody lantern, we were in plain view of anyone who approached us from any direction but the canal. I crawled over to the patrol leader and suggested we send two men back to the house to cover our rear. The squad leader just shook his head and told me not to worry about the house. He said we would need all our firepower up front if the Cong came down the canal. Our intelligence sources had said that there was a good chance for some enemy movement on the water that night and he wanted to be ready. I crawled back to my position and lay there with a slowly growing sense of anxiety in my belly.

As we waited, minutes seemed to go by like hours. Aches became pains, itches became rashes, and stiffness set into every joint. The sounds and calls of the jungle night began to intensify. Huge bats, of the heroic proportions reserved for horror movies, flapped through the air and lent another ominous sign of impending evil. Somewhere behind us, we thought where our earlier chow stop had been, a mortar barrage began to impact. The explosions sent the bats and birds hustling from one tree to another and temporarily sllenced the nocturnal jungle conversations.

About that time, a unit somewhere off to our left came under attack. The chatter of the machine guns and the crump of the exploding mortar rounds came through loud and clear. We all gazed off in the direction of the sounds and gave our attention to the distant battle. Occasional sprays of tracer rounds could be seen arching lazily up toward the moon. The orangered tracers from American automatic weapons and the green tracers from the communist guns flew upward in a graceful exhibition of light. The elegant display belied the lethal deeds being done beneath their illuminated arches.

It wasn't long before helicopter gunships came beating the air over our position, headed in the direction of the firefight. Then we heard an old C-47 circling in the dark above us. We knew it had to be a "Puff the Magic Dragon." The old World War II cargo planes had been converted into flying gun platforms; they carried the electronically controlled rapidfire machine guns called miniguns. The miniguns could spew out thousands and thousands of rounds a minute, compared to hundreds of rounds a minute for conventional machine guns. I have seen a minigun turn a cinder-block house into a mound of dust on just one pass. At night the tracers coming from a minigun made a solid streak of fire all the way to the earth. It looked as if someone were pouring red-hot iron from a cauldron up in the sky or as if a dragon were breathing flame down on its victim; thus the name "Puff the Magic Dragon." The stream of red-lit bullets is even more impressive when you recall that only every fourth round in a belt of machinegun ammo is a tracer round.

The presence of the Puff bothered me. I hoped those air support guys knew where they were supposed to shoot, and I hoped it wasn't in our direction. I was worried about small errors because we were pretty close to the position under attack. Our proximity was accentuated by the fact that the parachute flares being shot up by those guys kept floating down almost on top of us. The eerie blue-white flares floated by just above the treetops, trailing white smoke and illuminating us in their harsh pale glow. One of the flares snagged in a tree nearby and burned itself out as we lay there, petrified. I was afraid we would be hit by some stray air attack, and I was convinced that some Cong unit sneaking through the jungle would come along while we were lit up by one of those damned flares and blow us all away.

By this time, I was almost sick with apprehension and misery. Everything seemed to be wrong. I thought we had set up in a bad position; I thought the Cong had probably found us by now and were probably up there in the brick house getting ready to blast us; I thought our own aircraft might come over and reduce us to molecules due to a minor mistake on somebody's plotting board. I was convinced we would never make it through the night. I began to practice the survival method that has been tested through the ages: I started with the little prayers and made my way up to the big ones.

The Puff continued to circle overhead and pour out its streams of fire. The miniguns fired so fast that the individual rounds couldn't be heard. Instead of the rapid chatter of a regular machine gun, each spit of the Dragon sounded like a long moan from an injured spirit. The sputter-pop from the firing of the helicopter gunships added to the battle symphony; mortar fire lent its percussive impact, and I pressed even closer to the ground at the throaty swoosh of artillery rounds flying by overhead. The sights and sounds of the adjacent night battle drew all our attention, and for a while we hardly paid any notice to our own stakeout. The air support apparently turned the tide for our guys, and the sounds of the battle died to a dull mutter. Only the occasional pop-pop-pop of rifle fire could be heard for a while, and then the sounds died off altogether. Now we all lay there in the damp grass, trying to see through the darkness and hear through the thick silence. We looked at our neighbors nervously, wondering if we were going to be the next to be hit.

The rest of the night progressed without incident. The chatter and squawk of the jungle birds and monkeys gradually returned and the big bats started swooping around again. Eventually it was my turn to keep the "Starlight" watch. In 1969 the Starlight scope was still a classified instrument. Using special light-intensifying technology, the scope gave the user a see-in-the-night capability far beyond normal human limits. One could squint through the single ocular of the scope and see the surrounding darkness illuminated by an eerie green glow. Since the scope used the light from the moon and stars to operate, the brighter the night the better the scope worked. On pitch black nights, the scopes weren't much good at all.

We had only one scope on our patrol, so each man was assigned an hour to be on watch with it. The man with the scope was responsible for watching the tree lines, the front of the brick house behind us, and the canal in front of us. Any suspicious movement was to be reported to the patrol leader. One of the things we had been taught about using the scope was that one should never allow something to so startle him that he give in to the urge to remove his eye from the scope and try to see what was going on with both naked eyes. Not only was it unlikely that anyone would see better without the scope than with it, but in moving his head and having to readjust his eyes to the darkness, the watchman would probably lose whatever it was he had in the field of the scope in the first place. I had been taught that lesson, but I hadn't learned it very well.

Rather than watch the canal, our assigned ambush zone, I kept a closer watch on the jungle around us and on the abandoned house behind us. The moon had gone down, but the clear and starry night gave enough light for the scope to work very well. I kept my eye glued to the ocular and watched the surroundings with nervous anticipation. I expected to see a platoon of Viet Cong come creeping up on us at any moment. I would occasionally sweep the canal with the scope, but I had given up on our staging a successful ambush. I was more worried about surviving the attack that I was sure was coming. I moved the scope slowly as I watched the jungle through its pale green glow, and my view moved over to the canal bank and down to the water's edge. I looked all the way down the canal to the right as far as I could see. Nothing there.

I swung the scope back toward the extreme left to view the jungle and the canal bank on that side of our position. I had my eye to the scope as I swung it rapidly from my right back to my left. I wasn't really paying any attention to the rippling green water in the scope's field of view; I was more interested in the trees. A form in the water moved rapidly across the scope's field. I was mechanically moving the scope back to the right to check on it before I realized that what I had seen was probably a person. Suddenly, there he was again. An icy clutch squeezed my chest. A Vietnamese man was standing there in waist-deep water! He was directly in front of me, craning his neck to try and see over the canal bank. An ammo belt was slung across his chest.

I couldn't believe it! I was so shocked at actually finding something out there that I just froze stiff. I was probably fixed for only a second, but at the time it seemed like an hour of indecision. When I did move, my reaction was to jerk the scope away from my disbelieving eye to try and confirm the sighting by using two eyes. Predictably, I saw nothing in the darkness. I was only halfway through the motion of removing the scope when I knew I had made a mistake. I quickly put the scope back up and looked out at the canal. I saw only a widening circle of ripples where I was sure I had seen a man seconds before. Desperately I scanned the water, the opposite bank, and the jungle that approached the bank. At the same time, I was cursing myself for my stupidity. Now I didn't know if I had really seen a man or if it was just a figment of my imagination.

There are hundreds of tales of green soldiers seeing things in the night, and of entire engagements being fought with only one side actually being present, the other there only in the overactive imaginations of the troops. I asked myself if I was just jumpy because the tension was getting to me. Was I seeing things? No, dammit, I knew I had seen a man standing there looking straight at me. I quickly convinced myself he was the scout for the Cong unit that had come to wipe us out. He must have seen me when I made my sudden movement and had taken a quick dive back under the water! I was sure we were done for and I was so damned scared and confused that I just squatted there in a stupefied daze, staring slack-jawed at the place where there had once been a man.

We had been on fifty percent alert for the last couple of hours, so my partner was asleep. He was the same Spec-4 rifleman I had started the evening with, an experienced veteran of many nights like this and apparently completely at ease with his environment. I didn't want to wake him without knowing what I had seen. I didn't want to have him think, "Here we go again with another green, dumb-assed lieutenant," which of course I was.

I worked harder at trying to convince myself that the whole thing was just a flight of wild imagination. A cold sweat dampened my forehead and upper lip. My palms were clammy and my tongue was dry. In the end my rationalizations were fruitless. I was still sure that I had seen the man in the water and that he had gone back underwater when he saw me with the scope. I thought about crawling over to tell the patrol leader, but he would want to know why I hadn't opened up when I first saw the man, or at least why I hadn't sounded the alarm. My ego insisted that I not go to the patrol leader. I was too afraid of appearing the fool.

I went back to work with the Starlight scope, trying to find some other evidence of Cong presence in the jungle around. Anxiously I searched the trees, the canal banks, the house, then back to the canal again. As time passed I became more and more apprehensive. I was sure the man had seen me, had confirmed our location to his buddies, and was now in the process of plotting our demise. My nerves were as taut as the skin on a banjo head. The sounds of nocturnal animals moving about the jungle floor sounded like platoons of infantry. The banana leaves rustling in the wind sounded like the movement of men through the vegetation. I learned why green troops are notorious for blasting away at absolutely nothing in the night shadows.

As time went on, I began to feel more and more guilty about not alerting everyone, but now I told myself it was useless since I had nothing to show them, and they would think I was imagining things anyway. Indecision and fear rendered me totally ineffective. I was doing nothing and saying nothing. I prayed I was wrong about the whole thing. I prayed I was just scared of the night shadows. Still, I kept sweeping the area with the scope, never putting it down during my entire watch.

When it came time to give the scope to the next fellow on the Starlight watch, I crawled over to his position, wakened him, and told him I had seen "something suspicious" out in front of us and for him to keep a close watch for any unusual movements in the jungle. I roused my partner from his slumbers and told him the same thing. It was his turn to be on watch at our position now, and I didn't want him to let his guard down. I wrapped myself in my cold, wet poncho and lay in the grass facing the villa behind us. I was determined to keep an eye on that place myself.

I spent the rest of the night in a state of stomach-twisting tension, always just a millisecond from pulling my trigger at something. As the gray light of dawn began to creep into the eastern sky, I began to feel a first ray of hope that we might survive the night after all. The other men began to stir and I could eventually make out all the men in the other positions along the canal bank. The patrol leader made his way from position to position, telling us to pack up and get ready to move out to our pick-up point. While everyone was arranging his gear, I decided to creep back up to the villa and have a final look around. I felt uneasy about walking into the jungle with that thing at our backs and not knowing whether it was still empty. I went into the edge of the jungle and approached the house from the side. I crawled onto the porch and lay there listening.

A few yards down below me on the canal bank the patrol was gearing up to move out. A mutter of voices and an occasional clank of metal on metal could be heard, but the sounds seemed muffled by the foggy envelope of the gray dawn which gave a spectral appearance to the whole scene. I listened for any sounds coming from inside the house. I heard none. I stood up by the front doorsill and gathered my nerve to move through it. My hands were shaking as I held my rifle close to my chest. Sweat popped out on my forehead. I was scared shitless again.

I lunged through the doorway and twisted violently as I hit the floor waving my M-16 around and trying to see and cover the whole room at once. I was ready to fire at the slightest hint of movement. Luckily for the roaches they froze where they were; they were the only thing there to shoot at. I let out a great sigh of relief and fell back on the floor, a move that released the roaches and sent them scampering off to their nooks and crannies. I got up and checked out the rest of the house and the jungle behind it. I didn't see even the slightest hint of human presence.

By now I was almost convinced that I had fooled myself about the man in the water. I was beginning to believe that he and his supposed comrades were just figments of my imagination. I sauntered back down to the patrol and harnessed up for the move back home. Standing on the bank I noticed that the canal was at the nadir of low tide. The water was now four or five feet below the edge of the banks, and mud flats bordered the central stream that had filled the channel the night before. Through the haze I could make out marks in the mud over on the other side of the canal. As we moved away in single file back toward the jungle, I craned my neck to check out the markings. As we walked by the area I stared intently at the pasty gray mud. Footprints! There was no doubt about it: a man's footprints ran from the grass at the top of the bank down to the water's edge. The last visible prints were under the very edge of the water and presumably came out to the middle of the stream or even all the way over to the near bank. A man had been in the water since the last high tide, and the prints led to the exact spot where I had seen him with the Starlight.

I pointed the footprints out to the patrol leader and said in my most nonchalant manner, "Looks like we had a visitor last night." I still didn't want to let on that I had seen anything myself, but I did want the patrol to be on the alert. A favorite and highly successful guerrilla tactic was to set up an ambush where the enemy was likely to be paying little attention, where his discipline would be lax, and when he thought he was home free. A small unit ending an all-night ambush patrol is always infected with the "all done" attitude and is a prime target for an ambush itself. The men are just looking forward to getting back in, getting dried off, and getting some sleep. The tendency is to drop the alertness and discipline that is necessary for proper action and reaction in combat. If the enemy is alert and aggressive he can make coming in one of the most dangerous parts of an ambush patrol.

The patrol leader pointed out the tracks to everyone and issued a warning for us all to stay alert and spread out as we made our way back through the jungle. The light banter and relaxed attitude evaporated into the damp morning air. Tension inched its way back into our bodies and as we moved out in column, our eyes strained to see through the jungle thicket. We moved along the side of a jungle path, staying in the jungle itself and fighting our way through the brush and vines.

The patrol leader knew enough to keep us off the well-used trail. Most ambushes are set to cover some common route: a canal, a trail, or a road. To move down the middle of a path where the going is easiest is to invite slaughter. The safest but most difficult way to move a unit is to make a new route about five to ten meters off to the side of the original path or road. In a jungle setting this maneuver may be enough to move the patrol out of the kill zone of an ambush and may even force the ambushers to abandon their position without firing a shot. An ambush position is usually extremely vulnerable to all approaches but the one it is designed to cover. A quarry's approach, if it is off by even a few meters, can sometimes screw up a carefully planned operation.

We stayed in the jungle shadows and moved cautiously alongside the jungle trail. When we finally got out of the underbrush and into the more cleared areas, I could see the relief on all the other faces and feel it in my own. We had come to an area of rice paddies, small fields, and a string of small hamlets. We all began to relax again and the "all done" syndrome reemerged. The sleepless night, the nervous tension, and the morning trek in the jungle had left me in a state of mental numbness. The lack of apparent need to stay alert any longer made it very difficult to pay attention to what I was doing or where we were going. I just wanted to get there so I could sit down and rest.

I was stumbling along pretty carelessly when I came upon my first encounter with a monkey bridge. The water in the small canal that ran through this particular hamlet was at low tide. The single-pole bridge was eight or nine feet above the rivulet of water at the bottom of the canal. The black, brackish mud stretched ten or fifteen feet to either side of the central stream. The canal bottom was an unhealthy-looking expanse of pasty, grayish-black ooze.

I watched the other GI's go over the rickety bamboo pole. A second, reed-thin pole was tacked up for use as a handhold. The problem was that the little strip of bamboo was not strung high enough to be of any use to us Americans. Trying to bend down to reach it seemed to cause as much imbalance as just trying to balance on the bridge pole without it. Everyone before me made it over. I was the last to go and had to do it without the handrail, such as it was, because the middle strand of it had collapsed when the previous fellow had pulled too heavily on it. He had almost fallen off the bridge, too, but had managed to right himself and make it to the other side.

I held my M-16 out in front of me the way a high-wire artist uses a balance beam. Twisting and leaning from one side to the other, I slowly made my way out along the bridge pole. When I was exactly in the middle, I heard a harsh snap and felt the pole lurch beneath me. I flailed my arms, trying to keep my balance, and had almost succeeded when there came another crack and the pole gave way completely. I plunged feet first into the canal, the bamboo bridge crashing around me. My glasses were spattered with a gray coat of foul-smelling goo. I couldn't see anything. I was jammed up to my hips in the gelatinous mud of the canal bottom. Above the waist I was almost completely covered with the splatter of gray muck. My rifle ended up about an arm's length away, muzzle down, stuck into the canal bottom all the way to the trigger housing.

Once everyone saw I was all right, they really began to whoop it up. There I was, stuck in the mud in a village canal, absolutely covered with shit, disease, worms, and the general effluvia of decades of village life. I couldn't move. The mud had a suction grip on my legs and I couldn't budge an inch. The guys up on the bank were still staggering around in fits of laughter as I pulled and twisted and tried to unlock the grip on my legs. The patrol leader finally threw me a length of rope, so I tied the end of it around my waist, grabbed the glop of mud that was once my rifle, and told them to haul away. Three of them pulled on their end of the rope and I pulled and struggled on my end to free my legs from the sticky mud. Our efforts finally succeeded and I was hauled up on the bank like a sodden log. When I stood up I still had about twenty pounds of stinking mud clinging to me. I looked like shit, I smelled like shit, and I felt like shit.

During the remainder of our walk back to our pick-up point no one could come near me. I was miserable and even glad for the lack of company. The patrol ended at the prescribed point where we caught a deuce-and-a-half (an army two-and-a-half-ton truck) back to Dong Tam. On the ride back I was really in black despair. My first combat patrol had essentially been without serious incident, yet I felt I had done a hundred things wrong, some of them potentially fatal. Even the plunge into the canal seemed to be a rude reminder of my incompetence and vulnerability.

I wondered what in God's name would have happened if we had actually had to fight. My stupidity alone probably would have been sufficient to get us all killed. What happened to all my training, I asked myself. What about that great-leader-in-battle bullshit? I couched my head between my hands, distressed by my own incompetence. I didn't see any way I would survive a year of this stuff. The certainty of my own demise was bad enough, but I felt almost as bad about the possibility that I might cause the deaths of some of the men around me. I had always had the confidence that I could do this job right, but now I had a mental whiplash from the sudden realization of my own vulnerability.

My anxiety was partly due to inexperience. I didn't yet know how quickly people learn from their mistakes, especially when their lives depend on it. I was very apprehensive during the next couple of patrols, but I did discover that I was rapidly getting the hang of things. I could make the proper decisions. I could use my training. I could carry my own weight. When I left the Ninth to go on to my team assignment in Kien Phong I had only a few operations under my belt, but I knew a hell of a lot more about combat and a lot more about myself than when I arrived.

I not only learned things about myself while I was at Dong Tam, I learned a lot about other Americans and how they got along with the Vietnamese people. I learned at first hand about the generally abysmal relations between Americans and the Vietnamese villagers. Most American soldiers had never really thought about how fundamentally different the Vietnamese culture, or any Oriental culture for that matter, is from our own. Most servicemen on a one-year tour of duty could never bridge that gap between East and West.

To get along in Vietnamese society it is important to be calm, unfailingly polite, and sensitive to how the particular Vietnamese you were dealing with fits into the social order. It should be no surprise that most GI's at war often are not polite even by American standards, and their sensitivity can be somewhere between that of a tank tread and a helmet liner. That callousness became the source of many problems, typified by an incident that happened at Dong Tam toward the end of my week with the Ninth Infantry.

I was returning from my last night patrol along with the ten other grunts in the squad. It was early morning and we had been walking along a small road for about half an hour, each one of us a tired, shapeless lump of olive drab militaria trudging along the roadside. After our all-night operation in the jungle, we were looking forward to getting back to our pickup point where we could rest our feet and maybe even get a little sleep. Earlier we had passed through a small village where the people were beginning to stir outside their hooches in the early morning light and to fuss with their morning cooking fires. As we continued walking along the narrow road back toward Dong Tam, the morning traffic of cyclos and bicycles gradually increased. Many villagers were heading for their jobs on the American post or for the morning market in Dong Tam village.

Later in our march we approached what appeared to be an American artillery battery revetted against banks of sun-baked delta mud. I could see some Americans working around the 105mm howitzers, and others were coming and going from the temporary shelters that had been erected in the area. When we drew alongside the camp, we came upon a group of five or six young GI's who were standing by the road and calling and waving to the young Vietnamese women who passed by on their bicycles. The women were hurrying by, attempting to ignore the rude soldiers.

Suddenly, one of the men, a swaggering young PFC, rushed out into the road and grabbed an old woman who was pedaling by on a rickety old bicycle. Laughing boisterously, he pulled the woman from her bike and pushed her to one side. The GI mounted the woman's bike and began to pedal away, taking with him the old woman's market supplies that were tied in a bundle behind the seat. The young American's friends were calling jokes to their pal on the bicycle and laughing loudly at the plight of the old woman, who was reduced to pleading for the return of her property, wringing her hands in nervous yet angry embarrassment.

Now that pissed me off. In her own village, among her own people, the old woman would have always been treated with dignity and respect. It was one of the few benefits of growing old in traditional Vietnamese society. Yet out here by an American army camp she could be accosted by an insolent private and be treated as a joke for other American onlookers. All this was being done in front of other Vietnamese villagers who were also passing by. That served to intensify the old woman's shame.

As we approached the group the soldier on the bike had turned around and was pedaling back by the old woman, shouting down her pleas with derision and sarcasm. He was looking over his shoulder and laughing with his friends when his chest ran right into my rifle butt. He fell with a grunt and the bike toppled over at the side of the road.

"Get up, you, whatever your name is," I said with as much venom as I could muster. "What the hell do you think you're doing? What kind of stupid trick is this?"

The private struggled up off the ground, but he was still trying to get his bearings. It took him a second to sort out what had happened. He looked back at his friends, who were still chuckling and grinning at him. Then he looked at me and snarled, "What's it to you?" Spite was written all over his face, and without looking at them directly I knew his fists were balled and ready.

I looked at him coldly and said, "There's not going to be any trouble here, private, so just calm down and give the old woman back her bike."

By now the young soldier had figured out that I wasn't an officer from his unit; in fact he could see from my shoulder patch that I wasn't even from the Ninth Division.

"Who the hell are you?" he asked sarcastically. He paused a second and said, "I was just playing a little, it don't hurt nothin'." He stuck his chin out and glared at me, defying me to do anything. I saw trouble written all over him, so I went immediately to the bottom line.

"I am an officer in the United States Army," I said harshly, "and I'm giving you a direct order. Pick up that bike and give it back to the old woman."

The private continued to glare at me. I didn't know what I was going to do next if he didn't respond. The men I had been out with on patrol were all standing behind me, but the glum look on their faces told me they didn't like this whole thing one little bit. The private glanced around at them, back at me, and said, "Shit!" He turned and went to pick up the bike. The old woman had already started to come over and get the bike herself, so the GI didn't really have to take it anywhere. When he picked it up he shoved it at the old woman out of anger and pure meanness.

"That's enough, Childers," said someone behind me. "Get on out of here before you get in real trouble." The speaker was an artillery lieutenant who had walked up from the direction of the American camp. Private Childers sneered at the old woman again as she tried to regain her balance on the bicycle, then he turned and cast an insolent gaze over this other officer and me.

"Move along," repeated the lieutenant as he nodded back toward the artillery revetments.

Young Private Childers walked over to his friends and the whole group ambled off, throwing us mutinous glares and muttering among themselves angrily.

"Are those guys yours?" I asked the lieutenant.

"Yeah, they're just bored."

I was nonplussed at his lackadaisical tone. "Don't you discipline people for acting like that? I haven't been around here but for a few days," I said with a tone of angry confusion, "but doesn't the Ninth have directives against screwing around with friendlies? Christ, you people must know this kind of shit gets you killed!"

"Calm down, you don't have to live here." The lieutenant had seen my MACV shoulder patch, too, and knew I wasn't from the Ninth Division.

"I don't have to live here to know that's not how to win the goddamned hearts and minds of the people!" I said with exasperated sarcasm. "That old woman is going to tell her whole fuckin' village we're all a bunch of assholes, and they're going to be all too glad to believe it! That damned private ought to be put up on charges!"

The artillery officer didn't say anything for a moment. He first looked down at the ground, then stared out into space somewhere off my right shoulder. Finally, he said, "You're right, there are directives against bothering the civilians. And I know this kind of crap causes us a lot of trouble. But it's unmanageable, we can't do anything about it."

"I don't know why the hell not," I said. "Reduce the bastards that do it, take their pay! What the hell happened to ordinary discipline?"

"Look," the lieutenant said, "we have enough trouble with our guys as it is. If we tried to charge every man that had a run-in with one of the locals we would just piss everybody off even more. Our guys would do even less than they are now! Believe me, these men just see *slopes*. They don't see good or bad, they just see slopes, and they don't like any of them. If I can get my guys to tolerate these people and maybe be nice to a few of them, I figure I'm ahead of the game. If I started handing out Article 15's just because a guy is a shithead and doesn't like the natives, I'd probably be fragged within a week."

I had heard of troops "fragging" their officers—disgruntled soldiers would throw a hand grenade into an officer's billet with the officer still in it—but I had never heard it come up in a serious conversation. I was a little taken aback to hear this lieutenant mention it so earnestly.

"I don't know what it's like where you're from," said the lieutenant, looking down at my shoulder patch, "but these guys are bored, nobody wants to be here, we got a morale problem you wouldn't believe, and none of us want to muddy the water more than we absolutely have to. Our guys read the newspapers. They resent being stuck over here to die for nothing."

I didn't know what to say. I had not spent any time in the field in Vietnam other than this week with the Ninth. The guys I had been going out with seemed normal enough, but I had only been with them while on patrol and when everything was intense and businesslike. I realized I didn't know what they were like while they were in camp. I didn't know what they talked about, what they liked, or what they hated. I really didn't know what it was like to be involved with the American army. The narrow glimpse I was getting here made it look like a sick army, and I was glad I wasn't going to have to be around it much longer. It wasn't that I didn't want to be with Americans, it was just that I didn't want to have to deal with all the problems those poor suckers were stuck with.

Finally I just shrugged and shook my head in resignation. "Well, it's your problem," I said. "It would be just too damned bad if that old woman's husband, or son, or brother ever decided to join the Cong to try and get through your wire so he could blow your ass to hell. It could be that people like your dumb-assed private there would provide most of the reason."

As an American who later lived with the Vietnamese people and who to some degree unavoidably "went native," I may have jaundiced views; but I have never recovered from the appalling view I got of the conduct of many of my countrymen toward the Vietnamese people. It is certainly true that my impression is based only on a limited number of observations since I did not normally work around large groups of Americans. Still, the observations were so consistent that the impression has stayed with me like an old sore. Every time I went back to areas where large numbers of GI's were stationed, I saw incidents of Vietnamese civilians being treated with contempt and disrespect. It was as true in Da Nang and Saigon as it was in Dong Tam and Can Tho. I was convinced it was a problem everywhere.

I do not claim that all American soldiers were mean, thoughtless louts who went around the countryside trashing the natives. I am sure most of them tried to do their difficult duty while preserving as much of the Vietnamese people's dignity as possible. Far too many, however, were harsh with their judgments, obvious in their contempt, and expressive of their dissatisfaction. Their attitudes were corrosive and terribly chilling to the ever-sputtering sense of cooperation between the natives and the American soldiery. As a result, I was often grateful later on that there were no American units in my district, or in the entire province for that matter. The increased firepower and scrounging grounds they might have offered would have been nice, but the effects of the GI's on the local population would have wrecked my own efforts at bringing some sort of peace and calm to my villages.

Chapter 2

T HE Huey helicopter's door gunner waved good-bye as it lifted away from the small dirt landing pad amidst a blowing cloud of dust and grit. I squeezed my eyes shut and leaned into the propwash, still too green to remember to hold on to my hat, no matter what. One hand gripped my M-16 and a bandolier of ammunition and the other held the strap of my duffle bag; the hat sailed off somewhere behind me. I couldn't even look to see where it went until the grit and sand stopped blowing in my face, but knowing my luck, I figured it had been blown into the large canal I had noticed nearby as we landed.

I opened my eyes when the grit stopped blowing and quickly took a look around me. A Vietnamese village stretched out behind me and a few people were standing in the single street looking curiously in my direction. In front of me were the earthen walls of a fort, and striding toward me was a tall, thin American dressed in a Vietnamese camouflage uniform with a blue Vietnamese beret perched jauntily on his head.

"Welcome to Tram Chim, Lieutenant," said the man with an easy southern accent. "I'm Sergeant Anderson." He stuck his hand out rather than salute.

"Thanks, Sergeant," I said as I reached for his hand. "I'm Lieutenant Donovan. I'd like to be able to say I'm glad to be here." We shook hands as we chuckled over my weak joke.

"Hey, Short Round," the sergeant yelled to someone over my shoulder, "go pull the lieutenant's hat out of the wire." I looked behind me and saw a small Vietnamese boy who had come up from the village scamper into the concertina wire to retrieve my hat. He had it in no time and brought it to me with a shy smile.

"Thanks" I said smiling at him. *"Tên yí, em?"* I said, asking his name.

"My name Short Round, *Trung úy*," said the boy, referring to my Vietnamese rank. His brown face was split by a large, white-toothed smile.

"He's one of the village kids we pay to run errands for us sometimes," said Anderson."He speaks pretty good English, too, just to have picked it up by hanging around."

We all stood there for a second without saying anything and just looked at each other. Short Round seemed to be awaiting other instructions and Sergeant Anderson just seemed to be waiting to see what I was going to do next.

I nodded toward the mud walls of the fort and said, "So that's home, huh?"

"Yes, sir, that's it," he said with a wry expression. He reached for my duffle bag and said, "Come on, let's go in and I'll show you the place. Everybody on the team is in today so the introductions will be quick and easy, too. See you later, Short Round." We both nodded good-bye to the youngster and walked toward the fort.

After we crossed a small bridge and passed through the fort walls, Sergeant Anderson led me to a hut in the center of the compound. It was a bastardized construction of plywood, palm thatch, and rusty old tin. A tall radio antenna at one corner was the only evidence of the twentieth century I could see. As we approached the hooch another American came to the door and leaned against the frame. He was wearing rubber sandals and a pair of jungle fatigue pants, but his thin upper body was shirtless. He wasn't just thin, he was gaunt. He squinted out at me in the bright tropical sunlight and I sensed the instant appraisal that was going on in his head.

"Captain Jackson," said Sergeant Anderson as we approached, "this is Lieutenant Donovan. The chopper just dropped him off."

Captain Jackson, whose name I recognized as being that of my new commanding officer, didn't bother to come out into the sunlight. He waited until I got up to him before he stuck out his hand.

"Welcome to Dong Tien District and Team 32, Lieutenant," he said matter-of-factly. He turned his head and called back into the hut, "Hey, team. Guess what just came in off the chopper?"

"What?" asked a disinterested voice from within.

"Fresh meat," said Jackson.

SOUTH VIETNAM WAS MADE UP OF FORTY-TWO PROVINCES, each of which had assigned to it a large American "Province Advisory Team." The province team had all sorts of military and civilian advisors assigned to it and was usually headed by an army colonel—the Province Senior Advisor, or PSA in army parlance. Provinces were made up of districts. Each district had a District Senior Advisor, usually an army major or captain. The DSA's led the smaller district teams, which usually lived out in the district towns or villages. Each province team also had several five-man Mobile Advisory Teams assigned to it. These MAT's, or MAT teams as they were redundantly called, lived out in the villages and hamlets with the Vietnamese people and tried to help them directly with both military and civic problems. The mission of the MAT teams fell under the rubric of the CORDS program, Civil Operations and Revolutionary Development Support.

The MAT teams were similar in many ways to the more publicized "A-teams" of the Special Forces, but with only half the men and almost none of the money and equipment. MAT teams consisted of two combat arms officers (meaning officers whose specialty branch was infantry, armor, or artillery) trained at the Special Warfare School plus three experienced noncommissioned officers who were, respectively, a light weapons specialist, a heavy weapons specialist, and a medic. I was on a MAT team. I had been assigned as assistant team leader, MAT 32, Tram Chim village, Dong Tien district, Kien Phong province, Republic of Vietnam.

Dong Tien district was bordered on the west by the wide, mud-hued Mekong River. A few kilometers to our north was the Cambodian border, and the district stretched eastward out over the vast flatlands known as the Plain of Reeds. I had seen the broad stretches of grassland and jungle as I flew out in the helicopter. The plains reached away as far as the eye could see. The verdant tableland was crosshatched with a seemingly random array of canals and ditches, each reflecting the sunlight like silvery threads against a green mantle.

Small hamlets and villages were scattered here and there, and dark green patches of jungle broke the monotony of the grassy savannah. Dong Tien district was far from the major centers of attention in Vietnam, and Tram Chim village was literally in the middle of nowhere. The nearest American ground combat units were at least a hundred miles away. It seemed to me that many well-worn phrases accurately described the place: the back of beyond, the outer limits, east hell, or when I was feeling especially glum, even that over-used expression, the heart of darkness.

CAPTAIN JACKSON MOVED TO ONE SIDE AS SERGEANT ANDERson and I dragged my gear into the team house. "Come on, Lieutenant," Anderson said, "I'll show you your bunk and then give you the nickel tour of this joint." I dropped my pack and rifle on the bunk where Anderson had thrown my duffle bag. All the bunks were together in a small room filled with a disorganized-looking assortment of personal gear and paraphernalia. I followed Sergeant Anderson back out into the larger common room of the team house and was introduced to the rest of the team.

An older-looking fellow, tall, sandy haired, and wearing only black pajama bottoms, strode over from where he had been cleaning his rifle and shook hands. "I'm Sergeant First Class Chambers, sir. Walter F. I'm the heavy weapons man."

"Glad to meet you, Sergeant," I said, shaking hands. "Where are you from in the States?"

"Alabama, sir. And I'm short, too," he said with a grin. "In three months I'm Alabammy bound!" He chuckled as he folded his arms over his chest and rocked back on his heels. "I retire then, too. I'll have twenty-two years in and I'm not plannin' to make any more visits to Southeast Asia. It's bad for an old man's health, I hear."

A black man came out of the small room that served as a kitchen for the team house. He walked over and introduced himself with a faint smile on his lips and welcome written in his eyes.

"I'm Master Sergeant Herbert Watson, sir. I'm the team medic. Unfortunately, I'm not short at all. Welcome to the team."

"Thanks, Sergeant," I said as we shook hands. "Where're you from?"

"South Carolina, sir," said Watson. "And you?"

"Georgia," I said.

"Georgia!" said Sergeant Anderson. "Well, I'll be damned. I'm from Georgia, too!"

I laughed. "Well, you never know where another Cracker is going to turn up, do you? Where in Georgia?"

"Cordele. My wife and kids are there right now waiting for daddy to come home."

"Crackers, palmettos, and sandspurs! Is that all I can get on this team?" asked Captain Jackson from the doorway. He rolled eyes in mock exasperation. "Aren't there any bonafide Yankees left in this army anymore? What's a boy from downstate New York supposed to do?"

"Come on, Lieutenant," said Sergeant Anderson. "Let's leave the man in his misery and I'll show you the rest of the place."

Captain Jackson grinned and said to Anderson, "Don't show him the sauna and the tennis courts just yet—he might get the wrong idea about the kind of place this is."

"Oh, don't worry, *Dại úy*," said Anderson, dropping in the Vietnamese word for "captain." "I won't show any of the good stuff!" He laughed as he turned and signaled to me to follow him. We walked out to the middle of the sun-baked compound and stopped. "Well, Lieutenant, this is home," said Anderson as he gestured toward the walls around us.

I looked around. We were standing by a large sandbagged mortar pit which looked in considerable need of repair. In front of the pit were two palm-thatch huts and off to our left was another. Beyond these small buildings were the walls of the fort. They were made of packed earth which had been turned to a concrete hardness by the constant baking of the tropical sun. The fort was constructed in the shape of a triangle and on each of its points was perched a small tin-covered guard post. I wondered who was stationed here besides the MAT team. "What are the hooches for?" I asked.

"Those two are the troop barracks for the Popular Forces

assigned to the compound," said Anderson, pointing to the two hooches in front of us. "This one"—he nodded to the hut off to our left—"is the headquarters hut for the district chief. You won't see anybody stirring in there right now because it's siesta time." He was right. I didn't see any activity except the slow fanning movement of a single man in one of the little guardhouses on the wall.

I knew that it was the habit of the Vietnamese not to work or even fight in the heat of midday unless they could absolutely not avoid it. I could feel the reason why. It was two o'clock in the afternoon and the sun beat down mercilessly on the dry, packed earth. There was no shade in the compound outside the buildings, and even in the buildings the air was still and calm. The oven-hot air hovered over the ground like a suffocating blanket. There was no electricity to power any fans, let alone air conditioners, and I could tell that just trying to think cool was going to become a major pastime.

"Come on," said Anderson, "let's go up on the wall and look around." We walked over to the nearest wall and climbed up on the knee-high ledge that allowed us to look over the top. The top of the wall was only about chest high to Anderson and me, so we climbed up on it and stood looking over the interior of the compound. Beyond the opposite wall of the fort and some one hundred yards distant I could see the first hooches of Tram Chim village. Just outside the wall was the helipad where I had landed. The fort was built right on the edge of the Dong Tien canal, the major water "highway" through the district. The other two walls were bordered by a moat filled with barbed wire "tanglefoot" and punji stakes, sharpened bamboo spikes that would impale any foot or body that fell upon them. Beyond the moat was another encirclement of concertina wire, a form of loosely coiled barbed wire. The only way to get across the moat was over a small bridge made of pierced steel planking that Anderson and I had walked over to get into the fort. There was a small break in the canalside wall, too. Through it you could go down to a short dock that stuck out into the big canal. Each wall of the fort was about fifty yards long, enclosing an area about half an acre in size. The only thing in the compound that offered relief to its barren, parched appearance was a large white statue of the Virgin Mary. I didn't know who had put it there and kept it clean, but they also had green plants growing all around its base. An interesting touch for an army post, I thought.

I let my eyes rove over the compound for a while and suddenly realized something was missing. "Where does a guy go for a shit and a shower around here?" I asked. I saw neither latrines nor makeshift shower stall.

"Right now we bathe in the canal with the natives. We're supposed to be getting in some lumber and a fifty-gallon drum to make a shower stall with, though. God, I'll be glad for that!" He said with a tone of disgust, "You don't know what kind of grunge will get you in that canal."

"What do you use for a latrine?"

"Well, we can't dig a pit. It would flood over during the rainy season, and our water table is just a foot or two underground anyway." Anderson pointed off to our right and said, "Just behind the team house over there are the shit cans. We take fifty-gallon oil drums and blow them in half with detcord. Build a wooden cover for it that has a hole to sit over and you have a shit can. Every week one of us has to take the cover off, pour in the kerosene and torch the shit. We rotate the duty," he said eyeing me carefully, "officers included." He drew in a deep breath through expanded nostrils and said, "I don't think you'll care for the duty, if you get my drift."

"Great," I said flatly. I turned away from the compound and looked out over the wall behind me. The flat plains extended to dense tree lines in the distance, but the nearer expanses of land consisted of rice paddies and some fields with other crops. "Is everybody in the village a farmer?" I asked, wondering how they worked in this muggy heat year-round.

"Either that or a fisherman, or both," said Anderson. "It looks flat and dry around here now, but just wait a few months. This whole place will be underwater come October. Then everybody's a fisherman."

I looked back over at the team house and pointed to the tall radio antenna beside it. "Does that two-niner-two keep us in contact with province headquarters pretty well?"

"It's spotty," said Anderson. "Late at night we can usually talk to province, but sometimes we can't get through to anybody, anywhere. The district team at Tan An is about fifteen miles away and sometimes they can relay messages out to us that we can't pick up from province. We've got two Prick-

25's, so we keep one hooked to the antenna and use the other on our operations."

PRC (pronounced Prick)-25 radios were the small backpack field radios used by army companies and platoons to communicate with each other. The communication range was limited and the radios required a fresh battery every twenty-four hours. I wondered how we talked with anybody on that radio way out here; where did we get the batteries; how often were we without any communications at all? A dozen questions came to mind just about radios. I realized already they were going to be a vital lifeline requiring some care and attention.

"We get a chopper out about once a week, too," volunteered Anderson. "It's called the 'swing ship' because it makes one swing around the province and then it's gone. It will bring out folks like you, our mail, our supplies, and, unfortunately, the colonel every once in a while."

I was about to ask about the colonel when I heard Captain Jackson yell from the team house, "Hey, Andy! Bring him on back. I want to brief him myself before you get him all screwed up!"

"Well, you've about seen everything there is to see from up here, anyway," said Anderson as he climbed down from the wall. "Come on down. Captain Jack wants to fill you in." I climbed down from the wall and walked back to the team house with Sergeant Anderson. When we walked inside, Captain Jackson was standing in the doorway to the kitchen.

"Come on in the kitchen, Lieutenant. The only decent table we've got is in here and I can spread out some maps and show you what's going on."

We walked into the small room where Jackson already had a map spread out on the table in the center. I noticed that the so-called kitchen had one propane gas-powered refrigerator, the only nonmilitary twentieth-century convenience I had yet seen, and a small bench with two kerosene camp stoves. Some shelves on one side held cans of food and condiments and two old-fashioned kerosene lamps. Jackson tapped on the map with his finger. "You can see that Tram Chim is right in the middle of Dong Tien district. All of our major hamlets are located along the Dong Tien canal here." I watched intently as his finger traced along the straight blue line running across the green and white map. "Or along this branch canal that comes in right out there in front of the compound."

"What's the population here?" I asked as I gazed down at the map.

"Something over thirty thousand in the whole district. Most of them are farmers and fishermen, but you'll find a few shop-keepers in each village, too. You'll see soon enough that life is pretty primitive out here for most of these people. Subsistence living plus a little cash from growing rice or fishing is about all that most people look for."

"Any Americans around besides us?"

"Not in this district," said Jackson, "but there is a district team down at Tan An, about fifteen or twenty miles away as the crow flies. We officially operate under them because Dong Tien doesn't even have a district team. This MAT team is the first group of Americans these people out here have ever had around on a steady basis."

"Do we ever go to see the folks at Tan An?" I asked hopefully.

"Once in a blue moon the DSA from down there will risk trying to get up here by road, but none of us have ever been down there."

"Oh," I said, trying desperately not to think of this place as the end of the earth.

"Don't think we're completely isolated," said Jackson, smiling. He pointed again to the map. "The canal taps into the Mekong here at An Long. The U.S. Navy has a converted LST, the USS *Benewa*, stationed upriver close to Hong Ngu. She's a base ship for what the navals call the 'brown-water navy.' They operate these river patrol boats, or PBR's, all up and down the Mekong. Sometimes they'll come up into the major canals like ours if we ask them to and help us set up ambushes, or ferry troops, or"—and he spoke with more expression now—"sometimes even bring us some decent food from the ship's galley." He nodded meaningfully toward the sparsely stocked shelves in the team kitchen. "You'll find that getting food through army channels isn't easy."

Jackson went on. "Each PBR has four or five men on board and they usually come in groups of two or three boats, so sometimes we might get to see as many as ten or twelve Americans at one time. Hell," he said, grinning, "if it weren't for the navy you'd think we were in this thing by ourselves."

"Do we get much help from the province team?" I asked, thinking of the well-kept compound I had seen back in Cao Lanh, the province capital. There were two hundred or so Americans there, and they had a compound with running water, electricity, and even an air-conditioned clubhouse to sit around in and shoot the bull.

"Are you kidding?" Jackson laughed. "Those guys are thirty miles away and every one of them is just sitting in an office. All they want is their reports coming in on time. We've been dropped out here to run our own little war, and they expect us simply to survive the best way we can." Jackson leaned across the table as he balanced on his knuckles and said, "Out here you have to get up every day and just do what you think's best. Never look back. Too much thinking can get you killed."

With those last comments Jackson suddenly seemed very intense, almost angry. He stared at me with a look that seemed to challenge me to gainsay him. Uncomfortable, I turned from the table covered with maps and documents and walked over to a window at the back of the kitchen. I stared outside toward the rear of the compound for a while, waiting for him to say something else. When he didn't I turned back to him and asked a question that was one of many on my mind. "What about the local VC? Do you get much trouble out of them?"

"Ah," said Jackson as he rocked back on his heels, "the brave men and women of the National Liberation Front." He paused for a moment and stroked his chin as if trying to think of what to say. "Well, as you know the Viet Cong are run out of the so-called Central Office for South Vietnam, or COSVN. From there the North Vietnamese and the NLF oversee, and to varying degrees direct, local VC activity. The Cong have a District Mobile Company in this district, and they seem to have pretty good communications with the North Vietnamese Army units over in Cambodia and with COSVN, probably through their contact with the NVA."

"But what about activity?" I asked. "Do you get very many attacks or tax squads, or press gangs?"

"It seems to run in cycles," said Jackson. "We'll go through a flurry of attacks for a while, then they will lie low and we would never see them if we didn't go hunting for them."

"Why is that?"

"It seems that one of the main missions of the local VC is to make a way for the NVA and larger Viet Cong units to slip through here from Cambodia and to get deeper into the country. When they're busy doing that they don't want to stir up the water by getting us mad at them. When the traffic-cop job eases up they start up the attacks again."

"We were told back in the States that the quality of local Cong units varies a lot. Are these guys any good?"

"I think the local leaders are pretty damned good," said Jackson with a grudging grin. "The local bosses come across as true believers, at least according to our intel reports. I think they know the grand plan from Hanoi and I think they think of themselves as dedicated communists. The local VC grunts, though, I don't know. I'm not sure most of them could tell a communist from a fascist. Two of the VC local force squads, for example, one up here by Khu 12"—Jackson pointed to one of the northernmost hamlets on the map—"and one that operates here out of An Long are more like bandit gangs and ne'er-do-wells than bands of guerrilla fighters."

Sergeant Chambers walked into the kitchen and began stirring around by the kerosene camp stoves. "Want a cup of coffee?" he asked as he lit one of the oven eyes.

"Sure," I said, surprised that such an amenity existed.

"Tell the *Trung úy* what your assessment is of the local VC while you diddle around over your makings," said Jackson.

"Well," said Chambers as he continued to try to get the lid off his olive-drab coffee can, "the District Mobile Company is a bunch of slick little bastards. And they don't give a goddamn what they do. They'll rob a bunch of folks here and shoot a bunch of folks there, and generally stir up trouble where they can, but they're hard as hell to catch when they do it. They travel light and can kick your ass if you aren't careful! I don't know how much they know about Ho Chi Minh or being a commie, but I do know they want to change the government in Saigon and they want the Americans out of the country. They ain't above murder and terror to get the job done, either."

Chambers paused to sniff the coffee grounds before he continued with a chuckle, "Shit! The NLF says they would like to have an election if it would be free and fair. That'll be the day! Those government boys in Saigon are afraid of fair elections and the Cong are afraid of any kind of election at all! They run their politics at the end of a gun barrel, at least that's all I've seen around here."

"We have NVA to worry about too," broke in Jackson. "One of our main activities is supposed to be 'border interdiction.' There are two regiments of North Vietnamese Army just over the border in Cambodia. They and some Main Force Cong units operate out of a sanctuary area over there. They are constantly trying to move back and forth across the border. If we can catch them coming into the country through our district we're supposed to slow them up as best we can and let the big units deeper in the country know what enemy traffic might be coming. They don't expect us to stop major units with our PF platoons, but they want us to let them know when something big is coming through. The major way we try to slow the traffic down or to force it out of our district is to hunt down the local VC units. When we screw up their operations it makes life difficult for the boys across the border."

"And have you been successful?"

"It comes and goes," said Jackson. "The major routes the Cong and NVA use to get through the district are here along the district border where the jungle is thick, and here in the middle of the district where they get a straight shot to the interior on a good, fast canal system." Jackson traced the routes on the map. "We know they use these areas, so that's where we spend a lot of time on ambush operations. When we get lucky and make some good contacts they ease off for a while or try to shift to some other traffic pattern. We stay busy just trying to keep up with where they might be trying to come through next."

"And what about the VCI?" I asked. "Does there appear to be a full local complement? Is there really a local 'shadow government'?"

"In some of our villages the Viet Cong Infrastructure is more intense than in others," replied Jackson. "We try to keep an information net in each hamlet and to use the Phoenix program when we can to locate and isolate the VCI. I know there is supposed to be a VCI for every government official, and that they are supposedly just waiting for 'liberation' to walk in and take over the government jobs, but I think we do pretty well at keeping them on the run.'' He paused for a moment. ''You never know, though. That's the thing, you never know. The most friendly guy in town may be the VCI village chief. What it really means is that you can't trust anybody!''

Sergeant Chambers had his water boiling and was now rattling around in the corner trying to find another coffee cup. Sergeant Anderson came through the door and asked, ''Do I smell coffee?''

''Yeah,'' replied Chambers, ''but you can't have any unless we find another cup.'' Both men started looking around the nooks and crannies in the kitchen.

''So how does the team spend most of its time?'' I asked Jackson, nodding toward the two men.

''We go about fifty-fifty, I think. The military assistance part of what we do consists of training the villagers in small-unit tactics, ambush operations, and village defense. In short, we're just trying to teach them to defend themselves against the Cong. Most of our civil affairs effort is spent in just trying to get the village chiefs and their cronies to understand what a bureaucracy is! A lot of these guys are practically illiterate. It's hard to get across the idea that filling out forms is simply a part of life in a modern government. The village leaders are often old folks, they are fishermen and farmers, and they just aren't form-filling-out kind of people. We try to get across the message that if the forms aren't filled out and if requests aren't made, then the schoolteachers won't come, the health clinics won't get supplies, the roads won't be repaired, and so forth.''

''Do they really get help if they do fill out the forms?'' I asked, remembering that the central government didn't have a good reputation for meeting the needs of the rural areas.

''Well, that's another problem. Our chiefs aren't too interested in going to a lot of trouble to ask for help when they know from past experience that Saigon doesn't give a damn about them anyway. I can tell you this from considerable observation, Donovan: the people in this district don't give a damn for the Saigon government because that government never does anything for them. The Viet Cong thrive off of Saigon fuck-ups.''

* * *

THE INITIAL BRIEFING JACKSON GAVE ME MUST HAVE GONE on for two hours or more. I had hardly had time to catch my breath since I stepped off the chopper and I felt my brain would turn to Silly Putty if he showed me another document or warned me about yet another problem I was sure to encounter. Toward the end nothing was sinking in. I must have had that glassy-eyed look of the drifting student because Jackson looked up at me and stopped cold in the middle of an explanation about how we got schoolteachers. "I guess you've had about enough of this for the time being," he said agreeably. "There's a lot here to absorb and you'll just have to live with it for a while before it starts to come clear."

"Yes, sir," I said, trying to clear the fog from my mind. "I think I'll catch on to it all after I've been around awhile."

"I tell you what," said Jackson as he pushed back from the table where he had been sitting, "let me suit up and grab my rifle and we'll take a walk down to the village before it gets dark. At least I can show you the local landmarks and you can see what kind of people we're living with."

"Sounds good to me," I replied. I was grateful for the chance to get outside and do anything besides listen to more details, details, details. I was anxious to look around outside the fort, too, so I followed the captain from the room and waited anxiously while he put on his fatigue shirt and jungle boots. He grabbed his hat and his M-16, and as he headed for the door he said, "Bring your rifle, *Trung úy*. It's policy to never leave the compound without a weapon. You never know what will happen out there."

I went over to my bunk and picked up my M-16 and a bandolier of ammo. Jackson was already walking out into the compound so I hurried after him, feeling stupid trying to trot along after him, sling arms, and get the bandolier of ammo over my neck at the same time.

I caught up with Jackson out in the compound and we walked on out together. The village-side gate was the terminus of a small dirt road that ran down to the village. The first of the village hooches were about a hundred yards or so from the fort and I could see that the road ran on into the village and formed what was apparently the main drag through town. It was a straight road, and for as far as I could see small houses made of grass and thatch were jammed in next to each other on either side of the street. The hooches on the right-hand side of the road were squeezed in between the road at their front door and the canal at their back. Many of these hooches had back porches over the water with a small sampan or two tied up to the wooden stilt pilings.

"Doesn't look like much from here, does it?" asked Jackson as we walked toward the village.

"You mean it looks better up close?"

"Worse," he said abruptly. "This road runs all the way through the village, I guess maybe three-quarters of a mile or so, with these hooches stacked in on either side. Practically all of them are made of bamboo and grass; and you'll see a lot of them in pretty poor repair, too. Down in the center of the village where the market is there are a few shops and houses made of masonry block, but they belong to the village big boys. The Catholic church and school are permanent structures, too, but that's about all we can boast in the way of construction."

"How many people live in the village?" I asked.

"Oh, I guess between four and five thousand. Most of the hamlets along the canal here have fewer than that, but we draw a bigger crowd because the school, church, and district headquarters are here. That's not many people for a small town, you might think, but there are big problems here with public health. All these hooches are concentrated together like this and everybody shits and pisses in the canal. Then they go and bathe and brush their teeth in it. I guess that bothers me a lot right now because we're having to do the same thing until we can get the supplies to build our shower stall."

As we walked into the village itself I could see the poor condition of many of the hooches. Worn and unrepaired thatchwork left holes in the sides of some huts. Army ponchos seemed to be the universal repair kit for these holes, and some houses had two or three ponchos stretched across a side or over the roof. Poverty was evident in other ways. Kids playing in the street were often clad in worn and torn shirts, adults were dressed in simple peasant "pajamas," and an occasional cyclo or small motorbike was the upper limit of conspicuous consumption.

I was impressed with the villagers in spite of the poverty

they lived in. They were an attractive people; the kids were cute, and many of the young women were Oriental beauties. Everyone seemed friendly, too. Men, women, and children smiled and stared at us as we walked down the street. Many of them spoke politely to Captain Jackson, the kids running along beside us, gawking at me. I supposed it was because I was the new American in town, so I smiled and tried to make a good impression.

"It'll take you a while to get used to the people," said Jackson as we strolled down the street. "For the most part we're all pretty friendly with each other and get along well. You'll find that they are curious as hell about everything we do, but in general they are quiet and courteous people. They don't have much, but they are hospitable with what they've got.

"You might be amazed at how well they get along without any of the modern conveniences that we take for granted in the States. Look around—you won't see any water spigots or flush toilets. There's no running water. See any wires? There's no electricity. No cars, either. No social services, and damned little medical care or education. Hell, most of these people have never been fifty miles from home. Some of them have never been out of the district! As a rule they have few interests in common with folks in Saigon or Hue, and the bureaucrats in those places are still trying to figure out how to deal with people out here. I don't know what will come of it all."

As we walked down the village street I saw pigs, chickens, ducks, and an occasional dog walking around freely in the street, rooting and pecking here and there for a bite to eat. I stared at a sow as she strolled into one of the dirt-floored hooches as if she owned it. Jackson laughed at my look of consternation. "Nature's vacuum cleaners," he said. "They keep the place cleaned up."

"Yeah," I replied, "but who cleans up after them?"

"That's another problem, but here you can eventually eat the janitor. There's something to be said for that!"

When we got to the center of the village Jackson showed me the market. "This is the only significant thing the government has ever done out here that I'm aware of." He pointed to a large open-air structure. It was essentially a rectangular concrete pad with a tin roof supported by simple concrete pillars. The whole thing was probably seventy-five yards long by twenty-five yards wide and was filled with people selling food and wares of all kinds. As we walked by the stalls people nodded and spoke pleasantly. There were stalls with shoes and sandals, simple shirt and pants outfits, vegetables, live chickens and ducks, and freshly caught fish, shrimp, snakes, and turtles. In one of the stalls a man was selling huge gray rats. They looked like wharf rats to me, and they were apparently freshly caught and killed.

"Don't tell me," I said, "the rats are a local delicacy, right?"

"No, they're a staple. They grow by the thousands out in the rice paddies, so the men trap them. They are a common meat source around here. It's like country folks back home eating the squirrels or rabbits they hunt."

"I can't wait," I said, glaring suspiciously at the string of dead rats.

"You won't have to," said Jackson, "I think Sergeant Watson is cooking tonight. He told me earlier that the ration was rats and U.S. government snap beans. That and a little chlorinated water to wash it down with will show you the absolute finest in our cuisine." Jackson laughed out loud as he turned and headed back in the direction of the fort. I smiled weakly as I strode to catch up with him.

As we walked back I saw other things to ask about. Large mats of open-weave bamboo were laid out in the sun for the drying and salting of fish and rat carcasses. Large crockery pots were pushed under the eaves of houses and were used for the storage of salt and dried fish and rats. Every hooch had at least one small sampan drawn up by it. Sometimes a house on the canal side of the road would have four or five pulled up under it. I guessed that some of these belonged to neighbors across the street who didn't have "beachfront" property.

"It looks like everybody and his brother has a sampan," I said.

"Yep. You'll see an occasional motorbike around here, but they aren't much transportation once the road is flooded. This road is the only one in the district, by the way. It runs along the canal all the way to the Mekong, where it joins Route Four. That's supposed to be an international highway connecting Saigon and Phnom Penh, but out here it's more like a country lane than a highway. Anyway, our road here is flooded over most years during the flood season and you can't go anywhere if you're depending on wheels. The only year-round mode of transportation is by water. Anybody who really needs to get around has got to have a sampan. You'll see everybody from little children to old folks poling these little skiffs along the canal.''

"Do we travel by sampan, too?''

"Sometimes. You'll learn to hate them with a passion, believe me. We're just too big for most of those little boats and it kills you to sit frozen in one all day for fear of turning it over. It makes me ache just to think about it.''

Jackson was just a fount of welcome information. I decided to stop asking questions. I had heard hundreds, maybe thousands of small bits of information this one afternoon, and little of it made me glad to be here. I needed time to digest it all, to think about the sights and sounds of this new place. I was close to being overwhelmed by the strangeness, and I wanted to get my feet under me before I went on to learning more.

Captain Jackson and I returned to the compound without much further comment. It was close to dark when we got back to the team house and Watson was indeed cooking the evening chow. Jackson had been right: it was rats and green beans. The rats were chopped up Oriental-style and braised in oil and some kind of flavoring sauce. I took my first bite with caution, but it was actually good! By the end of the meal there wasn't a bit of rat left on anybody's plate.

As darkness fell one of the men went around and lit the kerosene lanterns. There was one glowing in the kitchen, one by the radio, and one in the common room. Sergeant Anderson pointed out that any room with a lit lantern had to have its doors and windows blacked out. "We usually just hang a poncho over the window or door," he said. "That seems to work well enough. It blocks the breeze, though, and it gets hot in here pretty quick most nights, so when you leave a room for the night and no one needs the light anymore, turn it off and take down the poncho. We need the air."

Not long after dark everyone but Anderson was climbing into his bunk. Sergeant Chambers threw me a can of insecticide spray. "Let your mosquito net down, then spray inside it with this. That will kill everything you have trapped inside.

Then just be careful when you crawl under the netting to get in the bunk. Sooner or later you'll learn to get in and out without letting any blood-suckers in with you.''

I thanked him for the advice. I had already sprayed myself with insect repellent, but it wasn't having much effect. Immediately after dark the air had come alive with mosquitoes, moths, and at least a dozen other kinds of pesky insects. The bugs swarmed around the lamps, and if you were sitting by one to read or write they crawled into your hair, flew down your shirt collar, and even got into your mouth. The mosquitoes were the worst. I counted twenty-four dining on my arms in spite of the thick spray of repellent I had just applied. Swatting at them brought no relief; for every one that moved off two more dove in for their try at a capillary.

I slid cautiously under my mosquito netting and lay back in my bunk. Sergeant Anderson was out in the common room on radio watch; the others were in the bunk room going to sleep. "It's early to bed, early to rise out here, *Trung úy*," offered Sergeant Chambers from across the room. "There ain't a hell of a lot to do for entertainment, anyway, so you might as well get the sleep while you can."

"That's right," said Jackson from the bunk above me. "Get the sleep while you can. It's a rare night we are all here in the compound at the same time."

I lay quietly in my bunk. I thought briefly of home and family, but I cut the thought short. Thinking of home made me feel worse for being so far away. I listened in the black quietness and could hear only the breathing of my teammates. I got some satisfaction from the fact that there seemed to be no mosquitoes inside my net with me. There were no mosquitoes, but there was also no air moving through the fine netting to relieve the muggy heat. Light breezes simply don't move through a mosquito net, so you just have to lie there and suffer the fevered air.

I had had a long day, so despite my discomfort I began to drift off to sleep. The bunk above me suddenly squeaked and Captain Jackson leaned out over the edge of his bunk. I could barely make out his face in the darkness, but I heard him whisper softly, "The rats around here are night scroungers and they get pretty brave. If one runs across your chest, don't jerk. They'll bite the shit out of you."

"Rats?" I protested. "They can't get inside the mosquito netting."

"Just wait," whispered Jackson. "They'll gnaw their way through."

I don't think I slept an hour the whole night.

Chapter 3

I HAD been in Tram Chim for two days, mostly learning how to avoid heatstroke, how to bathe in a canal while standing shin-deep in bottom slime, and other assorted aspects of camp life in the tropics. Late in the afternoon I was sitting in the common room of the team house trying to memorize the Signal Operating Instructions handbook. The booklet contained all our current radio code designations and I needed to know them in order to know whom I was talking to on the radio. Captain Jackson, or "Captain Jack" as everyone called him, leaned out through the kitchen door and said, "*Trung úy,* come on in here. You've got your first operation tomorrow."

My stomach lurched as I stood up. My first operation on the team. Dozens of questions flashed through my mind, refusing to wait the few minutes for Jackson to lay everything out. I wondered who I would be going out with, where in the district we would be going, what the purpose of the operation would be. I walked into the kitchen and saw that the maps were again spread out on the table.

"You'll be taking out the Tram Chim PF platoon on a search and destroy back into these sanctuary areas," said Jackson, pointing to a wooded area on the district border directly south of the village. "Don't worry, it's the simplest part of a three-part operation. You've also got a good platoon there. They have a good platoon leader, so if you listen to him you should stay out of trouble. Don't try to give too much advice on these first operations, Dave. Just watch how they do things and get the feel of the territory.''

He pointed to the map again. ''Sergeant Anderson and I will go out with the Regional Forces company and swing off to the left here and sweep from east to west. Your platoon will essentially be in a blocking position in case we flush something up. You'll be there if they try the old trick of running along the district boundary lines.''

I stared at the map and tried to take in all the specifics of the pincer operation he had wax-penciled on the map grid. I tried to sound positive when I spoke. ''Yes, sir. I've got to get started sometime, so I guess this is as good a time as any. Who's going with me?''

''From the team?'' asked Jackson without looking up. ''Nobody. Chambers will stay here to man the radio and to watch the compound. Watson is going to stay with the Vietnamese headquarters unit to help the Viet medics in case we take casualties. Yours is the shortest part of the operation, so I imagine you can handle it alone.''

''Dai úy,'' I said nervously, ''this is my first operation out here. I don't know these troops and they don't know me. I think I should have someone with me in case we get into trouble!'' I was more than a little shaken by the prospect of going out alone, especially on my first operation. I had always been told it was stated policy and just good common sense to always send men out in pairs. That way a man always had a partner to rely on if things got hot. A seriously wounded man can't call in his own medevac and he can't coordinate tactical air support, and there was always the fear of an American being left behind by panicked native troops. I didn't like this at all.

''There's nobody to spare, Dave,'' said Jackson as if he were explaining simple math to a first-grader. I stared at the map, trying to think of something to say, something rational that would deliver me from this fix. I couldn't do it, though. My Southern upbringing and all my military training screamed against arguing with the authority or, perhaps even more, letting it appear that I was too afraid to take on an appointed task. I nodded my head glumly and said, ''Yes, sir.'' I left the room, concerned not only for myself, but about Captain Jackson. If this was an example of his decision-making, I wondered how he made other decisions, and if I was going to think they were as bad.

Later in the afternoon Sergeant Chambers and I were sitting on the wall of the fort after having checked the Claymore mines scattered in the barbed wire tanglefoot. Chambers picked at his teeth with a stick as he spoke. "I hear you pulled a solo for tomorrow."

"Yeah, it looks like it," I replied.

"It's not the first time, *Trung úy*. The *Dai úy* has a medal on his mind and he pushes pretty hard sometimes. He's getting short and he thinks he needs a Bronze Star, at least. He's a Pointer, you know. He wants in for a career and he's got to get his ticket punched."

I squinted as I stared out across the compound. I said nothing for a moment, not knowing if I should acknowledge the complaint or not. "I don't see how sending me out alone has got anything to do with him getting a medal," I said flatly.

"We're not supposed to use these troops like he does sometimes. He'll pull a lot of PF platoons and the RF company together in a battalion-size operation with all of us spread out all by ourselves. These PF's and RF's aren't trained for that. Captain Jack is supposed to coordinate big operations with province so we can get the help of an ARVN unit or two. He won't do it because he keeps hoping he will catch the local Cong off guard and really clean up. If that happens he wants all the glory for old number one. At least that's what me and the guys think."

"Aw, it can't be that bad, Sarge," I said, forcing a grin. "He seems pretty straight to me so far. He just figures this operation tomorrow is going to be a dry run and I won't be needed for anything but walking anyway." We left it at that and walked on back to the team house. It nagged at me, though, that the men seemed to have such a bad opinion of Jackson.

I knew the RF's and PF's were of limited value for big offensive operations. The RF's and PF's, or Regional Forces and Popular Forces, were the two types of local militia we worked with. The RF's were organized in company strength and were used all over the district, whereas the PF's were organized by platoons and generally were to be used only in their village area. I wondered if it was true that Jackson was overreaching with these poorly equipped troops. My teammates were senior NCO's, and I had always kept myself safe and on the right track by listening to experienced noncoms. These guys were saying that our captain, our *dại úy*, was on the verge of becoming a loose cannon. It made me very nervous.

Early the next morning I met with my PF platoon at the edge of the village. The platoon leader and I discussed the operation for the day and decided on the line of march and the estimated time to each checkpoint. Jackson and Anderson joined up with the RF company and struck off on their part of the operation. It took about two hours of steady walking across the plains and canals to get into the thick tree lines along our district border. We took up our positions and waited for the RF company to come up or for them to flush some Viet Cong in our direction.

We had been in position for two hours. My PF platoon was spread out along a tree line that faced a large open meadow. A canal ran through our position and that was the escape route we were supposed to be blocking. I could talk with Chambers back at the team house by radio, but I could never get Jackson up on the net. Chambers relayed to me what information he had about the RF company movement, but he didn't really know where they were either. As noon approached, boredom and hunger began gnawing at my attention. I became drowsy sitting there in the brush with my back propped up against a big tree. I was about to stand up to keep from snoozing off when I heard the rapid spatter of an automatic weapon out to our front. It couldn't have been over a hundred yards away. I gripped my M-16 and rolled over on the ground, facing our front.

Suddenly they were on us. They hit our left flank first, so they must have come up the tree line from that direction. There was a heavy barrage of gunfire and two or three loud explosions all within about fifteen seconds' time. I looked toward the gunfire, but could see nothing through the thick vegetation. I heard the platoon leader shouting to some of his men to move over there and give some support to the left flank. Two Vietnamese militiamen ran behind me toward the fighting. I turned to follow but when I got up I could see only one of the men dancing through the bushes. The automatic weapons fire seemed constant and all around us. Suddenly the man in front of me jerked and stumbled forward as if he had caught his foot on something. When he fell he lay completely still. I immediately dropped to the ground and crawled over by the trunk of a tree. In spite of the firing and shouting that was going on all around, I could see nothing but the one man lying on the ground about ten yards in front of me.

Something exploded just on the other side of the tree. The blast rolled me over, and my left leg was burning. I couldn't tell if I was hit or if the leg was just tingling from the concussion. I never stopped to think; I just flipped back over to my original position. Suddenly a man wearing an NVA pith helmet came running through the bushes at me. He was firing an AK-47 one-handed from his waist. In the other hand he held a grenade. He was firing wildly over my head with uncontrolled bursts from his rifle, but he managed to lob the grenade with his other hand and disappear behind the dense brush. The grenade landed not three feet from me. It hit with a light thud and rolled slowly in my direction. Suddenly my world was silent except for the persistent hiss of the grenade fuse. It's funny what you can remember when you have to. I knew it was a homemade grenade; I could tell that from the crude "pineapple" casing. That meant I didn't know if it had a two-second or a twenty-second fuse, whether it would go off like a weak firecracker or like a mortar round. Without ever really stopping to consider my action, I reached for the grenade and flipped it back toward the place where the enemy soldier had disappeared. After about two seconds the nearby explosion sent shrapnel slapping through the forest, and I had no sooner looked up than the pith-helmet man came running from the bushes again. This time he held his assault rifle extended in front of him with both hands. He was firing in short bursts, and the rattle of its firing sounded incredibly loud at such short distance. The ground around me was jumping with the impact of the rifle rounds. I couldn't move for fear of rolling into a round that would have otherwise missed me. The soldier was coming at me full speed. The spike bayonet was flipped out from his rifle barrel.

I was screaming at myself inside to hurry, hurry, but it seemed my every move was in slow motion. I finally got my rifle barrel up and squeezed the trigger. I hit him with my first burst when he wasn't ten feet from me. The man spun like a top, and the AK-47 flew through the air like a piece of loose debris. The man hit the ground on his back and bounced as though he had landed on a mattress. He drew one knee up and raised one arm slightly off the ground. He dropped the arm after a second and didn't move again.

The firing continued around me, but this was the only man I had seen. I didn't even know where my friendlies were anymore. I was completely disoriented. I got up and moved toward the sound of the firing, still off to my left, and had gone about twenty yards through the bushes when I came upon the platoon leader and one of the militiamen. They were both dead. It was strange. The lieutenant was covered with blood and was a gory mess. The other man was just as dead, but with only a small clean bullet hole in his abdomen.

"Dead men"—the thought flashed through my mind—"and either one of them could have been me. Who survives is a matter of luck." The firing had died down for a bit as I made my way through the brush, but now it started up again. Several automatic weapons were barking back and forth a few yards in front of me. At that moment, I didn't know if the guns belonged to my guys or to the Viet Cong, so I crawled cautiously toward the sound. I was surprised to suddenly come out on the canal bank. I had thought the canal was somewhere behind me, and now I realized I really was totally disoriented. That made me doubly glad to see a small group of militiamen spread out behind a large earthen bank about ten yards in front of me. They were firing over the top at some target on the other side, and didn't seem particularly disturbed by the return fire I could hear popping off somewhere out there in front of them. I ran over and dove down beside them as a new burst of fire kicked up some dirt in front of the mound and sent other bullets whining by overhead. They might not seem disturbed by the firing, but I sure as hell was!

All four men stared at me for a moment, then broke into big grins and pointed over the edge of the mound. They wanted me to look and see what they had. I cautiously peeped over the top of the mound. An open area stretched away from us, and in the middle of the clearing, about fifty yards away, was an old bomb crater. There were people in it. I couldn't tell how many, but two of them suddenly rose up on their knees and started firing short bursts of 7.62mm at us. I scrunched back down again and looked around. We had these guys trapped, that was for sure, but I wondered where the rest of my platoon was. I wondered where Jackson and Anderson were, and where the platoon radioman was. I wondered if anybody here knew what was going on. I sure as hell didn't.

I just lay there for a while, looking into the trees behind us, trying to figure out what to do once we took care of those guys out in the crater. Nothing particular came to mind, so I turned to the men and spoke to them in fractured Vietnamese.

"These men cannot escape," I said. "Call to them and see if they will surrender." One of the men nodded and stuck his head over the edge of the mound. He called out to the men in the crater and told them to come out, we wouldn't kill them. His answer was a spray of automatic weapons fire. The militiaman slid back down next to me, smiled, and shrugged. He drew his finger across his neck in a throat-cutting motion, and I just nodded my head.

I could now see four or five of our other men in the trees behind us. They too would occasionally fire out at the crater, and I realized this was the only action left. Whoever the group was that had run into us, they had all been killed or had escaped, except for this miserable band trapped out in the crater. I was about to suggest another *chiêu hồi* call when I heard the familiar coughing sound of an M-79 grenade launcher being fired. The sound came from the woods behind us, so I presumed it was one of ours. In a matter of a second or two, the grenade round hit out near the bomb crater. The explosion sent up a cloud of dirt and dust but caused no damage to the enemy. It was about five yards short of the crater. Another round was fired from behind me, and I quickly looked out toward the crater to see where it would hit. I guessed all the Cong soldiers were hunkered down deep in their hole because none was firing and I couldn't even see tops of heads. Our man with the grenade launcher was good. The next round landed right in the pit. With a loud crump and an eruption of smoke and mud the grenade landed right in the middle of the group of enemy soldiers. The men with me all saw the same thing, so they almost immediately were on their feet and charging out toward the crater. They didn't tell anybody, they didn't coordinate any lifting of fire, they didn't even wait to see if anybody else was still firing from behind us, they just jumped up and took off. They fired from their hips as they ran toward the crater, but the shots weren't very controlled and I think they were just depending on the fact that everyone in the crater was probably dead or incapacitated. They were right. The militiamen got to the crater without a round being fired in return. Being hesitant to take off so willy-nilly, I came up from behind them and joined them at the edge of the pit. There were three men at the bottom of the shallow crater. One had a huge hole blown in his side and the other two were speckled with the tiny shrapnel holes made by the serrated wire wrapped on the inside of an M-79 grenade round. There were three AK-47's at the bottom of the pit, and one of the men had a chest pack of B-40 rocket rounds. Blood and mud were oozing together in the mire at the bottom of the big hole.

Two of the militiamen scrambled down into the pit and collected the weapons. A latecomer walked down as cool as you please and went through the dead men's pockets. I didn't know if he was looking for money or items of military value, but frankly, I didn't care. I had other things to worry about.

When everybody came up out of the woods it seemed we only had about half the platoon, so I asked one of the men around me, "Where is the *Trung sĩ*, the platoon sergeant? Where are the rest of the men? Where is the radio?"

It turned out that the men guessed that the platoon sergeant and the other half of the platoon had gone on without us, but it was unclear whether they had just gone home or whether they had gone off chasing the Cong. I still had no radio, I still didn't know where the hell Anderson was, and I still didn't know what the other half of the platoon was doing. I decided to get the hell out of there while we still could.

We found three dead friendlies in the woods behind us, the platoon leader and his companion and the man I had seen go down earlier. There were six dead Cong, the three in the pit and three scattered back in the woods. We had two walking wounded. We tied our dead to poles and carried them out like sides of pork. It was a long walk back to the village and we still had plenty of daylight, but I didn't know how many Cong Jackson had flushed and where they might jump out at us again. It was a tense afternoon.

The longer I walked back toward the village, and the longer

I thought about this stupid operation, the madder I got at Jackson. Shit! I could have gotten shot! Without anybody there to help me. Without a radio. Without a prayer for a medevac. Where would I be now if that had happened? I'd be dead, that's what! All because Jackson wanted his big operation. I swore to myself that I'd be damned before I'd agree to this kind of screw-up again.

We staggered into the village late in the afternoon. Word had gone before us that we had suffered casualties. I guessed some of the men had run ahead to spread the word, and the women were already keening in the street. I didn't know who belonged to whom or what to do with the bodies, so I just hoped the platoon sergeant would do the right thing. At the edge of the village the men laid the three bodies down on the road, faces up, hands down by their sides. Family and friends were soon gathering around the bodies and the moaning and wailing began in earnest. I didn't have the slightest idea what to do and I was really pissed at being left alone to handle the mess, so I just walked toward the compound.

Jackson and Sergeant Anderson had already returned. I walked into the kitchen where the captain was and said curtly, *"Ḍi úy,* I think we fucked up today." Jackson looked up at me, his eyebrows raised in irritation. I continued, "My platoon got shot up. We had three KIA and two WIA. You said this would be a cakewalk." I paused, waiting for him to say something. He didn't, so I continued, "You sent me out alone and said there wouldn't be any trouble. Well, I'm not buying that shit anymore, let's be clear about that!" I glared at him a moment, thinking he might speak up. He just looked at me. I blew air between my pursed lips and said, "If you want the rest of my after-action report I'll give it after I've cleaned up." I turned on my heel and stalked out of the room.

Jackson never asked for the after-action report. In fact we never mentioned the operation again, period. I never did figure out where he and his element were all day, or what they did while we were trying to keep the Cong out of our hair. I did learn a lesson about preparing for operations and carrying them out. I also learned to be wary of my team leader. If he was a loose cannon as Chambers had suggested, I wanted to make sure I didn't get smashed between his wheels and the deck.

* * *

As THE WEEKS WENT BY I HEARD MORE AND MORE COM-
plaints about Captain Jack. All of our NCO's were experienced soldiers—they didn't tend to gripe about minor
personality problems—so when they came to me it was difficult to slough them off as if they were a bunch of privates
bitching about the duty roster. These men had legitimate
grievances. Jackson was not an able administrator simply because he did not put much effort into it, and his poor judgment
made him a poor combat leader.

Playing the role of the supportive assistant team leader was
a difficult task, but I didn't know what else to do. I tried to
change some of the captain's ideas and to offer alternative
suggestions, but in our situation there was little one could do
to control a senior officer who had set his mind on something.
Captain Jack could observe and officially comment on our
behavior, but there was no one to comment on his. There were
no officers around senior to him, and he had no peers to hold
him in check. We were alone and he could do as he damn
well pleased.

For the team members to control a team leader was nearly
impossible. If I or one of the team's sergeants lodged a complaint, it would be his word against ours. Since I was new to
the field, new to the job, and a junior officer to boot, I felt
helpless. I didn't think that making a complaint would do any
good, so I spent considerable effort in trying to keep the rest
of the team settled until Jackson finished his tour. It was not
an easy job.

Captain Jack began sending out three-man ambushes at
night: three Americans, no Vietnamese. He thought we had a
better chance of making a contact if we operated without the
villagers. We could move more quietly and operate with more
flexibility if we didn't bother with the local units. In essence
he wanted us to abandon our mission to train those units in
exactly the type of operations we were conducting on our own.
No one was happy with the situation, even though our ambushes and night operations were very successful. We hit several supply convoys, small Viet Cong squads from the local
area, and even the heavy weapons unit of the Cong's Main
Force battalion. The latter was just the sort of group a three-
man ambush shouldn't take on, but Jackson loved it. If the
whole battalion had come into our beaten zone he would have

had us open up on them. He was desperate for his medal; we were desperate to survive his search for it.

The tension began to run very high. The captain had us on patrol every day and on ambush every night. We rarely got a night's sleep, but had to catch catnaps whenever we could. Fatigue and unremitting pressure began to fray the edges of our nerves and tempers. The men were constantly complaining to me and I was trying to keep them steady on a day-by-day and case-by-case basis. Sergeant Anderson began to resort to the village beer and the hard liquor he had purchased back at a PX with his ration ticket. He had been a good man and a solid soldier for months, well before I arrived on the scene, but in a matter of a few weeks he became a real problem. Anderson never went out and got falling-down drunk, but every evening he somehow managed to get a little inebriated, just enough so that he was sloppy in his speech, his manner, and most dangerously, his reaction time. Finally no one trusted him to go out on combat operations anymore. When someone out in the dark is trying to kill you, you want the man watching your back to be fully alert, not dozing off into a drunken never-never land. Anderson's problem escalated rapidly, and he capped his fate one evening when he got into a bleary argument with Jackson. The sergeant was on the verge of assaulting the captain before Sergeant Chambers and I got them separated. The next morning Anderson was sent back to the province town on the mail and resupply chopper. He ended up being court-martialed for insubordination and "conduct to the prejudice of good order and discipline in the United States Army." He had been a good fifteen-year army veteran, but the situation we were in and the pressure from Captain Jack had finally cracked him.

The wear and tear was having its effect on us all, Jackson included. I think exhaustion and the frustration of our work plus his usual level of bad judgment finally pushed the captain beyond being merely a bad officer to being a disastrous one.

The final act began with one of those three-man night ambushes. Captain Jack, Sergeant Chambers, and Sergeant Johnny Robertson, Anderson's replacement, had successfully sprung an ambush on a squad of Viet Cong guerrillas, killing five Cong and capturing a boat, some documents, and two of the surviving guerrillas. Sergeant Watson and I had been the stay-behind crew. We had been keeping alternating four-hour shifts on radio watch all night long and were dead tired ourselves.

It was early morning, just at sunup, when Jackson, Robertson, and Chambers came back through the gates with their patrol and prisoners. They shucked their wet gear and clothes, drank some of our gritty hobo coffee, and tried to shake the knots out of their muscles. We all relaxed and slouched in our chairs in a state of seminumbness.

I sat back and just stared blankly at the wall, trying to let the fatigue drain off through the tips of my limp fingers. I tried to wish away the thousand little aches in my body that came from staying awake most of the night. Sergeant Watson went into the small kitchen area of our team house to make another pot of coffee. He and I had spent a good part of the night in there sifting through our last canister of flour. We were picking out the bugs and worms, a distraction which helped pass the time as we listened for a squawk from the radio.

Sergeant Chambers went over to his bunk to get some dry clothes and Robertson soon followed him. Captain Jack just sat there in a chair in his wet green underwear and stared malevolently at the two Viet Cong prisoners. He said something about wanting information from both of them.

The Viet Cong were sullen young men dressed in the standard attire of loose-fitting cotton pants and shirts, with rubber sandals on their feet. Their arms were tied behind their backs and they were bound together by a length of rope tied around their necks. The two guerrillas were told to sit by the door just inside the team house. Captain Jack began to interrogate them with the standard questions about their unit, their hideouts, and their arms caches. They gave the standard answers: that they were just fishermen who were innocently minding their own business when an ambush erupted around them. The documents captured with them clearly contradicted these assertions, but the Cong were going to admit to nothing. So much for that, I told myself, Jack'll have to leave the interrogation to the intelligence types back at the rear.

Jackson sat back in his chair and asked me to hand him his M-16. The rifle was leaning against the wall by my chair. I handed him the M-16, thinking he was going to clean it, a standard procedure we all went through after each operation. I flopped back in my chair and reached over to a table for a packet of photographs I had received from home on the last chopper run. I began to flip through them, trying to escape into the scenes of the family farm and the tall Georgia pines. I remember Captain Jack saying something else to the prisoners, but by that time I wasn't paying any attention to him.

BAM! A sudden explosion jerked me up in the chair. Jackson had fired his goddamned rifle! From the way he was holding the M-16 and the way he was looking, I immediately knew he had fired it at the prisoners. "Oh, my God," I thought as I looked quickly over at the two men. I thought he had shot one of them. Both of the guerrillas were still squatting there by the door, though. They were staring up at Jackson, fear drawn across their faces. A fraction of a second later I realized I was hearing a sound like water rushing from a pipe. I thought of broken water lines after a winter freeze. "That's strange," I thought, "we don't have water pipes here."

I had hardly completed the thought when I saw the whitish gray cloud drifting through the door and enveloping the two captured Viet Cong. For half a heartbeat I paused, uncertain as to what I was seeing. Then a realization struck that turned my veins to ice and my torpor to terror. Propane gas! That asshole Jackson had fired a round by the prisoners to frighten them. The bullet had struck the ground just outside the door and ricocheted into a cylinder of propane gas we had for running our small refrigerator. The tank had been punctured and was now spewing gas out in a great cloud. Everyone seemed frozen in his place; nobody was moving.

"Gas!" I yelled, breaking out of my stupor of incredulity. "Get outta here! It's gonna blow!"

I spun on my heel and headed for the door on the far side of the team house. Robertson made his move at the same time. We both reached the far door at the same time, but we had no trouble getting through. The propane had finally found a flame and exploded with a blast that sent both of us flying through the doorway. I was tossed through the air as if by some giant hand. I must have done a flip because I remember turning face up to the sun as I completed my arcing flight. I landed flat on my back and felt the air punched out of my lungs by the jolting thud. I lay there for a second, dazed by the blast, and when I finally moved my head, I was surprised to find I was still all right.

I staggered to my feet and shook myself to see if any parts were loose. I tried to clear some of the cotton from my brain, feeling my head with my hands to see if it was still there. I saw that Sergeant Robertson had gotten to his feet and that he was apparently unharmed also. The team house was already billowing flame and smoke, but we both started back to the door we had just been blown out of. As we got there the two Viet Cong prisoners came running out. They stumbled through the doorway, still bound together by the rope around their necks and with their arms still tied behind them. They were both on fire. Their clothes were scorched and smoldering; yellow flame flickered at the black edges of holes already burned through the cotton cloth. The fire was in their hair, too, sizzling and flickering as it sent up its sulfurous stench. Both men collapsed at our feet, lurching and jerking as they tried to escape the flames that ate at them. The nylon rope that held them together at the neck had melted into their skin. Robertson and I started beating out the flames with our hands. We threw dirt and mud on their heads as we tried to kill the fire. When the last flame was out, we left them smoldering on the ground and raced back into the team house.

Captain Jackson was still standing where I had last seen him. He appeared unharmed, so I presumed he had somehow gotten out of the house or behind some protection before the propane blew. He stared at me for a split second and reached for our lone fire extinguisher, a futile gesture since half of our wood and bamboo house was already a blazing pyre. I yelled something to him, I don't know what, and he turned to say something back. When he looked at me I saw the panic in his eyes, the haggard stamp of fear and confusion on his face. It was then that I remembered the mortar ammunition.

The preceding evening two navy PBR's and a converted landing craft called a Tango boat had come up our main canal. They stopped by the fort to give us a case of fresh fruit and some ammunition we had been trying to scrounge from them for over a month. The ammo was for our 81mm mortar. We had tried and tried to get the stuff from the regular Vietnamese supply channels but the system simply wouldn't cough any up for us. We needed a hundred rounds, a mix of high-explosive, white-phosphorus, and illumination rounds. Using the standard tactic of scroungers everywhere, we bargained with the navy for two hundred rounds. The navy, trying to either shame us or confuse us, brought us four hundred. We were ecstatic, of course, but we didn't have nearly enough room in our mortar bunker for that much ammo. I had the Vietnamese soldiers stack most of the ammunition in a thatch lean-to on the side of our team house. We wanted to keep the mortar rounds out of the rain while we dug another pit bunker to hold all the extra rounds.

That was what I remembered as I stood there in the burning house: almost four hundred rounds of 81mm mortar ammo were just on the other side of a flaming thatch wall. The next blast was going to make the first seem like a peewee firecracker.

The fire on the roof was dropping pieces of flaming palm thatch down on us. I grabbed Jack's arm and shouted over the roar, "The mortar ammo! Come on! The fire's gonna blow it! We gotta get everybody out of the compound!"

Robertson, Jackson, and I went out of there like a shot. Some of the militiamen were running toward the burning building as we ran out. Other men from outside the fort were coming inside the walls to see what had happened. We started shouting at them all to clear out, warning that the mortar ammo was going to blow at any minute. Immediately everyone began running back toward the village-side gate, scampering over the walls, or running through the canal-side gate.

The two PBR's from the previous evening had returned from their night operation and had docked for the morning just outside our walls. "The mortar ammo is gonna blow!" I yelled to a couple of the sailors who had come into the fort. "Get to the boats! Move, dammit, this place is gonna blow to hell!" The sailors headed through the canal-side gate, yelling warnings and instructions to their mates on the boats. I looked around for my other teammates; I saw Jackson climbing on board one of the PBR's. I didn't see Robertson, but I knew he had come back out of the burning team house. I didn't see Chambers either, but I did see Sergeant Watson. He was stumbling toward me across the now almost empty compound. He had had to run through the flames to get out of the house, and he had been caught in the first gas blast to boot. He had had no shirt on and was badly burned above the waist. His pants and boots were smoldering but were not on fire. At least they had offered his lower body some protection from the flames.

Watson walked toward me with a dazed, uncomprehending look on his face. He didn't seem to be in any pain, but his charred flesh made me grimace as if it were me who should hurt instead of him. He was a black man, or rather had been. Now the black skin of his arms and face was largely peeled up like dried, burnt parchment. The exposed flesh underneath was a nauseating pink. What had been thick curly hair on his head was now fused into a solid, shiny black helmet. I grabbed him by the belt loops, afraid to touch his skin, and led him to the PBR's. I boosted Watson up on the bow deck of the nearest boat and yelled over to Captain Jack on the other PBR, "Have you seen Chambers or Robertson?"

"Robertson got out, I saw him," yelled Jackson over the sound of the PBR engines. "I haven't seen Chambers."

The fire was now boiling over the entire team house. I figured it was going to blow the mortar ammo any second. The roar of the fire, the coughing of the boat motors, and the yells of the running people produced a tumult of noisy confusion. I had not seen Chambers, but as I turned to look back into the compound, I saw the two Viet Cong prisoners being led to the village-side gate by one of the local militiamen. They stumbled along, still roped together, clearly in bad shape. I still didn't see Robertson, but I hoped both he and Chambers had gone out the village gate with most of the Vietnamese. A few of the locals, like the sailors and Jackson and me, had run through the canal gate and were now climbing aboard the PBR's.

It took only a second for the sailors to have the engines revved up and the boats backing away from our small jerry-built dock. As the boats were moving, two young Vietnamese women were trying to reach the side of one of the vessels and swing themselves up on its deck. I was still standing on the dock, so I grabbed them one at a time, one arm around the waist and the other gripping a handful of buttock, and heaved them aboard the nearest one before it pulled away. Then I made a leap for the boat myself. My jump was short and I had a tough moment or two before one of the sailors was able to help me haul myself over onto the deck.

As our PBR was still backing into a turn to get us pointed upstream, the first explosion of mortar rounds ripped through the compound with a tremendous blast. Wood, thatch, mud, metal, and intact mortar rounds came raining out of the sky. The mortar ammo that had exploded had launched other unexploded rounds and sent them careering through the air.

Some of the illumination rounds were popping off in the air above us; some of the HE and WP were going off as they hit the ground. Rounds landing in the canal sent up large plumes of water. Near misses were dropping all around us. The rounds exploding in the air and on impact really scared me. They weren't supposed to do that; mortar rounds have a safety pin and a self-arming device that is supposed to prevent them from going off unless they have been fired out of a mortar tube. The combination of heat and explosion in our stack of ammo had apparently been sufficient to make many of these falling rounds so unstable that they were going off anyway. We could see some of the rounds as they came and we never knew if the ones landing nearby were going to be ones that went off or not.

Our pilot slammed both throttles full ahead and the boat surged forward. We almost ran down the other boat as it was coming out of its own turn. Both PBR's roared away from the fort, racing to get beyond the reach of the flying mortar rounds. Explosions were still blowing the inside of the compound to shreds, and mortar bombs and other debris continued to rain around us.

Suddenly the boat ahead of us reduced power and we almost ran her down again. I leaned over the side of our PBR to see what the devil they were doing. I wanted to get the hell out of there and no dawdling around. Two men were leaning over the side of the lead boat to reach out to two figures in the water. I saw immediately that the people in the water were Sergeant Robertson and Cô Ha, our hooch maid. Both of them had apparently gone straight into the canal and begun swimming upstream before the PBR's even started their engines. The lead boat had stopped to pick up the swimmers. That took nerve, with mortar rounds exploding overhead and on the canal banks on either side. Good for the U.S. Navy.

The sailors hauled in Robertson, then with two sailors hanging on to Cô Ha, who was still dragging in the water, the lead boat went to full power and practically jumped out of the water. Our pilot went back to full forward on his own controls and we followed in the spray of the other PBR. I looked back at the compound as we raced down the canal and saw another explosion launch another fan of mortar rounds high into the air. We ploughed straight ahead, trying to get outside the range of the falling mortar bombs.

Mortar rounds were being tossed around inside the compound, too. They exploded against the inside walls and the small buildings within the fort. Tin and timber kept flying up into the air along with the smoke, flame, and other mortar rounds. I guessed that some of the ammo was cooking off from the intense heat even after it had been tossed out into the compound by previous explosions. The fire was certainly cooking off our rifle and machine-gun ammunition—I could hear the rapid coughing and popping as the heat ignited it like a giant string of firecrackers. We were lucky the walls of the fort contained the low-flying bullets. Otherwise we would have had to contend with that hail of metal as well.

When we got outside the reach of the falling mortar bombs, both PBR's slowed and pulled over against the canal bank. Most of the people on the boats climbed up on the bank to watch the fireworks and the slow disintegration of the fort. Others tried to tend the burned or wounded, most of whom had only minor problems. Sergeant Watson was by far the most severely burned of the lot. He was sitting on a metal case down under the boat's cockpit. He just sat there staring at the bulkhead. I recalled that burn victims lose a lot of body water through dehydration, so I mixed salt in some water and handed it to him in a metal canteen cup. I sat there and made him drink it, but he looked so weak and lethargic that I was afraid he was going to die before we could get him any help.

I tried to see that Watson was as comfortable as possible before I went up on the deck to find if the navy chief had been able to raise any help on his radio. One of the sailors was working on the radio, so I climbed up on the canal bank where the other people were. The explosions were continuing inside the fort and none of the buildings appeared to be still standing. The big explosions that launched the large sprays of falling mortar rounds were apparently over, but the individual rounds continued to cook off in the heat.

I think Jackson was in shock. He was just staring back at the fort, not organizing aid for the injured, not trying to contact help on the radios, not functioning as a leader in any way. He looked over at me as I approached and said in a shaky voice, "What are they going to do to me?" It was clear that "they" were our army superiors and what they were going to do to him was something in response to this fiasco. Hell, he wasn't worried about us or our wounded at all. He was worried about his career!

I just turned and walked back to one of the boats. I climbed aboard and started working with the radio myself, trying to raise the province team on the army net. We were too far away from the province town, though, and I couldn't get through on the PBR's radio. The sailors were finally able to make contact with the USS *Benewa* out in the Mekong River, and the *Benewa* relayed our situation to the province team. We finally got confirmation that medevac choppers were en route to pick up our wounded and that help from the province team was being organized. A relief team would be on its way as soon as a helicopter became available.

Sergeant Chambers was still unaccounted for. I was very uneasy about that. We all hoped he had gotten out and had been able to make it to the village, but somehow that didn't seem likely to me anymore. No one had seen him since the first blast and initial fireball, and deep down inside I didn't feel there was much chance he had made it out unscathed. I was afraid that if he had gotten out of the team house at all, he must have been forced out the back into the part of the compound away from the canal and away from the village-side gate. If Chambers was only hurt and not dead, then I hoped he had been able to make it over the back wall of the fort and use that as protection from the blasts.

I walked back over to Jackson and said, "Captain, we've got to go back and look for Sergeant Chambers. He's the only one unaccounted for. The navals have all their men."

Jackson just continued to look at the compound in the distance and watch the exploding mortar rounds send their smoke and debris into the air. The punctuating *wham* of the HE rounds accompanied each skyward eruption, and even though the tempo of the explosions had slowed considerably, the small arms ammo still popped like popcorn in a pan. Smoke from the WP and illumination rounds that had cooked off billowed up out of the compound, forming a tall, dense, white column above the small fort.

Jackson's face was taut with worry. "No," he said hesitantly, "not yet. We need to wait a bit longer. It's gotta cool down some."

His hesitation pissed me off. I looked him dead in the eye and said, "Captain Jackson, sir, I request permission to return to the compound to look for Sergeant Chambers. He may need help if he's still alive." I spoke slowly and formally. I wanted Jackson to understand that somebody was going to do something. If it had to be me, that was o.k.

Jackson looked at me with a vacant, somewhat quizzical expression. I thought for a second he didn't know what I was talking about. Finally he shrugged and turned back to watch the fort. "All right," he said, "you can go if you can get one of the navals to risk a boat and take you back."

I went straight to the boat I had come out on and asked the chief petty officer to take me back to the fort. He was agreeable but had to put me on hold until he got permission himself from the *Benewa*. One call back to his ship and he had the go-ahead for the risky run. We were on our way. I pulled a steel helmet and a flack vest out of the forward gun tub and strapped them on. The chief had permission to make a run past the compound, but he was told not to stop. He was going to have to drop me on the fly. I began calculating my jump over the side since I was going to have to try to hit shallow water as the boat skimmed past the compound. I didn't think I would make much of a swimmer in a flack vest and steel pot.

The gray-green patrol boat quickly got up to full speed. As we approached the compound the fire, smoke, and explosions seemed more threatening than they had back on the bank. I began to wonder if Captain Jack had been right about that waiting business, but I was committed now and I'd be damned if I was going to go back. I asked the pilot to move more toward the left bank and to slow down as we went by the compound's walls. Just as we passed our dock, I swung out over the stern of the PBR, hesitated a second, and jumped. I hit the water like a flat rock and made a flip or two on the surface before I sank. My guess about where to jump had been

correct, though, and I came up in waist-deep water. I turned
to signal the PBR that I was o.k., but the boat's engines had
roared back to full power before I had even hit the water
and the gunboat was already far down the canal.

I crawled under some barbed wire at the canal's edge and
made my way along the wall toward the nearest entrance to
the compound. Explosions kept going off on the other side of
the wall, but when I got to the canal-side gate I stuck my head
around the edge of the opening and looked inside. The interior
of the fort had been blasted, churned, and burned beyond rec-
ognition. Even though I knew the place was being blown to
hell, I was still taken aback by the almost total destruction.
The team house had been burned to the ground and the ashes
had been blasted all over the place. Only a clump of charred
wood and tortured tin remained where the house had been.
The south end of the house, where we had stored the mortar
ammo in the lean-to, was completely gone, and a huge hole
in the ground marked the place of the former ammo stacks.
Burning debris must have fallen into the hole because smoke
was still pouring out. Mortar rounds were still down in there,
too. An occasional blast from the pit would throw dirt, charred
wood, and other debris out into the compound.

The other buildings were not burned but had been blasted
to pieces by the explosions. I noticed a few mortar rounds
lying around on the ground, many of them smoking, all of
them burned black. Suddenly one of them off to my left went
off with a loud pop. I jerked as though I had been shot. I
thought the sound was the first sputter of an HE round cooking
off and I wanted some cover before it really exploded. The
mortar bomb was just an illumination round, though, a flare
that had finally cooked off in the heat. Rich white smoke
spewed from the metal casing and billowed upward to join
with the other smoke pluming into the sky.

I lay against the outside of the fort wall and listened to the
popping of the rifle ammunition and the blast of an occasional
mortar round. I knew that once I went inside the compound
to look for Chambers, I would have to be sure to get behind
some cover and stay there. The rifle rounds still going off
could fly out in any direction and the shrapnel from the 81mm
mortar bombs could come in chunks as big as your fist. I could
end up casting a polka-dot shadow.

I screwed up my courage, pushed off the wall, and ran through the gate toward a drainage trench off to my right. I made a dash across the open area between the gate and the ditch and with a great leap took the last few yards through the air. I jumped just in time because as I landed with a splat in the muddy trench, a mortar round went off somewhere just to my left. Shrapnel zipped through the air and clods of dirt fell all over me. I thought I was scared before, but I wasn't; *now* I was scared!

I kicked my low crawl into high gear and made it over to an area where our navals had put up a small canvas tent to act as a sunshade. It was now hanging on one pole and was hardly more than a tattered rag. I crawled under it, trying to make my way to the back of the compound. I was floundering through the folds of heavy cloth, about to suffocate in the hot trapped air, when another mortar round went off not far away. The canvas popped and jerked as the shrapnel cut through it. I hugged the earth, trying to keep below the flying metal, but I felt a sharp tug at the back of my flack vest and a fiery sting across my cheek. I later saw where a sliver of steel had sliced into the fabric of my vest and embedded in the nylon packing. A small piece of shrapnel must have just grazed my face also because I had a scratch across my cheek, like the gouge of a large thorn. The bleeding was for dramatic effect only.

Another explosion followed quickly after the first, and the tent collapsed completely, the tent pole shorn off just above my head. I crawled on through the torn fabric and made it over to a small crater blasted out by a previous explosion. I lay in it, waiting, listening, and wondering if the pace of the explosions was going to pick up again. My ears were ringing from the concussions, my heart was pounding in my chest, and I was breathing like a winded horse. The midday tropical sun was white hot and I thought I was going to cook off like one of the mortar rounds. I had that thick-tongued feeling of thirst that comes with the combination of heat and fear. I tried to ignore it, but finally couldn't resist scooping up a handful of the brackish water that had already settled in the bottom of the crater. I sucked it into my mouth and spat it back out again. Just the wetness in my mouth gave me some relief, and I pressed back down into the bottom of the crater. The sense of aloneness was incredible.

I waited to see if the explosions would slow down enough for me to be able to get up and move on to the back wall of the compound. I hoped that I could find Chambers back there somewhere. The rifle rounds eventually stopped going off, except for the occasional pop from the ashes of the team house. A period of several minutes went by when no more mortar rounds exploded either, so I decided to make a run for the back wall. I ran past the smoking ruin of the old team house, clambered up to the top of the wall, and rolled over to the other side. I got up, shook myself off, and quickly looked down the length of the wall in both directions. I desperately wanted to see Sergeant Chambers; he wasn't there.

"Chambers," I called. Nothing responded but the faint crackle of drying embers and the solitary pop of a rifle round in the ashes.

"Chambers," I yelled again, "it's Donovan! Can you hear me?" Nothing.

I crawled on down the wall a bit to a spot directly behind the team house. I peeked over the wall into the compound and searched the tall grass behind the house, praying for a sign of Chambers. Nothing.

"Damn," I thought, "what now?" I decided to try to get a closer look in the ashes of the team house, so I crawled back over the wall into the compound. My attention was focused on the remains of the building. It was just a pile of smoldering ashes and I couldn't make out anything in it. I walked slowly toward the pile of blackened tin and charcoal, moving in a half crouch, wary of another explosion. When I was within about five yards of the smoking remains, a harsh *Pop!* and *Fzzzzzzzzzzz!* went off just to my left. I dropped like a stone, wincing in fear. It turned out to be another of those illumination rounds that had popped off after being cooked for a while in the fire and then thrown out by one of the explosions. It was about ten feet off to my left and I had not even noticed it.

I had been looking for Chambers so intently that I had failed to notice the mortar rounds lying about in the grass. The fact that the illumination round went off a few feet from me and I had not seen it caused a flutter in my stomach. If that had been an HE round I would have been atomized by the blast. I looked in the grass to see if any others were lying around. I was literally frozen by what I saw. The damned place was practically a carpet of mortar bombs! Many of them were still giving off faint wisps of smoke or steam. On some I could see a little spring hanging out of the forward part of the casing, a dead giveaway that the bore-riding safety pin had been jarred out by the explosions. That meant the mortar round might go off at the slightest impact. Heated up like they were, I figured the smallest vibration might be enough to set them off. A whole field of the fragile bombs lay between me and the wall of the fort. It was a miracle that I had gotten so far into the compound without stepping on one or kicking one, and now I knew I had to pick my way back out again. Knowing the bombs were there and to be avoided made the getting out much harder than the getting in.

I began making my way back toward the back wall of the fort, searching the grass ahead of me for the primed explosives. I carefully considered the stepping space between each of the bomb carcasses and deliberately estimated each gentle footstep I took. A sticky heat hung around me. Sweat trickled down my back and arms. I tried to breathe without gasping, but my racing heart kept demanding more and more oxygen. I was afraid any vigorous movement at all might send me off balance and into one of the mortar rounds that just needed one touch to set it off. Sweat stung my eyes and made it hard to see. I had to stop and wipe my eyes in order to check the final few feet of grass before the wall.

I stepped past the last couple of mortar rounds and slowly crawled up the compound wall. I was still afraid that a heavy footfall might cause one of the nearby HE rounds to go off with a blast. Once I got to the top of the wall I took a more studied look around the compound. The whole interior was littered with unexploded mortar rounds.

I circled the compound, calling for Sergeant Chambers, but I found no trace of him. I did find the two Viet Cong prisoners. They were lying close to the main gate. They had made it that far before one or both of them collapsed. Tied tightly at the arms and neck, each was bound irrevocably to the fate of the other. They were both terribly burned and, mercifully, dead. I presumed it was the initial blast and fire that had been the cause. I could see no shrapnel wounds or other signs that the subsequent explosions had done them in. They were just lying there like swollen hunks of raw meat, the flies already settling on their lips and eyes.

As I stood there looking at the two corpses I found myself thinking that Jackson was guilty of homicide. I couldn't sort out what degree or anything, but the men were his prisoners and he had killed them. He had not done it intentionally, of course, but firing that shot by them in the first place was illegal. He was trying to force some information out of them through intimidation, a violation of the rules of war. Firing close to the two Cong in an effort to scare them had turned out to be a deadly miscalculation. Jackson had ended up killing the prisoners he had only meant to frighten. Two deaths due to a negligent and illegal act—I guessed that was at least manslaughter, if not worse.

I had seen people killed before, people killed with little holes in them, people killed with big holes in them. This was war and people got killed in it. I also knew that miscalculations and accidents happened, so I wondered why I immediately felt so bitter about the loss of these two men. I was confused. I just stood there for a minute looking down at two blistered bodies, conscious only of a building resentment toward Jackson. I was about to move on in search of Sergeant Chambers when I heard the throaty hum of the PBR engines. It seemed the others had decided to return, so I went over to the wall of the fort by the canal to watch them come in.

The PBR's motored on down the canal past the fort and put in down by the village. I found an M-16 in the rubble of one of the shattered thatch buildings where the Vietnamese troops stayed, so I armed myself and squatted on the wall to wait. I watched Jackson and Robertson make their way up toward the compound, leaving the sailors to tend to the boats and Sergeant Watson. Both men stopped outside the wall as I peered down at them. Jackson looked apprehensive, and I imagined his eyes to be black with guilt.

"Is Chambers in the village?" I asked as I sat there on my haunches. I swatted the flies and squinted down at the captain for a reply.

"No," said Jackson as he shook his head, "he's not down there. You didn't see him up here?"

I slowly dropped my head to my knees, filled with disgust and anger. I took a long time releasing a lungful of air. I tried to control the emotions that came with acknowledging that we had probably lost Chambers too. "No," I said, shaking my head, "I haven't seen him. Come on, let's all look again."

The explosions had finally stopped altogether, and we could take a more careful look. Jackson went to look around the walls again, and Robertson was digging in the rubble of the other shacks. I crawled up on a pile of dirt and debris next to the burned-out team house and looked over into the jumble of smoking ash and shredded metal. I stared at the blackened mess for a long time, trying to pick out the remains of any identifiable artifacts. I recognized the skeletons of our M-16's and the AK-47's we had captured. I saw the burned box that constituted the remains of our team radio. I looked intently among the ashes for other recognizable items. Suddenly I was startled to see a charred head, and below that the blackened sticks that had been the arms of a man. The fingerless limbs were reaching upward as if asking for assistance. The head was aligned so that for a flash I thought it was looking right at me. I knew it was Chambers. I was shocked at just coming across him lying there like that, after looking for him so intently and not seeing him.

"Oh, my God!" I said with shock and disgust. Robertson and Jackson must have heard me because they both came over to where I was standing.

"What's the matter?" asked Jackson. "Do you see him?"

"Yeah, he's there where the kitchen was," I said with a nod toward the team house. "He must have been caught in the first blast." God, how I hoped he had been killed outright!

I turned and walked back to the village-side wall. Now I chalked up three deaths to Captain Jackson, and this time one of them was ours.

Jackson stopped functioning altogether. He stumbled around the compound, mumbling tearful comments to no one in particular. He kept coming over to ask me what I thought was going to happen to him. Each time I told him to just calm down, that I didn't know what was going to happen. Robertson and I posted some guards around the ruined fort and I got Jackson to go down to the village chief's hooch where he would be out of my hair. A little later two medevac choppers arrived to take away Sergeant Watson and two injured Vietnamese soldiers. We helped Watson aboard the chopper as best we could, but we had nothing with which to cover him. I winced to see the propwash blasting sand into his terribly burned chest. He was still conscious and able to function, so I held on to the hope that he would make it. As the choppers lifted off he raised one hand in a faint wave. I waved back and clenched my fist in the air, trying through the silent effort to somehow lend him strength.

Sergeant Robertson and I walked back to the compound to wait for the arrival of the PSA and the relief team that was supposedly en route. The navals had heard on their radio that a group from the province team were coming out in a Chinook helicopter to help us haul out everything salvageable. I presumed we were either going to be taken back to the province town until this affair was settled, or were going to be sent out on a new assignment almost straightaway.

When the big chopper finally appeared on the horizon, Sergeant Robertson came up and stood beside me on the wall of the fort. He fidgeted for a moment or two without saying anything, but finally he turned to me and asked, "What do we tell the PSA, *Trung úy*?"

I stared at the approaching chopper as I tried to organize my thoughts. I said, "I don't know. What do you think, Johnny?" I was still confused about my feelings toward Jackson. I hadn't decided whether I really thought he was criminally at fault, but I did know I was mad at him. I knew he was an ass. I knew he had turned into a dangerous incompetent. I also knew he was one of the team. He was one of us, one of the sufferers, one of the victims. The bond we all shared was one not easily broken.

Take the guys coming out in the Chinook, for example. They were from the rear. Even though they lived only twenty or thirty miles away, we considered them to be from a different world. They had a mess hall, hot showers, electricity, and even dry beds for a full night's sleep. In a sense, we looked upon them as an undercaste, pussies, men without the blood of warriors. In reality they were all our friends, and when we were back in the province compound for any reason, they all tried to be helpful to us. Even so, we held ourselves to be better men.

We weren't better men, of course, we just had different jobs. Still, people who are alone and in constant danger often

develop the consoling conviction that they are better than anyone else, that by their suffering they form an elite cadre.
Wherever such a group is found, there is also the tacit agreement that the brotherhood protects its own. The undercaste,
so the feeling goes, has no business in the affairs of the elite.
The true warrior class is strong enough to handle its own affairs. It sounds like a silly, improper, even dangerous attitude,
but it's there and it's as real as steel.

Robertson didn't answer my question. Maybe he knew I
was juggling for time, still trying to make up my mind about
what to do. Finally he shrugged and said, "He didn't mean
to blow the place up."

"Chambers is dead," I said bitterly.

Robertson didn't need reminding of that. He looked down
and spat between his feet. He looked back at me and asked
again, "What are you going to tell 'em, *Trung úy?*"

I knew Robertson wasn't pushing for an accusation. He had
been in the army too long; he knew all about the us's and the
them's. In Robertson's mind Jackson was one of us, and he
was willing to let the whole thing go as if it had been an
accident. As for me, I was still trying to settle my own
thoughts and check my memory of the incident. How much
of my memory was true and how much of it was tainted by
my disgust with Jackson? I knew that in a few minutes I would
have to give a complete report to one angry army colonel. I
had to have my story straight, without any quibbles or uncer-
tainties. Two things finally settled my decision: First, I was
glad to be alive and was prepared to be generous. Second, the
brotherhood bond told me I shouldn't turn in my own captain,
not after the dangers and struggles we had been through together as a team.

"O.k.," I said, "we'll tell 'em it was an accident. Captain
Jack was cleaning his rifle and it went off by accident. The
bullet hit the tank and so on. Don't mention anything about
his talking to the prisoners."

Robertson stared grimly back across the blackened and still
smoking compound, "All right, *Trung úy,* it was an accident." His shoulders sagged a bit as we both turned to walk
out to the big chopper landing noisily on our landing pad.
"Damn," he said loudly. Then with a lower voice, "It's too

bad about old Chambers and Watson, though. Thank God it wasn't you or me, eh, *Trung úy*?"

"Yeah," I replied with resignation, "thank God it wasn't you or me."

I went on down to the chopper pad and reported to the PSA. I told him what I knew about the "accident," and when the colonel asked, I pointed out where Jackson was holed up in the village. Robertson had gone ahead to get the captain, and to tell him that we were going to save his ass. When I saw Jackson and Robertson come out of the village chief's hooch and start walking out toward us, I left the colonel and went on back to the compound.

I helped two other guys with the grisly job of getting Chambers's remains into a body bag and loading it on the medevac chopper that had arrived to pick it up. The PSA told me to get on the chopper and escort the body back to graves registration in Can Tho. All the way there I couldn't help but think of the gruesome black thing inside the plastic bag at my feet. It was a morose duty to turn him over to the guys that hand out the CMH. Those initials ordinarily mean Congressional Medal of Honor, but for the dead they simply meant Casket with Metal Handles.

I got the medevac pilot to drop me by the field hospital that had received Sergeant Watson. I went in and asked the nurses on duty at emergency receiving about the burned black man who had come in a few hours before. They all assured me that Watson was doing well, that he was receiving the best of care and would probably be resting in Japan by the following evening. I was relieved to hear that, and asked them to pass on a farewell message from me and the team. I ran back to the waiting chopper and climbed aboard for the trip back to Cao Lanh.

I spent the next several days filling out forms and writing up reports about the incident. Robertson and I had to answer a lot of questions, but our stories must have been similar enough to satisfy the two officers assigned to investigate the case. By that time I had managed to subdue any qualms I had about not telling the truth about Jackson shooting at the prisoners. I smothered any doubts I had with the idea that my first responsibility was to the brotherhood bond, his being one of *us* and all. I also asked myself what good would come out of my reporting him, anyway. If he was found guilty of some crime and punished, it would only mean another life chewed up by the war. It wouldn't change anything that had happened; it wouldn't bring Chambers back; it wouldn't convert Jackson from a frog to a prince. I convinced myself that Robertson and I were acting properly. Jackson was an ass, but I rationalized that he hadn't really meant to kill anyone. It was a dirty war, I said, so let bygones be bygones.

My resolve to let the captain off the hook was shaken about a week later when we got word that Sergeant Watson had died of his burns after reaching Japan. Now I could tally four lives lost to Jackson's craziness, two of them American. I came within an inch of going to the colonel and telling the whole truth, but I didn't. Ever full of excuses, I told myself that now I just wanted revenge, that I was lashing out in anger without a care for the consequences. In the end I went back to my old decision. "Forget it," I said, and forget it I did.

Jackson was in considerable trouble with the PSA anyway. When the colonel and his party arrived at the village on the day of the incident, Jackson had not been functioning as a commanding officer. When the colonel talked to him it was clear that Jack had lost control of the situation a long time before. I think the colonel was disturbed at this sort of flagrant malfeasance on the part of a fellow West Pointer. It offended his sense of God's order of the universe. Jackson became *persona non grata* during the brief remainder of his tour. He was assigned some meaningless desk job at province headquarters where he could sit and sweat out his final days in-country. He never did get his medal.

Within three weeks, Robertson and I were sent back out to Tram Chim with a full team. I had been made team leader and had been appointed District Senior Advisor to boot. Our new team medic, Master Sergeant Dennis Fitz, from Michigan, joined us fresh from the States. We picked up Sergeant Charles Abney as our heavy weapons man from another district team, so he was an experienced hand I was glad to get. The new assistant team leader, Lieutenant Cantrell, was a brand new OCS graduate. He seemed to be a nice enough fellow and I figured that if he could survive long enough, his enthusiasm would temper, his judgment would improve, and I would have a good officer to fall back on.

The move back to Tram Chim kept me busy, and with all the pressures and problems requiring my attention, Captain Jackson and the ''accident'' were soon pushed to the back of my mind. Later on, the incident became just another card in the mental file that was cataloged in my brain as ''Vietnam War,'' labeled ''Do Not Disturb.'' In the many years since, when memories of that day have flashed into my mind, I have always refused to let them linger. I don't want to analyze those old thoughts and actions again. It is difficult to judge the decisions I made so long ago under circumstances so different from the present. I do know, however, that I am not always comfortable with them.

I sometimes awake from a dream where Jackson, uncensured and unrepentant, has been allowed to make yet another mistake. I never can remember what the dream was about, but somehow I know that more men have been killed. It's because Jackson has made another mistake, this time even more stupid, this time even more deadly.

PART TWO

The Kingdom

Now we're old and grey, Fernando,
And since many years I haven't seen a rifle in your hands.
Can you still recall the fearful night we crossed the Rio Grande?
I can see it in your eyes how proud you were
To fight for freedom in this land.

There was something in the air that night,
The stars were bright, Fernando.
They were shining there for you and me,
For Liberty, Fernando.
Though we thought we'd never lose, there's no regret.
If I had to do the same again,
I would, my friend, Fernando.

"Fernando"
Abba (1979)
A rock song

Chapter 4

My team and I had helicoptered back out to Tram Chim in early September after being blown out of the place in early August. The fort had been repaired to some degree, and the bulk of the loose mortar ammo that I had last seen carpeting the compound had been cleaned up with the help of an explosive ordnance team from the USS *Benewa*. We had to rebuild our team house and bunker and get the local troops to complete the repairs of the fort wall, but before long we were back in business as usual, immersed in our various jobs, complaining of shortages and of being forgotten by the rest of the army, and marching out on one combat operation after another.

And the rains came. God, did it rain! It rained several times a day, and sometimes the winds that blew unimpeded across the plains drove the rain before them in horizontal sheets. The rain would fly right through any open doors or windows to soak everything within reach. We had to batten down every opening to the team house before each storm, an exercise that became tedious from constant repetition. Closing all the ports kept out the wind and rain but kept in the stifling heat and fetid humidity that rose from everything. Sometimes the need for a breath of fresh air would overcome the desire to keep the rain out and we would open the bamboo thatch door a crack, accepting the spray that came in with the relieving breeze.

Sooner or later everything was wet from the constant rain. Mattresses mildewed, matches disintegrated, cigarettes went limp, socks rotted, feet turned soft and pasty white from always being underwater, and jungle rot ate away at everything between our navels and our knees. On combat operations we couldn't avoid getting soaked all over, from either the rain, the sweat, or a dunking. Damp, chafing clothing rubbed a man's neck, shoulders, groin, knees, and waist. The raw patches of skin encouraged the multiple forms of fungus and general crud that were just waiting for a damp, warm place to live. Since we could never get really dry or clean, our skin was constantly rotting off our bones just the way our mattresses were rotting on their bunks. Small abrasions or scratches would turn into festering sores that refused to heal. Just trying to keep our skin intact became a primary occupation. A dry, clear day was always good medicine because we could lie out on the bunker roof and soak up some sun. Unencumbered by any boggy clothing, I could just feel the rays drying out my body and closing up my wounds.

The clothing of the natives was adapted to the hot, wet climate. No one wore regular shoes or boots. Open sandals were the only footwear, and clothing was made to be loose-fitting and light. Men wore the black cotton "pajamas" of Vietnamese peasant fame; some of the older men wore a turban-like head covering. Women wore similar, though often more colorful, clothing. Only on special occasions did they wear the beautiful *ao días* seen so often in the cities.

Despite criticism from province headquarters, we sometimes wore the same garb the natives did. We liked it because it was such sensible clothing for the climate. Without socks and heavy boots, our feet would dry out in a matter of minutes. Wearing light cotton pants and no American underwear allowed our skin to stay drier than when we wore the heavier fabric of army uniforms.

Once the rainy season had begun I knew the floods wouldn't be far behind. The rains had actually started in early August and the land had been sinking ever since. Because the average elevation in the district was only about nine feet above sea level, it didn't take long for the water to overflow the canal banks. By October the whole world seemed to be underwater. Every part of the main road was flooded, and we lost two small but necessary bridges on the road to An Long. Tram Chim could no longer be reached by dry land.

Our helipad was covered and choppers couldn't land any-more, but the fort itself had been built on a slight elevation that kept us from being completely flooded during the season's peak. Even so, most of the interior of the compound was underwater at one time or another, and any ground not covered with water had been turned to an ooze of gray, pasty mud that had the adhesive property of flypaper. It stuck to everything, got everywhere, and bugged the hell out of everybody!

The hamlets in the district were built right on the banks of the canals to take advantage of the elevation offered by the high bank of packed earth left from the canal excavations. Even these houses and buildings were sometimes flooded, though, and families had to sling their belongings from the bamboo rafter poles and get used to sloshing around in ankle-deep water. It was that or live in their boats.

It was mid-October. My team and I had been back in Tram Chim for several weeks and our work had begun to take hold again. Lieutenant Cantrell and I handled a lot of paper-work and made the district rounds to hold meetings with the local chiefs. The NCO's taught various classes about tactics and weapons to the village militiamen, and we all spent a lot of time on operations trying to show in practice what we taught in our primitive classrooms. I had spent the better part of this particular day on a medical civic action program with two navy men, a dentist and a physician from the USS *Benewa*. I had arranged for the two men to come out on a PBR and hold a clinic with Sergeant Fitz, the team medic, in the marketplace of Tram Chim village. The program had been a big hit and by mid-morning we had had patients lined up for a hundred yards, the column snaking its way around the busy market square and back down the village street.

In the early afternoon I had left the area to attend to some other business, and now at mid-afternoon I found myself standing inside the compound with nothing particular to do for a few minutes before heading back down to the clinic in the village market. I was chipping away at the wall of the com-pound with my knife, marveling at how the sticky, gooey, Delta mud could dry down to such a hard, impenetrable sub-stance. Our walls of dried Mekong mud were like concrete.

I was startled by Sergeant Robertson's urgent call from the commo bunker. "Lieutenant Donovan! Hey, *Trung úy!*"

"Yeah, what is it?" I called.

"Province says that Captain Dunn and his RF's over in Kien Van are chasing a Charlie boat convoy. It looks like the boats might get away and cross over into our district. They want to know if we can get enough men together real quick and run up there to intercept. What do I tell 'em?"

"What?" I shot back sarcastically. "Where the hell am I going to scratch up a platoon at this time of day to just run off out in the middle of nowhere?" It sounded to me as though Captain Dunn, the senior advisor of our adjacent district, had caught a Cong convoy coming in from Cambodia. Now it was about to slip through their fingers and he needed some help. It wasn't going to be easy to get it to him. "Cantrell and Abney are out on an operation already! What the hell do they think this is, a damned troop depot?" Robertson just rolled his eyes and shrugged his shoulders. I stood there with my hands on my hips, looking in the dirt, wondering what the hell I could do. "Shit!" I said in disgust.

"Is that what I'm supposed to tell province?" asked Robertson after a brief pause.

"No." I finally said, "Hell, tell 'em we'll try to get up there with what I can put together."

Robertson turned and ran back to the radio and I ran to the little hooch in the compound where I knew I would find the commander of our Regional Forces company. I explained the situation to him and asked if he could help me get together all the spare men in the fort for a quick sortie up to where the VC convoy was supposed to be coming into our district. I was surprised by the little commander's quick acceptance of the challenge. Soon we were both running around the fort, gathering up men and supplies and rushing them out to the sampans that we would have to use to get up to the unpopulated district border area.

Within minutes we had gathered about fifteen men and were on our way in the cramped little boats. We moved along well considering that we only moved under pole power. The small boats cut their way with equal ease across the open waters of the canals and through the green thickets of reeds that grew up from land already under the rising floodwaters. As we approached the area we became more cautious. We would move a few hundred meters and crawl up on a canal bank to have a look around. Sometimes we would climb a tree to get a better view of things. The American pilot of a small single-engine spotter plane contacted me on our PRC-25. He had been with Dunn and his operation and he began directing us in to the escaping enemy convoy.

We paddled, we sat, we searched, we floated, we did everything but sight the convoy. We all became tired and nervous. I was sick of listening to the ever-promising pilot, who kept saying we would soon have the enemy in sight. I was beginning to worry about finding our way back home when suddenly, through the trees in front of us and across a flat field of elephant grass, I saw movement. My breath caught in my throat, my pulse quickened, exhaustion was completely forgotten. I grinned and said, "Now we've got 'em!"

The three large *ghes*, or sampans, were being moved along by their gasoline engines. We could hear them putt-putting in the distance, and after watching them for a while from our position down in the reeds, I could tell that there were several armed men on the deck of each boat. They were dressed in the traditional black pajamas and were keeping a pensive watch to their rear. They were also keeping an eye on the spotter plane which was lazily circling high up in the air behind them. The Cong boats were out of rifle range for us but I thought we would be able to take up an ambush position along the canal we were on and just wait for them to come upon us. After watching the boats for a few seconds more, however, I realized they were moving obliquely away from us, traveling generally from right to left across our front. To catch them we would have to abandon our boats and chase them on foot. Our only hope was to get some air support. That might slow the convoy down and allow us to close up on them.

I called back to the team compound by radio and briefly explained my situation to Sergeant Robertson. I told him to send a message to province headquarters urgently requesting some sort of air support. Province responded rapidly. They gave me all the air support they had available—the same little spotter plane that had been shadowing the operation all along. Its armament consisted of four rockets in its wing pods and whatever rifle or pistol the pilot had with him. Robertson had just finished relaying this good news when the spotter pilot came up on my radio frequency again, using our code designators.

"Red Banks Echo, Steely Canyon one-zero, over."

"Canyon one-zero, this is Echo-six, over."

"Echo-six, this is Canyon one-zero. I have just been on the other net to province. It looks like no other air is available. I have two willie peters and two HE's on my wings. Can I help, over?"

I knew we had to slow the boats down if we were going to catch them. They were moving away from our intercept point, not toward it, and we couldn't simply take off across open land running after the escaping sampans. For one thing, unless the boats slowed down we would never catch them, and if we did get close, the VC could shoot us down like little ducks in a gallery. The spotter pilot had told me he had two white phosphorous rockets and two high explosive rockets. I wondered if he really knew how to hit something with them.

"One-zero, this is six. Affirmative. Can you put two rockets in the lead boat and sink it? Maybe that would block the canal and give us a chance to catch up with the boats. If you can't stop 'em, they're going to get clean away, over."

"This is one-zero. Roger, I'll give it a shot. If I hit the little guy up front on my first pass, I'll swing back and try for the big one in the rear, over."

"This is six. Roger, one-zero. Go to it. Out."

We left a couple of men with our boats and began moving off through the elephant grass in the direction the Cong supply boats had taken. Somewhere behind the treetops I heard the approaching yowl of the small aircraft engine. Suddenly the little olive-drab plane was overhead, then beyond us. Smoke and a flash of fire erupted from beneath its wings. Two rockets darted from the small plane and disappeared over a tree line out in front of us. In an instant we heard the dual crump of their impact followed by a smattering of small arms fire. I guessed the Cong were shooting back. I could no longer see the plane, but I soon heard it circling back to our left. We kept moving in the direction of the target, not sure what the result of the strike was. I kept trying to call the pilot but I could not get a response from him on the radio.

The plane came back over us and fired again, this time using its last two rockets. The twin blasts of the explosions confirmed our proper direction so we went forward even more urgently. Finally the pilot came on the radio again. "Six, this is one-zero, over."

"One-zero, six. Did you get 'em? Over."

"That's affirm', six! I got 'em both, but you guys had better hurry. That middle boat is trying to get around the front boat I hit. When I hit him he went dead in the water but the middle guy is trying to get around, over."

"One-zero, this is six. Good job! We're on our way, out."

I waved my men on and urged them to move quickly before the remaining boat got away. Sensing the approach of action, their spirits picked up. We moved more rapidly now, but with greater alertness. Before long we could see the top portion of a beached, smoking sampan just short of a tree line about two hundred yards away. Everyone took cover while the patrol leader and I crawled forward to look the situation over.

The spotter plane had run out of both guns and gas and had called to say he was headed home. The pilot made one final pass just above the treetops. As he disappeared over the trees in front of us, I saw him holding his M-16 out his side window and firing at the boats below him. It was crazy and ineffective, but a nice touch, I thought.

We came under light fire as we moved in on the stricken boats. We returned the fire sporadically, but concentrated on keeping moving. We didn't want to let the remaining boat escape. As we approached the beached wreck, several men came out of hiding along the canal bank and approached us with their hands up. The firing soon died down altogether and we gathered a group of seven prisoners. I made sure the militiamen stayed spread out across the target area and that they kept their eyes open for other prisoners or an unexpected attack. We still didn't know where the other two enemy boats had gone.

When I got up to the canal bank itself, it was clear what had happened. About fifty yards farther up, a smaller sampan had suffered a direct hit in the bow. It had gone down off to one side of the narrow canal. The middle boat had apparently been small enough to squeeze by, even with the stricken boat in the way. The sampan had been able to continue on down the canal, where it had disappeared into a section of thick jungle.

We searched the wrecks for useful items and information. We found no dead VC and no weapons. We did have prisoners, however, and one of them had made the oversight of not disposing of an ammo belt still slung across his shoulder. That caused us to disbelieve his claim that they were all just innocent fishermen. In the wreckage of the boats we found two large cases of medicines from East Germany, Poland, and Czechoslovakia. We found a large packet of personal letters and official communications from various COSVN directorates and other Viet Cong headquarters. We also discovered some large bundles of shirts, pants, and camouflage cloth. When we searched the canal bottom, we recovered two AK-47's, the popular Soviet assault rifle.

Just as I thought we were about to wind everything up and begin the journey back home, I heard some commotion from the nearby tree line. I walked over to where a group of men were huddled in conversation and found that someone had dragged a man out of the canal. He was lying motionless on the bank, and I could see he had been hit by a piece of shrapnel. What had probably been a piece of razor-sharp metal had unzipped his abdomen right at the belt line. He was lying on the ground with his eyes closed, groaning softly. His wet, gray-white intestines were spilling from his wound despite his feeble attempts to hold them in with his hands. The militiamen were already drifting away. They didn't know what to do, and the sight was unpleasant. I knelt beside the man and thought to myself, "Oh, my God! Now what do I do?"

I knew immediately I was going to violate a key instruction about field first aid. You were never to use your own wound bandage on another man. Your bandage was for you if you got wounded. It was your own lifeline. Rule or no rule, I wasn't going to leave a man there with his guts stringing out of him. I sprinkled the wound with the yellow disinfectant powder and wrapped him with my bandage. If he was bleeding badly, I couldn't tell it; in fact I was surprised at how little blood was coming from inside the wound.

I called on the radio for a medevac chopper and informed the others that we were going to set up a perimeter and wait until the "dustoff" arrived. We put out a defensive perimeter and sent four men off on a recon patrol in the direction the supply boat had escaped. I wanted to make sure the other VC had actually left the area and were not just sitting over there in the trees somewhere, waiting to jump us at the first opportunity. There was no way I could leave a wounded man, gutshot at that, out there on the plains to die, but my decision to wait for the evacuation chopper did bring up some problems.

We didn't know how many men were with the boat that escaped. We had already rounded up seven prisoners from the two boats that had been sunk. We didn't know if others had escaped with the third boat or if they were perhaps still hiding in the woods, armed to the teeth. If they all came back to rescue their buddies we would be in a vulnerable position. There were only about fifteen of us, and with seven prisoners to watch, we would be in real trouble if an attack started. Evening was approaching, too. I knew that a favorite Viet Cong tactic was to locate a small, isolated unit around sundown and come back for the attack under cover of darkness.

We had rushed off from our village with only individual weapons and a basic load of ammo. We had no rations to eat, no entrenching tools with which to dig in, and no air support to call upon in an emergency. As the sinking sun bloodied the tropical sky, I became more worried about the possibility of an attack. I sent another recon section off into the woods to keep an eye out for any returning Viet Cong. My worry was intensified by the fact that we were away from the populated areas of the district and close to the Viet Cong sanctuary areas. The few Cong that disappeared with the undamaged boat might return with the whole Viet Cong district company. If we got hit by that bunch, we wouldn't stand a chance.

With the adrenalin surges all gone, exhaustion set back in. Minutes dragged by like hours. Everyone including myself became more and more anxious. We all wanted to get the hell out of there.

I was squatting by the wounded man. He was still quietly moaning, but would only open his eyes when he asked for water, which I refused him. Never give water to a man with a gut wound. It only increases the crud oozing into his abdomen out of any holes in his stomach or bowels.

I didn't know if the man could hear me or not, but I kept whispering to him in Vietnamese, telling him not to worry, a helicopter was coming to get him. I kept looking off to the darkening horizon for some evidence that what I said was true, but I could see nothing there. As the orange tint in the sky changed more and more to the blue-black of evening, and as the first star twinkled in the failing light, I began to think that staying and trying to help the wounded guerrilla had been a sucker move. I squatted beside the pallid victim and listened to his shallow breathing. I fanned the mosquitoes away from his face and slapped at the ones trying to fill themselves on my own blood.

I knew I had made a simpleminded decision. I had let heart win out over mind. I knew that normal use of small-unit tactics would have had us hit the boats, scour them quickly for useful equipment or information, and then get the hell out of the area. Yet here I was playing Florence Nightingale and risking the lives of my men in the process. I was on the verge of telling everyone to form up and move on back to our boats when one of the men rushed up, exclaiming, *"Máy bay, Trung úy! Máy bay!"* He pointed eagerly toward the southeast, and sure enough I saw a small blinking red light over the blackening but still faint horizon. At the same time I heard the reassuring whop-whop of the approaching helicopter. I was ecstatic, and I'm sure everyone else was at least relieved.

"Red Banks Echo, Red Banks Echo," the radio squawked with a rush of static, "White Knight three-zero, over."

I picked up the handset from the radio harness and squeezed the push-to-talk button, "White Knight three-zero, Banks Echo, go."

"Ahh, this is three-zero, Echo. Is your lima zulu hot or cold and do you have me in sight, over?" The "lima zulu," or landing zone, we wanted him to come in to was indeed cold. Not a shot had been fired in over an hour.

"Three-zero, this is Echo. We have a cold lima zulu. I do have you in sight. Bear five degrees right from your present heading and you should fly right into us. Range, maybe three klicks, over."

"Three-zero, roger. Five degrees right, three klicks. Wait, out."

As the chopper approached I began to feel better about myself. I was glad we had stuck it out for the wounded Viet Cong. I regained the confidence that I had made the right decision. I hurried back to where the man lay. I bent over to tell him that the chopper was coming in. He would be in a modern hospital within a few minutes. As I leaned over him, however, he released the air in his lungs in a ragged gurgle. His pale color instantly seemed to blanch even further. The transition was so stark and shocking that in retrospect I always imagine I actually saw a spirit leave his body. He was dead. Blank eyes staring through my head and into the infinity beyond. He was dead, I knew it even as I felt for a pulse at his neck. He was dead! I felt like I had been kicked in the chest. My throat tightened, my jaw dropped. I stared at him in disbelief. I grabbed his shoulder and shook him hard. "What are you doing?" I thought, frantically addressing the dead man in my mind. "You can't die now, not after we waited out here for you! It's not fair! I've saved you! *I've saved your life, goddammit!*"

I had not saved him, of course; he died at the moment of his rescue. Our wait and risk had been for nothing. I felt betrayed, as if a friend had turned on me after I had helped him out. I stared at the corpse and felt the anger churning inside me, anger at the dead man, anger at myself, anger at the whole situation.

The dust-off chopper had spotted us and was circling to land in the semi-darkness. I walked disgustedly over to the radio and called the pilot.

"Three-zero Echo, over."

"We have you, Echo. Can you put us down on some dry ground, over?"

"This is Echo, three-zero. The whiskey india alpha has just become a kilo india alpha. We won't need you now. Sorry for the trouble, over."

There was a tense pause before the pilot replied, "Roger, Echo. Sorry about that. Three-zero home bound and out." The chopper wheeled about in the air above us and headed back. With the fading thump of the chopper blades in my ears, I walked back over and looked down at the dead Viet Cong soldier. I had wanted to save him so badly! I had been feeling so good about it! Damn! I had never watched a man die slowly and up close. It was an ugly experience.

We left him there for his comrades or the buzzards, whichever found him first. Darkness was around us now and we had no time to bury him. We slipped away into the clear tropical night. I kept looking back at the lonely body until it was just a faint spot, mostly obscured by the darkness and the elephant grass. I was depressed all the way back to the village.

Sometimes that same feeling of depression still returns, especially when I see one of those blood-red sunsets that slowly succumb to evening. It was under that same sanguine sky that I heard the death rattle from that anguished man out there on the Plain of Reeds.

THE HIGH WATERS OF THE RAINY SEASON FORCED MANY OF our operations to be carried out in small fleets of sampans. We couldn't walk far through the floodwaters so we used the small village sampans as our mode of transport. The size of sampan we generally used was from twelve to fifteen feet long and about two and a half feet wide. They were the native version of the family car; every family had at least one. The agile little Vietnamese were experts at paddling, poling, and balancing in the small craft. We klutzy Americans could hardly sit in the damned things. The slightest movement would set the boat to wallowing and threatening to turn turtle. Even when someone else was doing the poling, the cramped position we had to tuck into just to fit in the thing would soon cause flashes of pain. After only a few minutes my back would start to ache, then my butt would feel as if I was sitting on a rail, then my knees would send up complaints, and finally everything below my waist would go numb from lack of blood. It was a miserable way to get to a fight.

The Infantry School handbooks never had any chapters on the tactics of sampan operations, so I made things up as I went. Our combat formations were makeshift, depending on the operation at hand and how many boats we had. No matter what, there's not much you can do tactically with a bunch of boats under pole power. If we came under fire from someone in a protected position, say in a tree line with a bunker hidden in it, we would be practically defenseless. I was always worried that a firefight would erupt with me frozen into position by some combination of joint pain and ischemia in the lower limbs.

At the peak of the flood season water really covered almost everything. Flying over my district in a helicopter was like flying over an ocean with trees scattered in it. We could fly for miles and literally see nothing that was completely out of water. When one is used to highways, bridges, and buildings with dry floors, that sort of thing takes some getting used to.

The army did make a concession to the unusual problems brought on by our rainy season. For example, our team's jeep was blown up during a mortar attack on our fort. Rather than replace the jeep, which we couldn't drive anywhere anyway, the army gave us a sixteen-foot-long Boston Whaler runabout. The boat and its forty-five-horsepower outboard engine came in olive-drab green. We installed a .30 caliber machine gun with a swivel mount and a steel deflector shield in the bow. On either side of the bow we painted a small American flag and the name USS *Proud Mary*. The name was inspired by a popular rock song of the time which extolled the virtues of working on a Mississippi River boat, the *Proud Mary*. Now we had our own *Proud Mary*, a ship of the line, forward gun deck and all. Not a fancy riverboat perhaps, but she was certainly a step up from the local motorized sampans which chugged along with such complacent lethargy. My district chief was green with envy when he saw us putter over in our new vessel. I had to go to great pains to explain to him why it was that I couldn't get him a boat just like mine. I don't think he was ever convinced that I couldn't get him one even if I wanted to.

Chapter 5

BEING a new District Senior Advisor revealed to me a whole host of problems I had not had to deal with previously. As an assistant MAT team leader I had been aware of many of the problems, but since they had been the team leader's responsibility I hadn't really bothered with trying to solve them. One of my major headaches now was trying to find supplies, not only military and civilian supplies for the Vietnamese villagers, but even subsistence supplies for my own team of Americans. MACV had made the decision that since MAT teams were to teach the local village and hamlet defense forces how to make the Vietnamese government and military system work, then the MAT teams should be provided for primarily by that same Vietnamese system. That would supposedly heighten our desire to make the system proficient. When we came in-country the army issued us our initial TA-50 equipment, an M-16 rifle, and a basic load of ammunition. After that we were supposedly on our own to survive with the Vietnamese. That made life in general, and combat in particular, a very different thing than what we'd been taught at the Infantry Officer Basic Course.

Since American units got first call on American tactical air support, medical evacuations, and even helicopter support, we only got help if everyone else was having a slow day. We would sometimes wait hours for medevac choppers, although we had been told back in the States that they were available within thirty minutes anywhere in the country. I have fought more than one guerrilla engagement where my only air support was a single-engine spotter plane with a couple of rocket pods mounted on the wings. I would have preferred a flight of F-4 Phantoms, but I always gave any airplane drivers who came by my heartfelt thanks. I was glad for any help I could get!

Guys who served with American units always found it hard to believe we couldn't even get simple things like sandbags or ammunition for our mortars. In the case of sandbags, our province chief kept most of those allotted to the provincial forces in the province capital itself. He wanted to make sure that he and his were well protected—to hell with the rest of us. There were other reasons for other shortages, most of them one form of corruption or another. In the end I was absolutely convinced that corruption was more harmful to the Vietnamese government than communism ever was.

American units always seemed to have plenty of food, too. Not so on a MAT team. My team was allotted thirteen cases of C-rations on our property books. We couldn't eat them, however, unless we kept an account book to show that whoever ate one of the C-rations had paid $1.15 for the meal. I learned that lesson early when an inspection team helicoptered out and wanted to see our thirteen cases. They also wanted to ensure that each case was stacked according to U.S. government regulations so that one inch of airspace separated all cases. Breathing room, you know. Army regulations and all that. The C-rations were only there for emergencies, anyway. We were supposed to eat them when we got cut off by massive invasions from across the border. Whether we would have to pay for our C-rations under those conditions was never established.

For everyday purposes, we could try to send a man back to the province headquarters to purchase food from the U.S.-run "country store." Team members were supposed to pool their money and buy enough food to last about a month. Inevitably, when our man got to the country store the shelves were bare except for the fifteen new cases of U.S. government #2 rutabagas and the overstock of canned green beans. We usually found it better to just survive with the local villagers. American army troops existing on rations of rats and rice or snake and water vine may seem strange, but believe me, you can develop a taste for anything. My favorite Oriental condiment is still *nước mắm,* a pungent Vietnamese fish sauce that many Americans could never quite stomach. Like I say, you can get used to anything.

Some of the weapons we had to use were also incredible. When I first arrived at Tram Chim, some of the local troops still had old World War II weapons. I was amazed by some of my early engagements where we had troops firing antique M-1 Garand rifles and Thompson submachine guns while being supported by old propeller-driven fighter-bombers. The whole thing seemed like a grade-B war movie. In 1979 I helped a soldier use a Browning automatic rifle in combat. Using that pre-1940 weapon in a military engagement in 1969 was as anachronistic as the Poles using cavalry in World War II! One of our hamlet defense groups was armed with nothing but 12-gauge pump shotguns. These short-barreled old scatterguns were designed for use in World War I and for riot control in prisons; yet here they were on the Plain of Reeds defending hamlets and rice paddies. I can say I was never issued a spear.

As THE RAINY SEASON DEVELOPED, OUR SENSE OF ISOLATION became even more intense. We could no longer be reached over land, the flooding around the fort made it difficult to get resupply by air, and the atmospheric disturbances made radio communication with Cao Lanh even more difficult than usual. We pushed ahead with our civic affairs work and our counter-guerrilla operations in spite of a brooding sense of aloneness. We felt as if a great weight had to be pulled forward, and that we were the only mules in the harness. That aloneness, that separation from other Americans and from life as we had always known it, brought on the strong inner tremblings of culture shock, a psychological malaise that produces casualties as surely as any bullet.

For some people, culture shock rumbled through their system the minute they stepped off the plane in Saigon; others were affected only in the most severe circumstances. In such an isolated outpost as ours one could quickly lose the psychological underpinnings that supported his normal personality. There were no friends, no family, no roads, no automobiles, no telephones, no electricity, no English language, no neighborhoods as we knew them, no American or European music, no radio, no television, no people who thought like us, looked like us, sounded like us, or even ate like us. Since all previous background and culturization had been suddenly rendered worthless, it was very difficult to establish any personal direction, purpose, or even hope. Good men and true have been rendered absolutely useless by the combined effects of constant danger and such rude cultural transitions.

It seemed to me that the best remedy for culture shock was hard work, so I made sure everyone stayed busy. I wanted to minimize the time anyone had to lie around and wonder what in the hell we were doing out here alone in the mud and the blood and the crud.

The efforts of my team to organize our villagers and militiamen as an effective counterpoint to the Viet Cong were carried out with increasing success. This angered the Cong, so they put a bounty on my head and on the heads of my teammates. I was told on several occasions by people I had good reason to believe that the price on my head was 100,000 piasters, cash. While that is only about $2,000 in today's money, it was a bloody fortune to a peasant out in the Plain of Reeds. We all found it difficult to move about freely and act normally when we never knew who would feel like trying to blow us away and collect the prize from the communists. The person who might try it could be one of the villagers who simply wanted the cash, or it might be one of the Viet Cong who had infiltrated the village units. It's a nerve-wracking thing, living with a price on your head!

Because of the need to be constantly on the alert, our reactions became finely tuned. When I was awake my eyes never stopped moving, whether over an apparently innocent crowd or through the quiet and shadowed jungle. With practice I learned to sense what was normal movement and activity on the quiet jungle path or in the bustle of a village marketplace. Abnormal activity, rapid movement lateral to the flow of a crowd, a waving frond in the jungle stillness, a moving shadow in the darkness, quickly got my attention. The acuity of my peripheral vision became so great I could almost literally "see out of the back of my head." My abilities to hear and smell also sharpened, and these combined with visual messages gave me an almost animal-like sense of safety or approaching danger. This was true for everyone on my team.

The pressures that developed from this constant alert were

numbing. At night one team member was always awake on radio watch. During a watch we not only listened to the field radio for the team's messages, we also guarded the rest of the sleeping team. If every team member was in the fort, each man pulled a two-hour watch through the night. Often two or even three of the five-man team were out on night ambush or patrol operations, which left only a couple of men to share an all-night shift of keeping each other alive and guarding the possessions of the missing teammates. Combined with exhausting full-duty days and the knowledge that you were miles from any help in case of trouble, those nights of subdued strain and boredom were as debilitating as a disease.

Even when we could have slept, we never really did. Any unusual sound awoke us with a start. To wake the next man for his radio watch, you had to tap him on the toe and take a quick step backward to get out of his way. The teammate would usually jump up from his bunk. Not really awake but functioning entirely on reflex, he was a dangerous man to be near. He might kick you or slug you, or take a bite off your nose. After a couple of seconds, he would be fully awake and acting as if nothing had happened. It was a strange phenomenon that occurred to everyone, but not one of us could ever remember his own waking antics. We only heard about them from our teammates.

We learned to trust no one, not even children. All mail and correspondence was to be burned after being read lest the Cong agents raid the trash and discover military or personal information they should not have. All beer or soft drink cans had to be crushed—if the cans were left whole the Cong would buy them from the local kids and use them as casings for hand-grenades. We wore our weapons constantly, even to a friend's house. We never went anywhere alone, always in pairs. We survived by being suspicious, a trait I have found difficult to set aside.

WE WORRIED ABOUT THE LOCAL CONG A LOT, AND WE HAD no doubt they were out to get us, but the majority of the villagers we encountered were very friendly. We were in such a remote region of Vietnam that the locals had not seen many Americans and were openly curious about everything we did. Everything. We couldn't urinate or take a crap without half the village turning out to watch. There were no bathrooms; the native crapper was just a single bamboo pole stuck out over a canal or a water-filled pit. To use this Oriental water closet you had to balance out to the end of the pole and sit on a small plank. There was usually a bamboo privacy screen around this little platform, but sometimes not. If a villager saw one of us Americans tenderly making his way to the defecatorium, they would call a crowd to watch. That can inhibit the bodily processes.

We would sometimes eat a meal in one of the open-air village cafes. When we did, groups of kids and adults would gather to watch our relatively clumsy use of chopsticks. In our team house and around our compound there were always two or three village militiamen staring at us, watching our every move as they calmly squatted in the doorway and smoked some of the god-awfullest tobacco ever to take a match. They would sit there and watch, always smiling, maybe murmuring to themselves on occasion, and while we tried to smile too, the constant observation damn near drove us crazy. We couldn't run them off because that would have insulted them and would have cut us off from the very people we were supposed to be helping. On the other hand we never knew who among them might be a Viet Cong checking us out. I swore I'd never go to a zoo again. I reckoned I knew too well how it felt to have to live in one.

On one occasion after a beer party at the local village chief's house I was invited to the thatched hooch of one of the willing village lovelies. The chief and all of his cronies were in high spirits and thought it would be great fun to watch the big white guy get it on with the princess. I declined with as much grace as possible, not that it was easy to turn down a free ride to the races, mind you, but I would have had to have been more drunk than I was and more perverse than I am to enjoy performing in public like a trained dog. I also admit to feeling that I had to maintain some sense of decorum as the senior American in the area. I wasn't at all sure that the army's list of my rights and privileges included free bounces in the bedding with every village girl that was offered me.

While the villages and hamlets in my district were poor economically, the people were always rich in courtesy and hospitality. I was constantly being invited into some tattered bamboo hut to share a simple meal or to swig a few bottles of warm Vietnamese beer. The simple food was always good, but the beer was awful. It was called *Ba mười Ba,* which means "Thirty-Three" in English. I have no idea why that would be the brand name of a beer. The label on the bottles had a picture of a tiger, and for that and other reasons we called it "tiger piss." We felt that name gave proper notice to the beer's label, its temperature, its color, and its taste.

At any meal in a Vietnamese house, the choicest morsels of food were always offered to the senior guest. That was often I, and as a matter of reciprocal courtesy I would pass it back to the host or on to one of my senior Vietnamese colleagues. Simple gestures like that went a long way in establishing friendship and cooperation, so I tried never to pass up an opportunity to have the villagers think better of me. Being a cautious fellow I always felt that a good impression might one day be the difference between life and death, so I indulged in graciousness whenever I could, especially with a simple thing like cigarettes, for example.

It seemed that every adult Vietnamese male smoked cigarettes. At any meal, party, or other male assembly, cigarettes were laid out on the table and shared by all. The host would put out his pack of Vietnamese cigarettes, even if he could usually afford only roll-your-owns. Since I always had the highly prized American cigarettes, I would put out my pack on the table also. Hands would invariably reach past the host's Capstans or Ruby Queens to my Winstons or Salems. A subtle but noticed act of camaraderie was for me to pass over my own American cigarettes and reach across for one of the host's. Those things were worse than the beer, but by my smoking them I showed the men that I was sharing as an equal. That was a critical message to get across if I was to have their willing support. It also showed that, when in an underdeveloped country, never underestimate the power of an American cigarette!

WE HAD ALWAYS PAID ONE OF THE VILLAGE GIRLS TO COME to the fort every day and try to keep our team house in some sort of order. She worked, or at least hung around, for eight hours a day, seven days a week, did the sewing and laundry at home, washed the dishes, cleaned the mud from the floors and boots, and generally kept the place in order. Most important of all, though, she made us smile. What a smile she had, too. Wall-to-wall, ear-to-ear happiness with perfect teeth that sparkled in the Oriental tawniness of her face. She was just a teenager, sixteen or so as I recall, but you could tell she was going to have that loveliness so common among Vietnamese women.

Her name was Ha, or more properly, Cô Ha, *Cô* being the Vietnamese word that translates loosely as "Miss." We always called her Cô Ha because we wanted to maintain propriety. Being from a small Southern town back in the States, I knew that appearances could be very important. That was certainly the case in our isolated, traditional Vietnamese village. I knew the potential problems of misinterpreted boy-girl relationships, especially when foreigners got involved. I didn't want the village fathers to get up in arms because they thought we Americans were getting too friendly with the village maidens.

Cô Ha had that vivaciousness and sparkling humor that are endemic in teenagers everywhere. Her pranks and jokes kept us amused when everything else called for crushing gloom. In times of dark depression she was often the only bright spark we could see. We didn't mind when Cô Ha would occasionally bring a friend with her to work. The laughter and giddiness of the two of them would provide a pleasant background to our otherwise somber circumstances. Her girlfriends had that sloe-eyed Vietnamese charm and a giggling curiosity about everything American. From the shy looks, the snickering that went on in the back room, and the occasional peals of laughter followed by embarrassed protests, one supposed they were indeed curious about many things, not all of them fittin' subjects for nice young village girls.

One day Cô Ha brought a girlfriend I didn't recognize with her. We had discouraged and finally forbade her to bring in friends from the outside whom we had not met. The Viet Cong were not above using young women to get into a fort like ours. They would have women cultivate the proper friendships, gain entrance to a compound, and then leave behind a deadly memento one day, say five pounds of plastic explosive hidden under the bunks. We didn't keep strangers out of the fort because I wanted to be mean and suspicious; I had just learned to be cautious.

Cô Ha was especially cheerful that day and her friend was equally animated, so I was reluctant to reprimand Ha and send her friend off. I mentioned the new girl to the others and told them to keep an eye on her general behavior. I had to admit that from the appearance of things this was just another young girl from the village who had come up with Cô Ha to get a closer look at the Americans.

Later in the day I noticed that Cô Ha and her friend were often in earnest conversation. During an especially intense series of mutterings and laughter, I could tell the new girl was urging Cô Ha to come over and ask or tell me something. Finally Ha got up and with much giggling and looking at the floor, she came over and asked me if I needed another girl to work in the team house.

"Why?" I asked in quick astonishment. "Are you quitting?"

"No, *Trung úy*," she said with a sly smile.

I was relieved. Ha did her job well, and we all liked her a lot. "Well then, tell your friend that I'm sorry but we don't have enough work around here for two girls. Tell her that if we did, we would be glad to hire her."

"But *Trung úy*," Ha said with laughter in her eyes, "she doesn't want to do what I do, she wants to . . . be a special girl."

I could tell from that last pause that Ha had been searching for words, but I couldn't figure out what she was talking about. I thought I might have misunderstood the whole conversation. Cô Ha was giggling again and was obviously amused at the look of puzzlement on my face. Ah! Now I had it. The girl didn't want to work full time; she just wanted to do extra work that Cô Ha might not be able to get to. Of course!

I smiled confidently and said, "I'm sorry, tell her that you can do all the work we have without need for help."

Ha dropped to a squat, hid her face in her hands, and shook with yelps of laughter. The other girl was squatting in the corner with a bemused look in her eyes. She looked at Cô Ha as if to urge her on.

"No, *Trung úy*," Ha finally got out between chuckles, "she

doesn't want to do the work I do. She wants to be the bed-girl for you and the others.''

My mouth must have dropped open because Ha broke into another fit of laughter. After a pause she said, ''Everybody knows you don't have a girl in the village, *Trung úy*. This girl will work here every day for the same pay you give me. She asked me to tell you this.''

You could have knocked me down with a gnat's wing. Sergeant Robertson, my light weapons NCO, had been listening to this whole conversation and muttered a prayerful, ''All r-i-i-i-ght!''

Now Ha and the other girl were really yukking it up. Sergeant Robertson was sitting there with a look on his face like a kid who just heard a fantastic fairy-tale. I was no longer confused, but I still didn't know what to say.

''Wait a minute,'' I said. ''You mean to tell me that she is willing to come in here and be the bed-girl for every man on this team every day of the week for forty dollars a month?'' Sergeant Robertson was grinning toward heaven and nodding fervently; I think it was his ''Thank you, Jesus'' routine. Cô Ha smiled and nodded too.

''Shi-it,'' I said to myself, ''what a bargain! And from a good-looker, too!'' I shook my head and somehow marshaled my resolve. ''No, absolutely not,'' I said firmly. ''Tell her thanks anyway, but . . . we can't afford the extra money.'' Sergeant Robertson went limp; he looked at me in disbelief. Cô Ha didn't look convinced either, so I thought I had better find another reason. ''And tell her that even though she is a very lovely girl, it is not allowed for us to have a bed-girl from the village. It would make much trouble for us. We can't do it, no way.''

''*Không xấu, Trung úy, không xấu*,'' Ha said as she turned away still chuckling. That expression translates to something like ''No sweat'' or ''It's o.k., don't worry about it.'' Ha and the other girl continued to talk and chuckle for a few minutes and then went on about the work they had been doing together. The failed proposition might as well have been an offer to make a new pot of coffee.

I was still flabbergasted. Cô Ha, who would never make or accept, so far as I could tell, any risqué advances, had without any detectable chagrin offered her friend as our own special whore. I kept going over the conversation in my mind, half-way convinced that I had misunderstood something critical in the discussion.

FROM WHAT I HAD BEEN ABLE TO TELL, THE SEXUAL MORES of the villages were very conservative; that was why I had been so surprised by Cô Ha and her friend. I never was absolutely sure that I understood the local attitudes correctly. While there was a lot of joking about sex among both men and women, I was never certain of the territory and never knew when I might say or do something that for some subtle reason was going to be offensive.

For example, it was impossible not to notice the women bathing in the canal that ran by our village. They would go down to the banks of the canal, ease out into the water, take off their clothes, and wash up. It was difficult to strictly observe the discipline of keeping all strategic body parts below the waterline, and horny GI's can perhaps be forgiven a mild interest in the proceedings. A cheerful shout or wave from such a group of women always seemed an invitation to at least go over and spend some time in pleasant conversation, yet I quickly learned that such a move would have meant big trouble. The women would have been embarrassed and the village men would have been angered. The social understanding was that women, or men for that matter, bathed in the open canal and everyone else pretended not to notice. If some bather of the opposite sex called a greeting or waved, the only appropriate response was to return the salutation in kind and keep on about your business. Men were not supposed to notice that the women were naked, and vice versa. My guys did not always obey the social rules. Late one afternoon Sergeant Abney and Lieutenant Cantrell, my assistant team leader, were sitting on the wall of the fort watching the boats in the canal ease their way through the brown water. Every evening there was a buildup of traffic in the canal as all kinds and sizes of watercraft made their way home from the day's fishing or the hot work in the distant rice fields. This particular evening a group of women came out from the village and went down to the water's edge by the wall of the fort. They were all laughing and gossiping and paying no attention to the local men or to the Americans up on the wall. The Vietnamese men followed convention and moved away or discreetly looked in another direction. Cantrell also followed protocol and went off to another area of the fort. Sergeant Abney ran off to get his camera.

Abney returned with his pocket Instamatic and started taking pictures like a tourist at the Eiffel Tower. To make matters worse, he drew attention to himself by calling and waving to the women in the canal. He was trying to get them to wave so he could take a picture, or so he told me later. The women were mortified that this guy was up there calling, waving, and actually taking pictures. They all ducked up to their chins in the water and showed considerable displeasure at Abney's acting like a teenager at a stag party. fortunately, Lieutenant Cantrell went over and hauled him away before the Vietnamese men in the compound could come over and register their ire.

When I returned to the fort later in the day and heard about the incident, I reminded Abney in no uncertain terms of the social rules regarding open-air bathing. I told him that he was never to show any attention toward the bathers again, and as a matter of fact, that it would be best if he stayed away from that corner of the wall entirely in the evenings. Some angry husband, fiancé, or brother could always turn out to be the very man we needed in an emergency. We had to accept the fact that we couldn't afford to lose a single friend.

MOST OF THE TIME THE VILLAGE WOMEN ACTED OUT THEIR expected roles of demure modesty. Usually when I least expected it, however, some woman would find occasion to break from the conventional mold. For example, sometimes women in the villages seemed to think nothing about coming out to watch one of us Americans take a leak. That was always good for a lot of grinning and pointing. At other times it was difficult not to notice the coy, enticing smiles from some of the young women around. It was very confusing to me, anyway, and being constantly horny didn't help settle things in my mind.

One evening Robertson and I had been invited to eat supper with one of the families in the village. We went and ate and stayed for a while afterward to talk with the old fisherman who headed the family. The little palm thatch house was lit only by a single kerosene lantern. The yellow glow from the glass chimney lit only a small circle around the wooden table in the front room. The old fisherman's daughter slipped into the room from the back and sat on a platform over in the corner that was used as the family's sleeping area. She was behind her father and a partition blocked her from his line of view, even if he turned around. She was an attractive girl, not over eighteen or so, whom Robertson and I both knew from having seen around the village. We had talked and joked with her and her friends on many occasions. I wasn't surprised, then, at her open and direct grin at us from over the old man's shoulder. It was what came next that surprised me!

Flashing an impish smile, she slowly pulled up her blouse and started gently squeezing and cupping her breasts, looking first at me, then at Robertson. She seemed to think it was a big practical joke to sit behind her old man and thrust her breasts at us in the low, flickering light. I think my mouth was hanging open; I know Robertson's was!

I tried hard to concentrate on what the old man was saying. I looked straight at him and tried not to be distracted. I didn't want to give him any reason to get suspicious and turn around. I was a little shaken, to say the least! If the old fisherman had seen his daughter carrying on like that in front of his guests he would have been apoplectic. Had he seen her, I wouldn't have been surprised if he had tried to kill her, or even us if he thought we put her up to it.

I made the sudden excuse that I had some business I had to get to back at the compound. I thanked the old man for his hospitality and pushed Robertson along toward the door. The old man's wife came from the back room as we were leaving and the daughter came over from the platform, blouse down but with a big "now what do you think about that?" smile on her face. They all came to see us to the door, where I mumbled a few pleasantries and dragged Robertson off in a hasty retreat. We both muttered our disbelief to each other all the way back to the fort. I kept looking over my shoulder, half expecting the old man to be coming after us with a gun. But the next time I saw the fisherman he was as friendly as ever. We continued to see his daughter down in the village and she would always give us a laugh, a toss of head, and a knowing smile that still seemed to say, "Now what do you think about that?"

SERGEANT ROBERTSON AND I HAD TAKEN A PLATOON FROM our Regional Forces company and had moved them *in toto* out into an area of the district where population was scarce and Viet Cong traffic from Cambodia was increasing. The authorities back in the province town wanted a new fort established out there to serve as a base for patrols.

In the Vietnamese tradition, when the soldiers moved, their women and children moved with them too. Families would load their pots and pans and a few bundles of belongings into small sampans and just set out to wherever the husbands were being sent. Sergeant Robertson and I went out with the RF platoon and their entourage to help plan the construction of the new fort and to see that the Vietnamese officers had no problems establishing their patrols and supply routes.

One day some soldiers I had been working with invited me to come along with them for their noon meal. Pham, one of the young men in the group, directed us all to the little tin lean-to his wife had erected to serve as their living quarters while the fort was being constructed. She had a cooking fire going in front of the small shelter and had prepared a meal of rice, fish baked in a banana leaf, some leaves of a green water plant, and *nước mắm*, the fish sauce that serves as the universal condiment of Vietnam.

Several fish had been wrapped in the banana leaf, ranging in size from fingerlings to a basslike fish that probably weighed a couple of pounds. The fish, as was usual, were not scaled or gutted prior to cooking. They had been caught by the subtle technique of throwing a hand-grenade into a pool of water. The explosion stunned the fish in the pool and they were collected as they floated to the surface, then immediately packed in the banana leaf and placed on the bed of coals. After a few minutes the meal was served by placing the steaming banana leaf wrapper on the ground and letting all who shared the meal squat around it with our bowls of rice. Everyone ate in common from the fish and the bowl of water vine leaves.

Each of us had cut his own chopsticks from twigs, and since we were hungry, we set right to work on the fish. Everyone just reached in and snagged a likely looking piece, dipped it in the *nước mắm,* and plopped it in his mouth. I had developed a taste for Vietnamese peasant food, and this wasn't half bad. The trick was to get some real meat in the grab with the chopsticks without bringing along a lot of scales or steaming fish bowel. The ploy became more difficult as the meat became more and more scarce. As the meal progressed, one had to rummage around amongst the fish intestines, gills, livers, and other biological accoutrements in search of a good morsel. In the end the only things left were the heads, scales, backbones, and the most unsavory of internal organs. Like I say, it wasn't half bad.

As the meal ended Pham was called away on some detail or other and the rest of the group lounged around his lean-to, talking with one another and with Pham's wife. I passed around some chewing gum that had arrived in my last "care" package from home. The conversation turned to the Vietnamese men's fascination with American women and the speculation about how they compared to Vietnamese women. I was drawn into the joking and laughter and noticed that Pham's attractive wife was also part of the good-natured give-and-take.

"Trung úy," one of the men asked in Vietnamese, "when you go to Saigon do you look for pretty Vietnamese girls to sleep with? In Saigon there are many pretty girls, no?"

"Oh, I look at the pretty girls." I chuckled. "But I don't sleep with them. Sleeping is a very expensive thing to do in Saigon."

Everyone laughed and Pham's wife giggled as she asked, "How much does it cost to make love to a girl in Saigon for one night, *Trung úy?*"

"I've heard that the *very* pretty girls can cost as much as one hundred American dollars for one night," I said a little wondrously. "That's too much for me. I'm just a poor soldier and must send my money to my family. Besides, my wife would be very angry if I slept with another girl, even if the girl were free!"

We all laughed again, and one of the men lounging on the grass said, "But girls are very cheap for Americans in Cao Lanh, *Trung úy,* and they are just as pretty as the girls in Saigon." He leaned over with a grin and added, "I can recommend an excellent place to you, and your wife will never know.''

Pham's brother, one of the other soldiers in the group, spoke up. ''He doesn't need to go to Cao Lanh and pay money. He can stay right here and get all the girls he wants for free!''

They all laughed and nodded their heads, but I rolled my eyes and shook my head in an exaggerated fashion to make the point that I didn't mess around with local women. ''No, no,'' I replied, ''I would have much trouble if I played around with girls in the village. Too many people would get mad.''

Pham's brother spoke up again with a smile. ''*Trung úy,* how can you live all the time without a woman? It would make me crazy!'' I was trying to think of a response when he continued, ''Ah-ha! Maybe the *Trung úy* doesn't think Vietnamese women are pretty, maybe he is just used to American women. Eh, *Trung úy,* do you ever want to go to bed with Vietnamese girls?''

''Uh-oh,'' I said to myself, ''now you better watch your words.''

''Of course, of course,'' I said aloud, stretching out my hand in protest. ''I think Vietnamese girls are very beautiful. It's just that playing around with the women here would probably cause me a lot of trouble.''

Everyone around the fire moaned in jocular protest and shook their heads. It was clear they all thought I was just making excuses. The group was joined by another woman, and she and Pham's wife joined in the joking and laughter. Then Pham's brother delivered the stroke that floored me.

''Trung úy, do you like Mỹ, Pham's wife?''

Grateful for learning her name at last, I looked over at her and said, ''Of course. She is very pretty and I thank her for allowing me to eat here today.''

Mỹ smiled and gazed off out into space. Pham's brother said with a grin, ''*Trung úy,* you like to sleep with Pham's wife?''

Pham's wife did not react, but her gaze shifted more in my direction. The smile still played on her lips and the other men were grinning and listening attentively. A little man was frantically running around inside my brain, trying to find an appropriate answer. I was surprised not only that Pham's brother had asked me such a thing, but that he asked me in front of Pham's wife and friends!

"Oh, no," I said with a weak smile, "I couldn't do that."

I'll be damned if Mỹ didn't look straight at me with a bit of pique in her voice and ask, "Why not, *Trung úy*?"

Now I really started to fumble around. Pham's brother was grinning at my discomfiture, and like the others was waiting with amusement for my reply.

"Well," I said, smiling and pausing to choose my words carefully, "Pham is a friend of mine. I would not want to make him angry with me."

Pham's brother shrugged his shoulders and shook his head good-naturedly. Mỹ still looked a little miffed, though, and I didn't want to leave a bad impression, so I said to no one in particular, "She is very beautiful, though, and I would love to meet with her if Pham were not a good friend of mine."

A slight smile played across her face and she turned to the job of cleaning up the litter from the meal. Still not knowing if I had said all the wrong things at the wrong times, I took advantage of the pause in the conversation and made up an excuse to go find Sergeant Robertson.

I've said before I never was sure I really understood the villagers' sexual mores and manners. I was confused by constantly conflicting signals. Finally, I learned that I could expect just about anything from anybody, and that I should be neither surprised nor shocked at anything. The men and women in our villages usually displayed a calm, conservative, even shy demeanor. Every now and then, though, some small incident like the one with Mỹ would happen, or someone like the breast-squeezing fisherman's daughter would come along, and I would have to work frantically to try and figure out what the hell was going on.

Chapter 6

RELIGION was an important part of the social life in our villages. It was also an important source of social strife throughout all of South Vietnam. Westerners who read newspapers or watched television during the 1960s remember the accounts of Buddhist monks and nuns burning themselves to death on the streets of Saigon. These acts were not performed because of some petty complaint or because of some new problems that had sprung up with the government. A long history of Buddhist-Catholic contention led to these scenes of tragic frustration.

Catholicism had come to Vietnam during the sixteenth and seventeenth centuries, and the church community continued to grow during the years of the French colonial administration. The Vietnamese most exposed to European influences were those who worked for or with the French authorities, and it was these people who most easily adopted the religion of their colonial overseers. Both French and Vietnamese priests and missionaries went out of the major cities and into the villages. As a result many rural villagers were also converted to Catholicism. Still, when the French left Vietnam, Catholicism was largely the religion of the urban upper class, the educated businessmen, the teachers, and the able government administrators. The people in the villages were primarily Buddhist or one of the other native sects. Thus there was a long historical association between Catholicism and political power that often caused the adherents of the native religions to feel left out of the political process. This unfortunate situation, the new versus the old, the European idea versus the traditional, formed a social lesion that would never completely heal and would eventually lead to open sores.

The welding of a European religion onto an Oriental society is done only with a difficulty not usually appreciated by most Westerners. Buddhism and Confucianism permeated Vietnamese culture just as Judeo-Christian thought provides the warp and woof of our own. Buddhism gives Oriental cultures a sense of timelessness not found in Western thought. Confucianism instills a respect for family, a reverence for ancestors, and an emphasis on an individual's harmony with the society around him.

Practically every house in my village had a small spirit house perched on a pole out in front. Grains of rice and smoldering joss sticks were placed in the spirit houses as ever-present offerings to whomever or whatever was keeping track. The local shades and vapors had to be kept appeased lest they repay irreverence with mean tricks and hard times. One had to be in harmony with the spirits as well as the neighbors.

Most houses also had a tall flagstaff out front, and on religious holidays everyone would run up a flag. The flags were of all colors, but red and yellow, the traditional colors for happiness and good fortune, predominated. On these special religious days the flapping colors and freshly painted spirit houses could turn even the most drab village into a bright place with a festive air.

The brand of Catholicism practiced in the local villages seemed quite different from the religion observed in the West. The Vietnamese Christian was hard pressed to totally eliminate Buddhist and Confucian thoughts from his religious life. They were too relevant to the way life was lived. Many Catholics in our village shared in some of the traditional, yet pagan, practices of their non-Catholic neighbors. Making an offering or a sign of respect to the local spirits usually just seemed to be the prudent thing to do.

The local Catholics also retained some of the "spiritism" of their non-Catholic peers in other respects. For example, statues of Christ or of his mother, Mary, were thought to house the spirit of the venerated person, an idea found in medieval European Christianity but not one in favor for the past several hundred years in the West.

A delegation of believers came to me one day and asked that my team move a homemade shower stall that we had just erected in the compound. The shower had been put up within the line of sight of a statue of the Virgin Mary, and if you happened to notice, the Virgin appeared to be looking right in our shower door. The delegation seemed convinced that Mary, the mother of Jesus, would be watching through the eyes of the statue, would perhaps see us naked in the shower, and would be insulted. Well, I damned sure didn't want to move the shower stall; it had been hard enough to put up the first time. My first reaction was to point out to them that the Virgin Mary certainly was not housed in their statue, but I knew I wasn't there to argue theology, and I knew whatever I said wouldn't change the attitudes instilled by generations of belief. We moved the shower.

THE CATHOLIC PRIESTS IN MY DISTRICT HAD A LOT OF SECU-lar power in addition to the religious authority of their office. It made our life very difficult when all that power was turned against us. The old priest in our village was one of two in the entire district, and he was virulently anti-American. He especially wanted MAT-32 out of his turf, and he spoke from the pulpit as if we all had horns on our heads and tails between our legs. I was convinced that he didn't like us mostly because we were a challenge to his authority in the village, but I occasionally suspected him of also being a dupe for the Viet Cong.

Prior to our arrival in the village the priest had been in a position to pull a lot of strings and to give strong voice to whatever he wanted the district chief to do. Tái, the district chief, was a Hoa Hao, but he listened to the priest because he knew that the priest had a large constituency in the district. He also knew that whatever the priest said to his parishioners would be believed, and whatever instructions the priest gave would be followed. In fact, Tái had been so accommodating to the priest's wishes on some occasions that it seemed the priest ruled the district whenever he wished to have his way. I suppose the local Hoa Haos and Buddhists knew how the Vietnamese Catholic priests ruled over their parishes, but to an American, and a Protestant one at that, it seemed a relationship straight out of the Middle Ages.

The largely unschooled population was taught to be completely dependent on the priest for its communication with God. The people were led to believe that anger from the priest was the same thing as anger from the Almighty Himself. Crossing the priest meant being cut off from the preeminent supernatural power, a terrifying prospect to the native villager, Catholic or Buddhist.

Our particular village priest sat astride this avenue of power and used it to enforce his will on the local Catholics. One example I remember for its pettiness more than anything else was that the priest made a rule that boys and girls could not hold hands in the village street. He told the young people that if they were caught holding hands, he would shave their heads. And he did, by George! Even more amazing to my mind, the people sat still for it! I also discovered that he could deal out corporal punishment and just plain physical abuse to those he supposed to be evil-doers. There would be no complaint from the faithful.

The priest was powerful also because he could do favors for the properly obeisant. He knew the priests and bishops back in the large cities. These urban clergy knew, or were sometimes even related to, important political figures and key bureaucrats. Through these channels the local priest could make a contact to have some action resolved in a parishioner's favor. This secular activity sometimes seemed to work and inspired great admiration from the local Catholic villagers. Unfortunately, this sort of direct access to the government was exactly what the Hoa Haos and Buddhists did not have and could see no hope of attaining. It was the sort of thing that made them, the majority, feel left out of their own government.

When I came along in the official capacity as an advisor to the district chief, the old priest was immediately resentful and jealous. He was opposed to almost any idea or government program that he figured came from the Americans. He was particularly opposed to the U.S.-inspired land reform program. It was rumored that this was primarily because either his church or he personally would lose large landholdings that had been improperly acquired. His government connections had reportedly stood him in good stead when this area of the country was first officially surveyed and deeded back in the mid-1950s. I never knew if all that was true or if he just didn't want the Americans causing changes in the local power structure.

His Sunday homilies were sometimes nothing but tirades against us five Americans. He would tell the men in the local militia units not to report to duty if an operation was planned and accompanied by American advisors. He told the people that if the Americans could be forced to leave the village, then all their troubles would be over. He could go back to taking care of everything just like in the old days. On Sundays the priest overtly preached noncooperation; the rest of the week he tried to covertly inspire sedition.

On one occasion I was informed that some of the men who were firmly in the old priest's grasp were interpreting his hatred for us to be the priest's way of saying that even our permanent elimination would not be frowned on. The plan they came up with was very simple: the Americans would just become very unlucky at surviving firefights with the Viet Cong. In the rush and confusion of combat it would be easy for one of our own troops to gun us down, and no one would be the wiser.

When I heard this I was furious at the old bastard, but I had almost no way to respond to his attacks. Everywhere in the world, taking on a preacher in public is a hard thing to do and come out a winner. I came within an inch of calling in the PRU's and having the priest eliminated under the dictates of the Phoenix program. I could almost convince myself that he was an operative for the Viet Cong. Most of his actions and attitudes fell right into their hands, and he was definitely a factor that needed to be eliminated for my own safety. I resisted the urge to have the priest assassinated, however; killing a man of the cloth went a bit beyond what I was prepared to do. Instead, we just made sure that some of our loyal Hoa Hao brethren always accompanied us on our operations. They acted as bodyguards and kept an eye on the occasional Catholic militiamen we suspected of being a part of the priest's coterie.

Either the priest or the priest's men lost their zeal for killing us outright, and the threat seemed to disappear after a week or two. I knew the old priest was still against us, though, and it was just a matter of waiting to see what he would do next. A long period of time went by without any problems from the padre. Oh, we heard of his standard rumblings and grumblings, but I had begun to hope he had decided to try to get along within the present system. I was wrong.

One day Cô Ha did not come to work and did not send any word about why she was staying out. This was very unusual, so the next day when I was in the village I walked by her hooch to find out what was the matter. She shared a small thatch hut with her brother-in-law and sister, both of whom were sitting in front of the house as I walked up. They rose when I approached, greeted me warmly, and asked me in. The inside of the house was dark compared to the bright sunshine outside, and it took a few minutes for my eyes to adjust to the dim light. It was only then that I noticed Cô Ha crouched in a dark corner. She pulled a scarf over her face and would not raise her head to look at me. I could tell she had begun to cry, a rare thing to see in the Vietnamese, even in the face of severe pain.

"Cô Ha, what is the matter?" I asked with concern. "Are you sick?"

There was no reply from the small figure.

I bent over and asked softly, "Why are you crying?"

Ha's sister looked at her grimly and said, "She has been hurt." She reached over and pulled the scarf from Ha's face. Ha's eyelids were puffed nearly shut. Her lips were swollen, and the scabbed lacerations made them almost immobile. Her whole face was some shade of black and blue. She looked up at me from her squatting position with pain and humiliation in her wet eyes.

"I'm sorry, *Trung úy*," she said softly, slurring the words through her stiff lips.

"What happened?" I asked, frowning in a mixture of surprise and anxiety. "Did you fall?" Sobs shook her body again and she hid her face in her hands. She would not speak. She was terribly humiliated and embarrassed by her condition, and my presence wasn't helping any.

Ha's sister looked down at her and said with a brittle edge of anger in her voice, "The priest beat her."

"What?" I asked in disbelief. Even considering the things

I had already heard about him, I couldn't conceive of a Catholic priest beating up a teenage girl.

I looked at Ha and asked her directly, "Did the priest beat you?"

Cô Ha nodded slowly. After a few moments of silence she told me the story. It seemed that the old man had been trying to get her to stop working for us for several weeks. He had ordered her to stop, in fact, telling her that it was a sin to help us. He said we were interfering with God's will for the village. She had refused, and the priest had become angry. Two days previously Cô Ha had gone to confession. The priest accused her of being a whore and demanded that she confess that she was screwing the American soldiers on the district team. He also insisted that she confess to trying to recruit other village girls to join her in our den of iniquity. When she refused to confess to those false accusations, the old priest became so enraged that he struck her, first once, then again, then a rain of blows on her face. The poisons of his own soul were poured onto a teenage girl whose only defense was a feeble protest.

I was so damned mad I couldn't talk. I turned on my heel and stalked out of the house. I didn't know what to do or who to go to. How do you deal with a miscreant man of God? The Vietnamese authorities at province level were all Catholics; I knew I could expect no help from them. My own people at the province team would not have the slightest understanding of why I was worrying about a priest. Hell, we Americans are for God, ain't we? Completely lost, I just wandered out into a rice paddy and sat there thinking about what to do.

Later that evening I thought again about calling in the Phoenix program, turning the PRU's loose to eliminate the old villain once and for all. I could think of a whole list of indicators that would convince interested authorities that he was working for the Viet Cong. Deep inside, though, I wasn't really convinced that was true. I knew for damned sure he wasn't working for God, but I figured that at the bottom of it all he was just a mean old man out to protect his selfish interests. I never could persuade myself to take any action against him, so in the end I just let it go. We always tried to keep abreast of the old man's plots, but officially we just learned to ignore him.

I sent *Bác-sĩ* Fitz down to patch up Cô Ha, and one morning a few days later she came back into the compound, ready to go to work. She still had a large bruise on the left side of her face and scabs still marred her cheek and lips. I got mad all over again, but she never uttered a word of complaint or recrimination. I don't recall that she ever missed another day of work—and of providing a little light and laughter to five soldiers who desperately needed it.

THE LOCAL CATHOLICS MIGHT NOT HAVE SEEMED TO BE mainstream Catholics like those I knew back in the States, but most of our local Buddhists weren't exactly mainstream either. They were for the most part members of the Hoa Hao (pronounced wa-how) sect, an offshoot of Buddhism most of whose adherents live in the Mekong Delta region of Vietnam. The Hoa Hao were strongly anticommunist. The Viet Minh, the largely communist Vietnamese guerrilla organization of the 1940s and 1950s, had murdered the sect's founder and the Hoa Hao remembered that with a passion. They developed a bitter hatred for the Viet Minh and their successor organization, the Viet Cong. Thus it seemed that Hoa Hao units were always made up of aggressive and brave soldiers. Being in Vietnam was not nearly so hard when I was helping a people so clearly willing to fight for their own rights and their own protection.

Unfortunately, the government was not too happy with the Hoa Hao and was not inclined to be helpful when it came to dividing up the government programs and various forms of village and hamlet assistance. It seems that in the late 1950s and early 1960s the Hoa Hao in the Mekong Delta and the Plain of Reeds had had enough of the central government's disdain and malfeasance. Ngo Dinh Diem, the president of Vietnam at the time and a stereotypical product of the Catholic mandarinate, ran a government noteworthy for its corruption and lack of concern for the peasantry in the countryside. The Hoa Hao finally decided they had had enough. They formed their own quasi-government and their own army. They were determined to defend themselves against the communists and from harassment by the Saigon government, too, if need be.

President Diem sent in some of his own army units to quell the mini-rebellion, but after a few clashes with the Hoa Hao units he responded to American urgings and perhaps his own common sense and struck a deal with the Hoa Hao leaders. He guaranteed an amnesty, government support, and incorporation of the Hoa Hao fighting units into the regular Vietnamese army. Diem was a sly fellow, though, and when things died down a bit, he began assigning the Hoa Hao units and their leaders to places outside their traditional Delta homeland. President Diem sent the Hoa Hao way up north along the DMZ where they were used as cannon fodder by the South Vietnamese generals—at least that's the way the Hoa Hao saw it—and they once again felt that their government had betrayed them.

When I arrived in 1969 the animosity toward the central government was still in the air. I had the feeling that the Hoa Hao leaders were biding their time, waiting for another opportunity to regain some degree of autonomy. For the present, however, the more unifying theme of war against the Viet Cong was requiring everyone's attention.

DURING MY FIRST FEW MONTHS IN TRAM CHIM, THE DISTRICT chief was a man by the name of Trần Trong Tái. He was a leader of the Hoa Hao sect in the area and he was an integral part of the local culture. He knew the people, and like most men of the Hoa Hao religion, he was willing to be aggressive against the Viet Cong guerrillas. The old chief and I got on well together and our partnership seemed to be well established. One day, out of the blue, news from Saigon told us our collaboration had ended. Rumor had it that the Saigon bureaucracy had suffered one of its periodic eruptions, and one of the bits of political lava being spewed in our direction was a man who was going to be our new district chief.

I immediately did some scrambling around on my own and made a few radio calls back to Cao Lanh. I wanted to find out what it was that caused Saigon to want to change my district chief and to get some hint as to what kind of fellow the new man was going to be.

It turned out that our new chief's brother had been involved in an aborted coup attempt. Following the old Oriental assumption of guilt by association, President Thieu had banished the brother's entire extended family from the Saigon environs. Our man, one Nguyên Đai Thụ by name, was coming to us like a Russian being banished to Siberia. The word was that my new chief was a perfect example of the Saigon government man. He had been a functionary in the military bureaucracy for fifteen or twenty years. Through a combination of lack of talent and lack of courage he had never risen to high command or responsibility. His family was of the old mandarin line, however, so he had been able to finagle choice assignments and had never actually been sent away from Saigon for any of his permanent military duties. Later I was to doubt that he had ever spent any significant amount of time outside of Saigon in his entire life. Thu had absolutely no idea of the problems of the people in the rural areas. In fact, it turned out that his culture shock at being sent to our district was perhaps even greater than that I had experienced when I first arrived.

The official word finally came down that the new man would be coming out from Saigon in a couple of weeks and that the old chief would be given another assignment in the district. When the village and hamlet chiefs got word of the change they were furious. In their view the insensitive Saigon government was sending out a citified Catholic bureaucrat to govern a rural Hoa Hao district. It wasn't right, by damn, and they weren't going to take it!

Village meetings were set up all throughout the district. The leaders sent word to Tái, the old Hoa Hao chief, that they wanted him and me to come out to the village meetings to talk with the people and listen to their complaints. The people had questions, they said, and they wanted to give me petitions to the government requesting that the current district chief and his government be left in place.

I agreed to attend, so every morning that a meeting was scheduled Tái and I and some bodyguards would board one of the small passenger-carrying sampans that plied the waterways from village to village. I wanted to reduce the military image of my job during these meetings, so I never took a rifle with me. Every morning I would put on my cleanest pair of jungle fatigues, strap on my service automatic, and top the whole thing off with my blue Vietnamese beret. The beret was one of those worn by the local militia, not the regular army, so I hoped it would help the villagers think of me as being on their side. I wasn't going out to work against the central government, but I wanted to make it as easy as possible for the people to see me as a friend, not as an American overseer or a lackey of Saigon.

The district chief, the guards, and I would leave Tram Chim in the first gray light of morning. The fishermen would be loading their nets into their boats and the farmers would be gathering up their implements before heading to the rice fields. Pulling away from the village, the bow of our boat would point down the main canal and cut the surface of the still water. Only the small putt-putt of our engine violated the morning calm. The waterfowl usually let us go by with little bother, and the water buffalo were completely contemptuous of our passing.

Watching the birds and the beasts of the Delta canals was one way of trying to ignore the cramps that would soon set in in my back and legs. Being larger than the normal passenger, I had to sit hunched up under the flat tin awning of the small passenger boat. Gliding along a canal so early in the morning and appreciating the quiet beauty of the place really gave me a sense of being submerged in Vietnam. I was seeing things, and animals, and people that few Americans ever saw, and I was experiencing things that hardly anyone else had had the opportunity to experience. I was still young enough to be idealistic about being America's representative to these thousands of Vietnamese. There I was, trying to be the brave cavalier, taking truth and justice deep into the heart of darkness! I loved it.

The boat would eventually reach the designated village and we would go to the meeting with the village elders. Quite often we would all just sit around a table set up in the middle of a cluster of small thatch houses. Sometimes a glass of warm beer or a pack of local cigarettes would be placed on the table as a show of hospitality. The village chief and his lieutenants would sit on one side of the table and the district chief and I would sit on the other. The other adult men would squat on the ground all around us. The women sat behind them, and all around the outside of the circle the village children would play their games or just stand and stare at me, one of the few Americans they had ever seen.

Exchanges of pleasantries were always necessary and a little more elaborate than most Americans are used to. Even the more earnest discussions, those about economic woes, political troubles, or the guerrilla problem, were usually carried on in a very polite, even stylized manner. Old men would approach the table, press their hands together—or less formally, simply clutch them together at their waist—give a slight bow or nod, and would begin some tale of trouble or woe they wanted me to hear. I always had to have a response, though I'm not sure it really mattered what I said. I often thought they just wanted to hear me say something in reply.

At first I tried to direct the people's attention back to the district chief. I was only supposed to be there to listen. The district chief was the proper avenue of complaint; I was just his advisor. The old men of the villages didn't buy that. They presumed I had the real power and they wanted assurances from me that something would be done about their problems. I guess the old men remembered the French colonial days, when the European men accompanying the Vietnamese officials were always the real decision-makers. The village leaders were used to that kind of system and they just presumed that things still worked the same way.

I was presented a sheaf of signed petitions at every village, requesting that the current district chief be left in his job and that the man from Saigon be sent somewhere else. At first I tried to get the village officials to turn the petitions over to the district chief or his staff so they could send the petitions on back to Cao Lanh. The villagers weren't interested in handing the petitions over to the Vietnamese authorities, though. They wanted me to take the petitions to the Americans back in Cao Lanh and from there to have them sent further up the chain of command if need be. I was told the villagers wanted the *Americans* to see the petitions; they didn't give a damn if the Vietnamese government saw the paper or not. The village leaders would say that they had always heard the Americans were fair and would listen to the people. They didn't expect any such thing from their own government.

I tried to explain my own low position in the American hierarchy, but they all seemed to think that I could practically walk right into the American ambassador's office whenever I wished and set him straight about what was really happening in the countryside. Nobody really believed my lack of authority. I finally stopped protesting and just started taking the petitions, nodding my head politely, and muttering phrases about seeing that the proper authorities would seriously consider their opinions.

Despite the fact that most of the meetings were so polite, an occasional petitioner had such a serious problem or heated opinion that the traditional sense of decorum was difficult to maintain. Once, an old man with a leathery, wrinkled face sat down across the meeting table from me. His long black gown with its high collar was of the old Chinese fashion, a style still worn by a few of the elderly villagers. The man's head was wrapped in a crude white turban, and his long gray beard and gnarled walking stick lent him an aura of wizened respectability. He was an alert old man, and his eyes still flashed and sparkled as he began to speak.

He was a Hoa Hao, he said, and he had fought the Viet Cong and the Viet Minh before them. He said he was not afraid to fight, even though he knew he was too old to be any good at it anymore. He was angry at the central government, he said, and he wanted me to know all about it. He began detailing his animosities toward the Saigon officials, and as he went down his list, he began to speak louder and louder. He became more and more agitated and started emphasizing his points by shaking his walking stick at me. The district chief, the village chief, and the other men kept their eyes directly on me. I guess they were looking for some reaction, but I made no comment and only occasionally would nod to indicate I understood what the old man was saying.

The old man's complaints were apparently shared by others in the audience. Some of the bystanders started adding their own comments to what he was saying; others began muttering encouragement to the old fighter when he hit on a point they particularly agreed with. As the litany of ire continued, the crowd got more and more agitated; the old man became more and more fired up. Soon he was talking loudly across the table at me and shaking his walking stick in my face. He was at the peak of his emotion when he arrived at the main point: it all boiled down to religion.

The old man complained about the government's mistreatment of the Hoa Haos in general, but in particular he was outraged that the administration had decided to replace the current district chief with some strange Catholic functionary from Saigon. He said it was just another example of how the

Saigon government ignored the needs and wishes of the people. The man paused in his tirade and stared at me across the table, daring me to try to defend the government policies. He wanted to know, he said quietly, how long I thought a government like his could rightfully continue to expect the people's loyalty?

I don't recall having a very good answer. I made some bland statement of reassurance and added a few more sentences of pure puffery, just trying to calm him down. After a few more mutterings the old patriarch stood up, gave a flex of the head and shoulders that was a mix between a nod and a bow, and proudly walked back to where some of the other village ancients were standing. They all ambled over to the shade of a big tree and stood there conversing while the hearings at the table continued. Everyone seemed pleased that the old man had had his say.

After the meetings were over each day and we were headed back to our fort in the water-taxi, Tái always congratulated me on how I handled the meetings and how I responded to the villagers' questions and comments. He could afford to be gracious since all the meetings were making him look better and better. Everyone was begging to have him left as the district chief. He was painted as being the greatest thing since salt, and I knew the locals wanted to keep him in as their chief rather than have to deal with some unknown quantity from Saigon.

Frankly, I felt bad about the whole affair. I liked Tái and I was under the impression that he liked me in return. I didn't want to have to go through another breaking-in experience with a new district chief any more than the villagers wanted to have a man from Saigon as their governor. The fact of the matter was, though, that I was going to have to accept the situation, like it or not. I knew my influence on decisions in Saigon was nonexistent. Hell, I had a hard enough time trying to make a dent on decisions made back in the province town, let alone Saigon! I figured from the very beginning that all these petitions and reports I was sending in were going to be for naught. I was absolutely right.

We never got a response from Cao Lanh or Saigon about all the paperwork we had sent them, but one day about two weeks after our first official notification of the change in our leadership the new district chief was helicoptered out to our village. Tái was made the Assistant District Chief for Military Affairs, a demotion he took with studied Oriental grace. It wasn't long before the new chief's wife and daughter came out to join him, and another man, the new Assistant Chief for Civilian Affairs, also arrived to begin his duties. Now I had three men to deal with where I had had only one before. That complicated my job, but I was determined to get along with the new man in charge and to make the best of a bad situation.

NGUYẾN DAI THỤ WAS A DISASTER AS A DISTRICT CHIEF. HE was a weak-willed, ineffectual man who did nothing but agree nervously with practically anything I said. He was a stereotype of what was wrong with the older Vietnamese officer corps. Thụ was a product of the French colonial army of Vietnam. In that army Vietnamese officers were not trained to be decisive, aggressive military men; they were trained to take orders from the French officers, and to be obeisant to these Caucasian masters in all social and military matters. When the French left Vietnam the Vietnamese army was staffed and led by an officer corps that had virtually no experience in making decisions or pursuing objectives in a determined manner. It was a deficiency for which they never made up.

When the Americans arrived, much of the Vietnamese military and civil administration eagerly transferred the decisions and responsibilities back to the new Caucasians. Their attitude seemed to be "The big rich guys are here now and they will take care of everything." It wasn't long before the paradox developed that the Vietnamese resented the pushy Americans for always telling them what to do, and the Americans resented the Vietnamese for never making decisions or showing any leadership in their own affairs.

As a practical matter this all led to the fact that I had an ineffective district chief. In the absence of his doing anything, many of the powers and responsibilities of the office fell to me. Technically, I was just a *Trung úy*, a first lieutenant, but more importantly I was the local *Cô Vàn Trướng*, the senior advisor to the district chief. In short, I had an amazing amount of power.

I was a twenty-three-year-old idealistic young army officer, left essentially alone to fight my own little war with my own little team of companions. I was determined and eager to do my best. Given free rein by a do-nothing but compliant district chief, I began to accept a growing list of duties and responsibilities. Military operations were performed as I directed; people were imprisoned or freed at my word; food and clothing from various agencies were distributed where I said, when I said; aircraft bombed or strafed at my command; curfews were established according to my wishes; villages applied to or through me for medical help, school supplies, building materials, and agricultural development assistance. I could even cause the summary execution of practically anyone in my district. In many ways I controlled life and death of thousands of the people.

The Vietnamese recognized the power I wielded, and after a while I began to expect the almost fawning courtesy with which I was treated. With no one around to give me my true measure, I began to accept my elevated status, and I began to use the powers in my hands as if they were mine by right.

Most of the responsibilities were not truly mine, but I knew the district chief would approve anything I did, and if I didn't do it, I had the definite impression that very little would get done. Perhaps it was only youthful American arrogance that made me take those powers that were outside my rightful reach, perhaps it was the almost mystical idealism with which I took on my whole task, but when I had the chance to get something done I by-God took it! Perhaps I was just a high-toned American, but in my dreams I was a cavalier for freedom, I was a warrior for Camelot. Even more than that. I was a Warrior King.

Chapter 7

THE rumbling gurgle of the PBR's engine was lulling me to sleep, and I had to fight to keep my eyes open. I stood in the cockpit of the small fighting boat and watched the canal banks for suspicious movement. We were still in the gray light of early morning after Sergeant Fitz and I had spent the night on an ambush position with a squad of Vietnamese militiamen; we had hitched a ride back to Tram Chim on the navy boat since the PBR, along with three others, was making a dawn sortie out in our direction.

It had been a mosquito-infested, leech-attracting night with never a sight of the Viet Cong. I was dead tired and not at all pleased with the operation. The militiamen had been entirely uninspired by the whole experience and had been more concerned about keeping dry and sleeping than in whiling the night away on alert for the enemy. Now I was just looking forward to getting back to the compound, getting out of my wet clothes, and dropping into my bunk for a few hours sleep.

Tram Chim village was still in the clutches of the early morning calm as we gurgled past its long row of waterside hooches. We finally approached the small dock just outside our compound's walls, and the chief petty officer piloting our boat sidled his craft up next to the dock. One of the sailors jumped off and secured the PBR to the landing. The Vietnamese men clambered out and were quickly off to their homes in the village. Sergeant Fitz slung his medic bag over his shoulder and climbed stiffly down on the dock. I thanked the chief

for the ride, climbed down to the dock, and gave the boat a
push back into the canal. As the throaty rumble of the engine
sounded from the waterline I watched the PBR pull away,
slowly at first, then quickly as it leaped up and darted away
like a speedboat. I waved after it and turned to go into the
fort. As I walked up to the canal-side gate I was surprised to
see Lieutenant Cantrell standing there waiting for me.

"Good morning, Jim," I said, somewhat puzzled at his
coming out to see me in.

"*Trung úy*, you're not going to believe this," he said with
consternation, "but we have a visitor."

"A what?" I asked thinking I had heard wrong.

"A visitor. He's a free-lance writer and photographer. Says
he's out looking for stories."

"How in the hell did he find us?" I asked sarcastically.
And with more curiosity, "How did he get out here?"

"Well, to tell you the truth, I think somebody sent him to
do a story on the Special Forces back in Cao Lanh, but since
they aren't up to much right now, they sent him out here. He
came out on the swing ship yesterday afternoon, so I guess he
has the colonel's blessing too."

"How long does he want to stay out here?" I asked. I could
just see us trying to live with an extra body jammed into our
already tight quarters.

Cantrell turned as I squished by him in my wet fatigues and
we walked on into the compound. "I don't know. He says he
just wants to find out what it's like out here, and with the gear
he brought I don't think he plans to stay long. He's mostly
just been asking everybody questions about what we do and
how we get along with the Viets. There he is now."

I looked up and saw a tall red-haired man step through the
doorway of the team house. He had a full dark beard that
seemed out of place after seeing nothing but clean-shaven
Vietnamese for quite a while. He walked up and stuck out his
hand. "Lieutenant Donovan, I believe."

"You got him," I said with a tired smile. "I hear you want
to stay with us for a few days."

"That's right. I'm Phil Roddenberry. I'm a free-lance writer
and photographer and I try to sell stuff to the wire services."
He paused for a second and gazed around the compound. "I
don't think anybody has worked this kind of terrain before, so

I'd like to try and put together a story. Write up something as to how you guys fit into the big picture.''

"If you figure that out, be sure to let me know," I said as I stepped on by him. I spoke over my shoulder, "You're welcome to hang out for a few days. I guess you know it's all on your own risk."

"Yeah, I know. Listen, do you mind if I talk to your local Vietnamese, too?"

"Hell no," I said as I cleared my weapon and threw the magazine on my bunk. "You talk with anybody you want to, but you might find it hard to find something out here that press people want to read about." I walked back to the door of the team house and took off my boots. I left them and the soggy socks outside where the sunshine could bake them dry, then I turned back to Roddenberry. "As a matter of fact, why don't you let Jim take you down there to see the district chief now. I'm damned near asleep on my feet and need to sack out for a while. You might as well use the time to good advantage."

"That's fine with me," said Roddenberry with a grin. "Let me get my pad," he said, looking over at Cantrell, "and I'll be right with you."

"No rush," said Cantrell laconically.

"Don't rush back, either," I said as I sat back on my bunk and lifted my feet off the floor. "I won't be fit company for a while." My eyes were closing as I lay back on the bunk, and I think I was asleep before they got out of the house.

Later that afternoon, after I had showered and shaved and put on some dry jungle fatigues, I took Roddenberry down to a beer hooch in the village and we had a talk over a couple of bottles. "How was your talk with Thu?" I asked, after taking a deep swallow of the bitter liquid.

Roddenberry shook his head. "I don't know. He was all smiles and helpfulness, but I don't know if he really told me anything or not."

I chuckled and said, "Our district chief is a careful man. He wouldn't want to spoil your trip by giving you any unpleasant news."

"Well, let me try a couple of questions on you, then. You set me straight."

"Shoot."

"What about free-fire zones? You ever have chopper pilots

or jet jockeys shooting up your civilians because they get caught in a free-fire zone?''

"We don't have any free-fire zones in this district. If anybody—that's navy boats, navy planes, air force jets, army choppers, anybody—wants to fire at something or bomb something here they have to call in and get permission from the district chief.''

"Why is that?'' asked Roddenberry. "Doesn't that waste a lot of time?''

"You bet it does,'' I said, "and it's frustrating as hell, but that's the system. We know where the friendlies are, where our patrols are located, where our ambushes are at night. I don't want some airplane driver with an infrared device or some of that other gadgetry to put an air strike on my head just because I had a night ambush out where he happened to be passing over.''

"Are the Vietnamese pretty good about checking on things and giving the clearances?''

"Well, this particular district chief has as much as told me to stop bothering him about it. He said that if I think it's o.k., it's o.k. with him. He doesn't like to be waked up in the middle of the night to make decisions,'' I said, grinning. "I think he knows that mistakes can be made, too. He doesn't want to take the risk of making one and getting some citizens killed. That would make him look bad. Despite all the publicized curfews, or free-fire zones if we had them, some of the locals are going to take the risk of staying out late or going into some area they shouldn't. Chances are that sooner or later they'll be mistaken for a group of VC and then they'll find themselves in the middle of an air strike. Somebody's bound to get killed. We tell people all the time to be sure and play by the rules. I don't want to get any of our people killed, but if a pilot flying over this district calls in and asks for permission to fire on something that sounds suspicious to me and I can't find any official notice of friendlies in the area, he's got permission to fire.''

Roddenberry pursed his lips and stared at me thoughtfully. "You made any mistakes yet?''

"Yeah, once. A navy recon plane called in one night and said he had a line of sampans traveling in the dark without lights. They were way out in 'Indian territory,' and we had no civilians or patrols in the area, so I gave him permission to fire. When we took a patrol out into the area the next morning, it turned out that the 'sampans' were actually water buffalo! God, what a mess! I filled out a chest-high stack of paperwork on that one. All the farmers in the district were claiming that some of the animals were theirs, and they all wanted twice the going price for payment! I was a real cattle trader by the time that was all over with.''

Roddenberry popped the top off his second bottle of beer and laughed as he leaned back in his chair. The little open-air shop was abuzz with flies and kids who had come to watch the two Americans drink Vietnamese beer. "Well," said Roddenberry as he plopped forward and propped his elbows on the table, "moving on to another sensitive area . . ." He paused as if he was considering what to say next, then he said quietly, "The Phoenix program."

This Roddenberry was good at his business, I thought. That question had caught me completely unaware, and he could tell he had raised the hairs on the back of my neck. The bastard couldn't suppress a wise little grin at my reaction. I stared at the tabletop, thinking about what to say and how to say it. Nothing particular came to mind, so I said, "What about it?" I didn't look up, but just played with the beer bottle on the table.

"Come on, Donovan," he said, "the Senate's been raising hell about this program that supposedly allows our side to assassinate anyone we think's a Viet Cong, or maybe just somebody we don't like. The word's out back in the States. The people want to know if it's true. Is it true? Do you have such a thing here? If you do, how does it work?"

I thought back to the Special Warfare School where the program had first been explained to me. I couldn't remember the classification level, but I did know it was sensitive information. I figured what the hell, since this guy asked the question, it would probably be best if I told him how the program worked locally. At least I could give him a straight story. I could imagine how such a thing could get sensationalized in the press, so I figured a calm discussion of the program wouldn't hurt anything.

"O.k.," I said, looking him in the eye, "the Phoenix program. I know it sounds bad, and it may be in some places, I don't know, but around here it's not much of a factor. I haven't used it myself, though I've come pretty damned close a few times. I might use it yet."

"Detail," said Roddenberry.

"Each province in Vietnam has what is called a Province Recon Unit, or PRU for short. They're mostly made up of ex-VC or NVA who have come over to the Saigon side. They are armed with Soviet and Chi-Com weapons, mostly AK-47's, so the other side is never sure who they are if they get in a fight. Our PRU's are run by the spooks in the CIA compound in Cao Lanh. They do do some reconnaisance like the name implies, but they are also the people who take care of the Phoenix program. Basically, what you've heard is probably true. I can contact the PRU's and have somebody taken care of. I mean I really can have somebody shot. An 'extreme prejudice' operation, I think they say." I paused for a moment to let that soak in, then I tried to moderate the message. "You gotta realize this is a war. Oh, we have these civil justice programs where someone accused of being a VCI is supposed to get his day in court. But despite our efforts to get the ball rolling, this justice system simply doesn't work like what folks at home are used to. It's corrupt, it's backlogged, it simply doesn't work. So, if I know that someone is a VCI, and if waiting to get proof positive that would stand up in court—witnesses, documents, and all that—might threaten lives or the safety of a village, then I can call in the PRU's. The PRU's and an agency man will come out, they will make their own decision about whether or not to hit the target, and if they do, they do it on the quiet. Sometimes they try to make it look like the VC did it so the local VCI will be confused and wonder what the hell is going on. Sow distrust and all that shit."

"Wait a minute," interrupted Roddenberry. "You mean to tell me you think it's all right to kill somebody just because you *think* he's a VC?"

"No," I replied, "I don't think it's all right, and besides that, I've never done it. I've come close a couple of times though; and I'll tell you what, it's mighty easy to sit there and dream about justice for the VC when the bastards are killing kids in *my* village. I wonder how much hollering there would be in Congress if those guys were sitting over here, never knowing when the local VC or VCI are going to blow up another school or another market!''

Roddenberry looked at me thoughtfully and finally said, ''Any other place or time, you'd say this was damned wrong. Man, you gotta know,'' he said, shaking his head, ''this ain't the American Way.''

''I didn't say I thought it was the American Way. I just said that it's there, and I said I've never done it. If I didn't have problems with it, I'd have already used it, and on some deserving bastards, too.''

Roddenberry snorted and said, ''Well, I don't think you are going to get much more opportunity to use it anyway. It looks like Congress is going to stop the whole thing.''

I shrugged my shoulders. ''Well, I can't say that it makes much difference to me. It's not a high priority item around here.'' I pushed back from the table, glad for a way to change the subject, and said as I stood up, ''We had better start walking back, time's getting on.''

We paid for our beers and walked out into the muddy street. Ambling lazily back toward the compound, Roddenberry continued to ask questions. I described the district to him, and I tried to explain some of the difficulties we had experienced in working with the government as well as in fighting the Cong. I told him about my own work in particular, and about the problems of dealing with a district chief who didn't want to do anything but wait out his time in exile.

''Well,'' said Roddenberry with a touch of sarcasm, ''if your chief doesn't want to do anything, it sure looks like you have your finger in every pie. How do you handle having all that power? What are you, two years out of college?''

I hooked my fingers in my pistol belt, smiled, and shook my head as I said, ''I don't know personality-wise, if that's what you mean. I really don't. I do think that having the power has made me really identify with these people. I think of this district as *my* district, not the district chief's. I think of these people as *my* people, the canals and rivers as *my* water, the sky as *my* airspace. The U.S. Army, Navy, or Air Force wants to do something in this district, they have to get my permission. I don't remember asking anybody for permission to do anything.''

''Pretty high-falutin' for a lieutenant, aren't you?''

"Maybe so," I said, "but there aren't any captains out here. No colonels or generals, either. It just so happens that I'm the top of the line. It could be me, it could be somebody else. The same job would have to be done."

"Yeah," said Roddenberry as we approached the compound and started across the bridge over the moat, "I reckon so. Tell me, do you think it's ever really going to do any good?"

"I'd like to say yes," I replied, "but every indication I get tells me that Saigon doesn't mean shit out here. If it's like this everywhere else in the country, I don't think they'll make it. The NVA mean business. Hanoi wants in, and I know my kind of people can't keep them out forever."

Roddenberry just nodded his head, and as we entered the compound he excused himself to use the latrine. I went on into the team house to check in with Cantrell and to see what was on for evening chow. Later that evening Roddenberry talked with some of the other guys, but he spent most of the time writing by the light of a kerosene lamp. I wondered what it was he was writing down and what he was leaving out. I wondered what he really thought about us all.

The next day I had to go with the district chief to make the rounds out to a couple of villages. We were supposed to check out the village offices and the local militia platoons. Roddenberry came with us and spent the day just watching and listening to what went on. That evening, his last at Tram Chim as it turned out, he and I sat out on the wall of the fort and looked out. It was cool up on the wall, and moonlight gave a vague illumination to the canal and the village. The only sound other than our own muted voices was the occasional call or baby's cry drifting up from the village. We talked for a good while about the war, the people, and how things seemed a lot different out here than they did from the headquarters of an American infantry division. Eventually, though, the talk turned back to power, and how it's used and how it's abused. Roddenberry made the common observation that power corrupts and waited on my reply.

"I think that's right," I said. "It's inevitable. It's hard to resist the little perks that come with a little power. You feel you deserve them. Then, as the power grows the perks grow too, and suddenly the perks corrupt."

"Well, Lieutenant Donovan," Roddenberry asked with a grin, "are you corrupt?"

"Not in the sense of doing something for perks," I responded. And after a pause I continued, "But I know I've gotten used to being the man in charge out here. I used to kick myself whenever I found I was actually expecting someone to bow and scrape, but I don't even do that anymore. The village girls smile at me, the old folks ask me into their homes, people who come for help seem to believe that I can do anything. People pay attention to me, they try to please me, I'm important to them. Thirty thousand people live in this district. I feel responsible for their safety and their welfare, I can't help it. I know they aren't really my people, I know they aren't really my responsibility, but inside I feel they are. I'm going to do my best for them, not for Saigon, not for Washington, but for them. That's my duty."

I could see Roddenberry's face in the glow of his cigarette. He kept on looking out at the village, faintly visible in the moonlight. The occasional wink of a lamp or a cooking fire would send a flicker up from the darkened huts, and from somewhere deeper in the village a dog began to bark. As if that were his signal, Roddenberry dropped his cigarette and put it out with the toe of his boot. As we climbed down off the wall he quietly asked me his last question. "So tell me, farm boy, how does it feel to be king?" I wondered for a second if he was joking, but I realized he wasn't. I thought for a moment, then I said with a wry smile, "So far as I can tell, kings must never really sleep at night, kings must never really trust anybody, and I know damned well kings are never really paid enough."

LIEUTENANT CANTRELL AND SERGEANT ROBERTSON HAD been up at dawn to take out a patrol in search of a Viet Cong "tax squad" that had been reported robbing and harassing farmers in the southwest area of our district for the past several days. Fitz, Abney, and I had been working around the team house all day, attending to various odd jobs and paperwork. After lunch *Bác-sĩ* Fitz had gone off to work with the Vietnamese medic, and Sergeant Abney had gone to the bunker to see if he could raise the team at Hong Ngu on the radio. We had some coded messages to transmit to them from province headquarters, so Abney got stuck with that job while I worked on the monthly reports. The dull work and the afternoon heat were soon having their narcotic effect and I could barely get enough strength to swat the flies, let alone make progress in filling out the seemingly senseless computer forms.

Suddenly I heard a ruckus out in the compound. Someone was shouting, then a shot was fired. I bolted upright. Two more shots. I was reaching for my M-16 and ammo when Abney yelled from the bunker, "What the shit's going on out there, *Trung úy*? Are we hit?"

"I don't know," I called. "Wait one!" I stuck my head out the door and looked over the compound. The hubbub was taking place by the village-side gate, but by the looks of the men in the guard posts there didn't seem to be any concern about an attack.

"I don't know what's happening," I shouted back to Abney, "but we're not being hit. It looks like some kind of dust-up out in the compound."

I was about to step outside and go over to find out what the problem was when the agitated group by the gate looked over at me and started moving in my direction.

The man leading the group was the militia officer in charge of the platoon assigned to our fort. From the look in his eyes and the set of his jaw I knew he was really mad about something. Immediately behind him came two other soldiers, dragging a protesting man in civilian clothes. Five or ten other men came along in a group behind them. The platoon leader stopped in front of the team house and called to one of the men in the back of the pack. The man came forward, carrying a fat little yellow dog. I was surprised to recognize Charlie, our team pet. I wondered what the dog had to do with all this. The platoon leader asked if the dog was ours.

"Yes," I responded, "that's our dog."

The platoon leader snarled at the man held prisoner. "You see, you crazy man?" he shouted in Vietnamese. "You have tried to steal the *cô vàn*'s dog!" He cuffed the man on the head with the back of his fist and turned back to me. "*Trung úy*, this man tried to steal your dog but was stopped by the guards as he tried to run back through the gate. I am sure he wanted to take the dog to eat. Most people don't have such fat little dogs. Look at him! He is not starving, he is just a thief.'' The hard-bitten platoon leader uttered the last word explosively and smacked the man on the head again. He glared at the cowering prisoner for a moment and then turned back to me. ''He should be punished severely for this, and especially for trying to steal a dog right under my nose! It is an insult! Who does he think he is?'' The platoon leader reached over and kicked the man on the leg.

I could see that the leader was in a rage more about the man trying to steal from us while he was in charge than about the actual theft itself. For some reason he took it as an insult and a threatened loss of face. He wasn't going to let this go lightly.

''The man is yours, *Trung úy*,'' he said. ''I give him to you. Do with him what you want. Nothing is too harsh for a dog thief.'' The platoon leader folded his arms and glared balefully at the prisoner. He seemed to be waiting for me to respond.

''Well,'' I said slowly, fishing for some response, ''what would you suggest, *Thiêu úy*?'' I had no idea what to do with a petty thief. I wasn't particularly mad myself, but I knew the thing to do now was to assuage the feelings of the platoon leader. He made several suggestions, the lightest of which was to put the man in the ''tiger cage'' and let him cook in the sun for a while, several days preferably.

The tiger cage was a barbed wire enclosure constructed by the local militiamen. It was almost long enough to lie down in and was just high enough to squat in. It was without shade and became very uncomfortable after an hour or so of confinement. This particular cage had been made to hold Viet Cong prisoners awaiting dispatch to the rear. After their capture the prisoners could be kept there for as long as several hours while we waited for the choppers to come pick them up. Sitting in the cage for a few hours was uncomfortable enough; sitting in it for several days would have been torture. Since some of the other suggestions were even worse, including having the man shot, I opted for having him put in the tiger cage. It would be a public punishment for the thief and would help the platoon leader save face.

I mustered a pissed-off-sounding tone to my voice and said, ''Put him in the tiger cage. No water. Let him talk to the sun.'' I stepped over beside the platoon leader and both of us glared at the thief, our arms folded and our faces grim.

The platoon leader issued instructions to his men, and they dragged the man away to the tiger cage. The officer turned to me and said, ''When you want him released, let the guard know. Since he tried to steal from you, you set his punishment.''

''No problem,'' I said. ''After he cooks in there for a few hours, he'll think twice about trying to steal someone else's dog.''

The leader nodded and turned to shoo his men back to their work. I walked back inside the team house and sat down at my makeshift desk. Abney had been standing at the door and had heard the entire proceedings. ''How long you going to let that little bastard cook out there, *Trung úy?*''

''I don't know,'' I said. ''I think I'll let him out at sundown. The *Thiêu úy* won't like it, but one afternoon out there is plenty for me. I don't want to end up killing the guy just because he tried to steal a damned dog.''

As the afternoon wore on, I managed to glance occasionally across the compound and check on the man in the tiger cage. He was squatting silently in the glaring sun, his only shade the shadow of the barbed wire strands which formed the top of his rude container. Other men walking by would occasionally call out a jibe or make a joke at the prisoner's expense. Sometimes the man would respond with a hot line of invective, sometimes he would simply stare away into space as if his tormentors were not even there. I imagined that it must have been much the same way in the States when we used to put minor miscreants in the public stocks for the afternoon.

Just before sundown I sent word to the gate guard to let the man go. I had heard that he was married and I knew that if he didn't come home that night, his wife and family would have no way of knowing what had happened to him. I figured the man had suffered enough discomfort and indignity for his misdemeanor, and I didn't want to push him to the point of inciting hatred. I always had to keep in the back of my mind the fact that I had a bounty on my head. If I made too many enemies in the village it would be easy enough for anybody to collect it.

I watched from the door of the team house as the man left

the compound, bowing and waving in my direction and thanking me profusely for releasing him. I thought jokingly as the man went through the gate, "Shit, son, you had better thank me. I could'a had you shot!" I amused myself with the thought that I was rather a liberal fellow for having held back the firing squad. I liked the idea of my being such a benevolent regent.

Chapter 8

T HE military operations we carried out with our RF's and PF's were done practically without any logistical or combat support. For example, we had no artillery in my entire district. So forget about artillery support; the best we could come up with was one 81mm mortar and an M-79 grenade launcher. Also, it was difficult to get helicopter gunships and "slicks," the lightly armed troop transport helicopters, to mount an air-mobile operation. We usually had to walk in to our fights and walk back again. If it was the wet season, we paddled in and paddled out in those damned little sampans.

Tactical air support from the U.S. Air Force wasn't exactly at our beck and call either. Naturally, their first priority was to provide support for the American army units. Unless they were really anticipating a day of light commitment to the Americans, they weren't about to send a flight of F-4's off to help some local-yokel Vietnamese unit out in the middle of nowhere and a hundred miles from any American troop concentrations. We were fighting in the same war, though; we were on the same side. When we needed help we needed help. Rationalizations about priority of need were not the help we needed.

Don't get me wrong, I have been terribly grateful to the U.S. Air Force. On the other hand, I have cursed every pilot wearing the blue, all their planes, and the sky they flew in. I have practically begged for air support, yelling into the mike of a field radio as I tried to overcome the noise of rifle and machine-gun fire. I would tell them to send Phantom jets, Huey helicopters, Spad biplanes, anything, but just send help. Some laconic voice would come back from across the miles and tell me they were trying to find something, but nothing was immediately available. Well, when you need air support, you need it right then, not sometime later. It didn't take much of this kind of procrastination to make me want to throw up my hands in disgust and just go home.

Whether I liked it or not, we had to march out on our patrols and ambush operations without any artillery and usually without any significant air support. Some of our men would be armed with modern M-16's, some would have old World War II-era carbines, and a few would have just a .38 pistol slung over the shoulder on a piece of string. Not one man in twenty wore a helmet, and not one in ten had a canteen. We were a ragtag army marching out of a ragtag village, seeking a ragtag enemy. It was war in its most basic and elementary form.

I think every man on my team recognized that so far as the regular American forces were concerned, we were out of sight and mind: we need not look to them for any significant amount of help. We got used to that after a while, and learned to make the necessary adjustments. We became expert scroungers and traders for some items, and for other things we just had to learn to do without.

There was one thing the Americans had that we could not scrounge and it was something we feared we might one day desperately need. That was emergency medical care, quick attention if we got shot. I think we all lived with the fear of being wounded and then dying due to the lack of care so readily available to everyone in the American units.

In a normal unit, the combat infantryman was probably never more than a few hundred yards from a qualified medic. If the soldier got hit, a medic could usually get to him in a matter of minutes. Not so in our case. More often than not, the team medic was not available to the men on the combat operations. He was often miles away from the military operations, carrying out other advisory duties. If one of us got hit, he would more likely be in the care of some fumble-fisted fellow grunt whose amateur efforts at first aid might be as dangerous as the wound.

Our remoteness from medical assistance made us extra careful in our own first-aid preparations. We began carrying two combat wound bandages in our web gear rather than the usual one. Each man was also given a styrette of injectable morphine, which was kept in a little waterproof container taped to his knife scabbard. If a man was wounded and the pain became unbearable, either he or his partner could administer the morphine injection. The law of the jungle was that you never gave another man your wound bandages or your morphine. He was not to expect yours, you were not to expect his. To expect another man to give you his own lifeline was not within the rules of the game.

Radio communications were often a problem, and our inability to talk with people in the outside world increased our general sense of isolation. Not only was it often impossible to contact our province team or even other district teams, but we often couldn't even talk with our own men. It was not unheard of to have patrols that would cover twenty or thirty kilometers in a day. If bad weather or weak batteries compounded the problem, men out on the operations would have difficulty maintaining radio contact with the team base. Sometimes communications would be totally cut off. In those situations if you were wounded or in any serious trouble, you might as well have been on Mars. We all recognized the potential for a replay of Custer and the Indians; it tended to make us very cautious.

The officers and men in our local village units recognized that we were together in our isolation and in the lack of help we could expect from higher government sources. The remedy that had been adopted by the native troops was to be sure not to push a contact with the Cong too far. Aggressive destruction of the enemy was not the prevailing philosophy. Rather, the view was more like "Let's get a few of them if we can, but there is no sense in any of us getting hurt in the process." Any desire to take assertive action against the enemy was blunted by the knowledge that additional military support would not be forthcoming should a really hot action develop. It didn't help that they also knew of the low quality of medical support provided for militia soldiers.

Well, I came to town green as a gourd and full of spit and vinegar. I had been told that it was my job to make fighters of my militiamen and I figured on doing just that. I intended to make it clear that listless pursuit of the guerrillas and lack-adaisical searches of their sanctuaries only encouraged their terrorism and banditry. I wanted to turn my militia into an effective fighting force, and I knew I couldn't do that by just playing like a local small-time king. My guys and I were going to have to train the locals to fight properly, and more than that, we were going to have to demonstrate with our own personal leadership.

ONE DAY SERGEANT ABNEY AND I WERE ON AN OPERATION with our RF company; it was a joint exercise with the RF company from adjacent Kien Van district and their American advisors. We were operating in the border area of our two districts and had been on the march all day. In the late afternoon we had a brief contact with a Cong unit of undetermined size. We gave pursuit and eventually trapped what appeared to be a Viet Cong company between ourselves and our neighboring RF unit. We faced the enemy company across a rice paddy. They were in a tree line on one side and we were strung out along the opposite tree line. I was pleased with our performance at that point; the operation was working in textbook fashion. We had trapped the Charlie unit even though we had problems with our adjacent friendly unit. It seemed they either didn't believe in using a radio or they had a faulty one; communication had been difficult all day.

As we closed in on the trapped enemy unit, we came under increasingly heavy fire. The men were spending more and more time on the ground and less and less time advancing. Finally all movement halted. The fire from the Cong unit had become very heavy. Crawling along with the RF leader, I tried to convince him to keep the men moving. He wasn't interested. The whine and crack of passing bullets made me wish that my head grew below my shoulders. I never felt I was down quite low enough, no matter how low I was. I could hear the constant spatter of bullets into the trees. Occasionally a branch would be clipped clean by a chance shot and provided clear evidence that getting hit by one of the little invisible zingers was going to be very unpleasant.

I knew we couldn't simply lie there. Unless we closed in, the Cong would slide out of our pincers movement. I was afraid and angry at the same time. I couldn't think of any safe way to get the unit moving again. I kept looking over at Sergeant Abney, who was as frustrated as I was. I kept yelling to him, "We've got to move up, we've got to move up!" Abney agreed, but he had already accepted the futility of getting the men on their feet again.

That was when I remembered the sometimes famous, sometimes infamous Colonel Anthony Herbert, a major when he had been my tactics instructor. He had been the most decorated enlisted man during the Korean War, and he had later received a commission and had become the archetype of the airborne-ranger army officer. I was just a cadet at the time I knew him, and I was impressed by his charisma, his leadership ability, and his military expertise. He had a great impact on my idea of what soldiering was all about and on my understanding of the responsibilities of an officer in the United States Army.

One day a couple of us cadets were having a conversation with Major Herbert about individual leadership. We were talking about what was to be done if troops under fire refused to move as ordered. After all, we thought, what can you do, shoot them for insubordination? Even if that was legal, and even that seemed questionable, none of us felt we were prepared to shoot our own men. Herbert had an answer for the situation. I lost a lot of sleep over it later because it laid bare in a very chilling way the danger and responsibility that are inherent in the duty of a combat leader.

Herbert said, "If your troops are down and won't move, you simply have to stand up and lead by personal example. You have to calmly walk over and talk with your squad leaders, urge the men up, and give a personal demonstration that the danger isn't as bad as they thought."

"But sir," I had protested, "we're talking about really heavy stuff coming in. What if the fire is so hot you can't get up? You can't just stand up in a hail of bullets! You'd be cut to pieces!"

Major Herbert looked me dead in the eye and said, "You know that every enlisted man in this army has to salute an officer when he goes by?"

"Yes, sir."

"You know about the O-clubs, the BOQ's, and other privileges officers are given in this army?"

"Yes, sir."

"You know that you'll get better pay and housing than enlisted men who often have twice the knowledge and ten times the experience you do?"

"Yes, sir," I replied again, beginning to feel somewhat chagrined.

"Well, in point of fact you stand the risk of having to earn every little perk you ever get. When all the chips are down, when the privates won't move and the sergeants won't move and fear has taken over everything, all the responsibility falls on your shoulders. That's why you have the commission and they don't. You took the rank, you took the privileges, now you have to pay your dues. You've got to stand up and by God lead those men! Nine times out of ten it's not as bad as you think. It's amazing what a little courage and leadership will do for good soldiers. You just remember this: the day you have to be the first one to stand up and say, 'Follow me,' that's the day you will earn every salute you ever get."

I cursed the memory as I lay there in the hot tropical sun, sweat stinging my eyes and automatic weapons fire drumming in my ears. I could feel Herbert standing there with that smug, I-told-you-so air. The lead was flying, the troops weren't moving. It was up to me to do something. Believe me, when you are running your own little war and you are your own little general, you can always find plenty of reasons for doing nothing. I had no direct orders to do anything and none of my superiors would have been the wiser if I just stayed put, but I could feel Major Herbert standing there looking right at me and saying, "Stand up and by God lead those men!" I stood up.

I looked at the Vietnamese lieutenant lying on the ground beside me and said, *"Thiêu úy, bấy giò chung tôi phāi đi, không?"* As I spoke I pointed to the enemy-infested tree line in front of us, trying to add to my insistence that we get up and move forward.

The lieutenant looked at me as if I were crazy. "Get down," he exclaimed in Vietnamese. "You'll get hit! We can't move up now, there is too much shooting from the trees." He kept motioning me to get back down.

The whine of bullets through the air, their flutter through the leaves, and the puffs of dirt they kicked up were giving me second thoughts about this standing-up business. I knew, though, that the Americans were fond of saying that the only thing Vietnamese troops really lacked was good leadership. I was determined to give it to them. I was *not* going to sit back down. I walked down the line of troops that had strung itself along an old abandoned paddy dike. They would pull at my leg or arm as I passed, trying to get me to lie down. I stayed up and told them they could do the same and not get hurt. The longer I stayed up, the more confident I became. I began to talk louder and with more assurance. My stride became a little less hesitant.

I began to realize that most of the Viet Cong riflemen were shooting high, a common error that many poorly trained fighters make. I was safer than it appeared. Sergeant Abney was taller than I, but he too got up and joined in my demonstration. I figured that sooner or later the Vietnamese officer would be embarrassed enough to get up himself. I knew that saving face was a powerful motivation for him. He wouldn't want to lie there and act the coward while the Americans were walking around as if nothing was happening. I was right. It wasn't long before the young lieutenant got up, albeit in a crouch, and began to demand that the others get up too.

"O.k.," I said to Sergeant Abney, "let's go get 'em."

We both stepped out across the mounded earth of the dike and began our slow advance toward the trees. The Vietnamese officer and his NCO's were now giving a tirade. The lieutenant in particular was trying to make up for his former timidity and was yelling at everyone. The men responded hesitantly, but they got up and moved out behind us. I looked over my shoulder and with great relief saw the ragged strand of men coming along.

Sergeant Abney and I motioned them on and slowed our pace until they came up to us. I told the Vietnamese lieutenant to keep his men from bunching up and to keep his lines straight. Abney and I went up and down the line, instructing the men to keep a steady but slow rate of fire going into the woods. At a time like that several things had to be managed properly. First, we had to return the enemy's fire, even if we couldn't see individual targets. It was hoped that this "suppressing fire" would encourage the enemy to keep his head down and decrease the amount of shooting he could do. Second, our rate of fire should not exceed the need (sometimes a hard thing to determine) since we wanted the men to keep moving, not stop every two steps to change magazines. Third, we wanted our men to conserve ammunition so they would have plenty of firepower left once they began the close-range, direct assault over the final few yards. That's when the rate of fire would have to be high. Even then automatic weapons fire would have to be in well-controlled bursts, not in indiscriminate, magazine-emptying sprays. If fire control is not firmly maintained, many men will run out of ammo right in the middle of their assault. In the excitement of the approach, they simply fire it all away.

Another concern was to keep everyone from firing over the enemy's heads. Most people have a natural tendency to shoot high. We wanted our troops to err on the side of the low shot, especially when firing automatic weapons. If green troops aren't trained to shoot a little low, they will end up wasting their bullets in the air and through the overhead branches. Next, we had to keep the assault line straight, especially since we had a way to go to get to the objective. We didn't want one group to get way out in front of everyone else or to lag behind. If an assault line gets too far out of whack there is a danger that the attacking soldiers will fire into their own comrades. Also, we didn't want one part of our line to get into the trees before the whole line was ready for the final leg of the assault; otherwise, the Cong could have taken us out piecemeal. We wanted everybody to get to the objective at the same time.

Yet another problem in this sort of movement under fire is that troops tend to group up during the approach to an objective. No one likes to be alone in time of danger, so we all tend to act like a flock of sheep. The combat leader's job is to keep people spread out and on line, not to allow the men to bunch up in tight little groups. Bunching up during an assault presents an easier target for the enemy; this can be lethal itself, but there is another problem. Men tend to lose their independent thought and action when they bunch up. When one man stops, everybody stops, and then everybody is hesitant to start moving again.

And so the list of distractions goes—hundreds of things crop up that have to be managed. Fear necessarily takes a back seat; one doesn't have enough time to be scared.

Becoming too preoccupied is dangerous, though. Loss of fear is usually accompanied by loss of caution. That can get you killed. Leaders sometimes become so preoccupied looking after everyone else that they forget to look out for themselves. It is a sad fact that people have to risk death by reason of duty or necessity, but too often they die by reason of forgetfulness.

I called the American advisor of our neighboring RF unit on the radio and told him that his unit should stay in a blocking position while we continued our assault. My guys were now up and moving, and I figured our neighbors would be only too glad to let us carry on. I wanted to make sure the Cong could not escape out the back door. While we pressed our attack I asked those other RF platoons to take up positions along the trails and canals that the Cong might use as escape routes.

My militiamen were steadily moving up, and they were putting down a slow fire as they advanced. Despite the training we had tried to give them, some of our guys didn't want to fire at all—they wanted to just run from one clump of grass to the next and leave the shooting to others. I kept after the Vietnamese lieutenant to keep his men up and shooting. He was doing his best and he eventually got most of the men doing their part. Finally we were into the tree line. I had seen two of our men get hit as we crossed the rice paddy.

As we had neared the trees, the enemy fire had actually slackened. I had thought that it was because our return fire had made them keep their heads down. In the tree line itself, though, there was no resistance at all. The enemy had vanished. There were two KIA's in the brush, but their comrades had disappeared.

I called the advisor with the blocking units and told him he should be alert for the escaping Cong. If he had his men set up in the right places, the Cong should fall right in their laps. We set out a perimeter defense around the evacuated Viet Cong position, searched the area for more people and equipment, and waited to hear the neighbors come into contact with the Cong. After a few minutes we heard a brief firefight break out somewhere off to our left, but that was all. Everything else was silent. The heavy contact never came.

I learned later that many of the RF's responsible for the blocking action had not really gone out to their assigned positions. The advisor told me he had discovered soon afterward that many of the men had just gone off toward the assigned area and laid back to while away a quiet afternoon. The Cong found it simple enough to slip by right under their noses.

My guys had done well and I was feeling good about their conduct. They had gone on assault while under pretty heavy fire. That was quite an accomplishment for a local village militia outfit! We all learned a lot from the experience: I learned firsthand that frightened men will respond to positive leadership; they learned that they could do what they had thought they couldn't. Even so, I'll always remember those first few minutes after I stood up and began walking up and down the line. I had no idea if the men would really get up and go. I was scared shitless, no bones about it, but I knew that our job was, to use an Infantry School phrase, to close with and kill or capture the enemy. Infantry that won't close is worthless. I wanted my guys to be worth something. I wanted them to *feel* worth something. I wanted them to know they could do a job that they had once thought they couldn't. We did it, and I was proud of it. I wished I could talk with Major Herbert again and tell him that he was right; sometimes you just have to be willing to stand up and by God *lead* those men.

SOME OF THE ATTEMPTS TO APPLY AMERICAN TECHNOLOGY to Vietnamese problems would be funny if they had not been so damned frustrating to deal with. The Hamlet Evaluation System and the Territorial Forces Evaluation System, referred to as HES and TFES, were two examples of such ill-advised Americanisms. The HES and TFES were computer printout lists of standardized questions sent monthly to every district senior advisor in the country. Among other things, the HES report had us determine how many televisions were in each village and hamlet (none—hell, we didn't even have electricity!), how many of the men were fishermen, how many were farmers, how many were in business, how many houses had tin roofs, etc., etc. . . . TFES wanted to know about the troop strength, morale, weapons, and equipment of the local district and village militia organizations. The intent of these reports was good, but like so many good bureaucratic intentions, the idea was weakest at the point of practical application. I saw DSA's give the reports they should have filled out themselves to their less informed and less experienced subordinates. Sometimes the instructions would be to just fill in the blanks with anything that seemed reasonable. Meeting the deadline for submission of the report was the important thing, not accuracy. Often, reports on hamlets were filled in when the hamlet had never been seen by the DSA or any of his team members. Instead of a firsthand look, the overworked DSA might take the word or opinion of a local Vietnamese official about the situation in some remote hamlet. While the Vietnamese colleague might in fact know of the situation in that hamlet, his motives in giving an opinion or an answer might have been viewed with some skepticism.

The Vietnamese authorities wanted all TFES and HES reports to be glowing and upbeat. The HES reports, for instance, formed the basis for the country-wide system of classifying areas as "pacified," "contested," or "Viet Cong controlled." There were actually four ratings, "A" through "D." An "A" rating meant that the village or hamlet was pacified; there had been no Viet Cong incidents in the area during the reporting period. A "B" rating meant that the area was essentially pacified but with some residual Cong activity. A "C" rating meant the area was contested by both government troops and the Viet Cong; typically, the government ruled by day and the Cong ruled by night. "D" meant complete Viet Cong control. This system allowed the construction of a great multicolored map back in Saigon which could be shown to the visiting generals, celebrities, and politicians. They would visit the posh air-conditioned MACV headquarters building known as "Pentagon East" and have the successes of the pacification program explained to them in great detail. By such simpleminded representations, the war-watchers could see the "A" color advance across the country. Everyone could tell that the pacification program was succeeding as the colors for "C" and "D" hamlets became more and more rare. There was "light at the end of the tunnel." Unfortunately, the simplicities of the system did not fit the subtleties of the situation.

On the Vietnamese side, district chiefs were put in a good light by an "A" rating. It meant they were doing a good job and could look to their province chief for future favor. The province chiefs, in turn, wanted their areas to be reported in with a heavy list of "A" ratings so they would appear to be successful back in Saigon or at the regional (I, II, III, or IV Corps) headquarters. Likewise, a DSA's and a PSA's job went a lot smoother if high ratings were given to most hamlets. As with the Vietnamese, it certainly looked as if he were doing one hell of a job if all of a sudden reported Viet Cong incidents fell off and hamlet ratings went up. It also made life much easier with your Vietnamese counterpart if you made him look good to his bosses. A district chief who took umbrage at your monthly reports could change your job from an absurdly difficult one to an absolutely impossible one.

When you are isolated and alone, with too little time to fill in reports accurately—too tired to care and with little belief that the statistics have any relationship to the life you are living anyway—it is easy to just put down the numbers that make life simpler. If I recall correctly, the month the infamous 1968 Tet offensive broke out, the country was reported to be over ninety-percent pacified. The Tet offensive showed that bullshit in the reporting system was to be measured in feet, not inches.

I HAD DRAWN THE UNENVIABLE DUTY OF BEING THE PROVince team pay officer for the month of November and had been sent back to Can Tho to pick up the payroll. I was spending the night in the Can Tho transient officer billets before collecting the payroll the next morning and flying back to Cao Lanh with more thousands of dollars in a paper sack than I cared to think about. The billets were in a four-story concrete block building set right in the middle of Can Tho. The accommodations were spartan. There was one shower per floor, four bunks to each prison-cell-type room. They did have plumbing, though, and I reveled in the warm water coming out of the shower tap. What a luxury!

That evening I went to the open-air bar on the roof of the building and got into a conversation with some of the other men staying over for the night. Most of the men using the billet were from various MACV units, men who had been sent back to Can Tho to take care of one thing or another.

There were five of us sitting at a metal table drinking bourbon and Shasta cola. The tall brown-haired lieutenant across from me was an engineer officer from Long Xuyen; I guessed he was on the province team staff there. The fellow sitting next to me was a red-haired captain from way down in Quan Long. He was a DSA in his province and we struck up an easy camaraderie. The third man was a quiet fellow in civilian clothes. He was either a police advisor on civilian contract or an Agency man. The fourth was a major from MACV headquarters in Saigon. He had been sent down to Can Tho to take care of some business at IV Corps headquarters and thought he was getting a taste of the boonies by having to sit up here drinking bourbon and warm cola.

The conversation wandered along many avenues and finally settled on the perception we thought the American people had of the war in Vietnam, and how they had come to see things that way. The fellow from Long Xuyen had spoken up and said he didn't think the Americans had any idea about the reality of life in the Vietnamese villages.

"What do you expect?" sneered the Agency man. "Most folks back in the States get their news from the damned TV! Those television reporters are all alike! They want to talk about flashy stuff and holler over the microphone while the guns are going off all around them. They want lots of action in the background just to make everything look interesting. That's how you sell TV time. It's not how you explain Vietnam to anybody."

The man from Long Xuyen agreed. "You know," he snorted, "the folks at home have this feeling that they're informed about things over here just because they watch the evening news. They don't realize they're only getting the tiniest little peep at what's really happening! How do you really tell people in Kansas about a war on the other side of the world when they're all there watching the TV from the dinner table? I don't think the folks at home get enough of the right kind of information, but, hell, I don't think they would know how to deal with it if they had it."

The DSA from Quan Long looked at the civilian across the table and said with a drawl, "Well, the folks back in the States may not be getting good information, but it's hard to bitch about that when even the government can't get any decent facts. Think about all the filters that are stacked in the information channel between us and Washington. Guys like me on a district team send information back to province. Province talks to IV Corps, from there to Saigon, and from there to Washington. At each step along the way people play games with the information. They filter out what they disagree with or what they think will put 'em in a bad light, and send on the rest. By the time it gets back to DC it's no wonder they can't make heads or tails of what's going on over here."

"That's right," I volunteered. "Everybody in the chain of command is so concerned about covering his own ass that nobody wants to hear any bad news. General Weatherday has come out to my team twice on his tours around IV Corps. Both times my PSA came out in a chopper the day before the general appeared just so he could hear what I intended to say. I couldn't make a clear report of anything that might have made the PSA or the province team look bad. If I had to report negative information, I had to understate it. Both times I stood there trying to give Weatherday a factual report with the god-damned PSA glaring at me over his shoulder, daring me to let any cats out of the bag. It pissed me off, but there wasn't a damn thing I could do about it."

The engineer from Long Xuyen spoke up. "You could just go ahead and tell the truth."

"And what the hell good would that do?" I asked. "The colonel would only play down anything he didn't like. Then, just as soon as the general left he would come back and eat me alive. I'd probably get relieved just so he could get some-body out at my team who wouldn't give him any shit. I'd be bounced off to somewhere else and the only thing I would have accomplished was to let some other goomba have my job."

"I've seen exactly the same thing happen you're talking about," said the DSA from Quan Long, "but most folks don't want to be a martyr for nothing. Hell, I don't think generals ever hear much bad news out at the district level. I suspect the province-level briefings are the same sort of emphasize-the-good-understate-the-bad kind of bullshit, too. Weatherday probably thinks things are going great all over IV Corps! When he goes around out in the field and hears nothing but great reports, it's probably pretty difficult not to believe them. I'll bet IV Corps plays the same game when they report to Saigon and Saigon does the same thing when they report to Washington.''

"I know that's exactly what happens between Saigon and DC," said the major from Saigon. "You wouldn't believe the jumping through the hat that goes on whenever General Abels has to go back and brief the president or the joint chiefs. We're generally supposed to make things look as good as we can, and if you don't play the game you can be made to look pretty bad." The major paused for a second before he said with a chuckle, "A lotta people know the building is burning, but nobody wants to yell 'Fire.' "

The conversation wandered off to other topics, but during the evening film that was shown later, I couldn't help but think back over what we had said. In actuality we were all part of the information network, or the misinformation network if that is more appropriate. Everybody hoped somebody else would pick up the pieces of the puzzle and put it all together, but at least at our level, we all passed off the responsibility to someone else. It is no wonder, then, that the American government operated in such a dense fog of optimism and unreal expectations with respect to the American effort in Vietnam. By the time the information from the field got up to the level of the policymakers, all the chatter and noise had been filtered out. Bad news was downplayed, good news magnified. I suspect many decisions were based on the glossy briefings of some brass hat who was more concerned about where he stood on the promotion list than he was with making sure the planners knew all the hard facts about the American position in South Vietnam.

Chapter 9

I т was a new day. Sergeant Abney and I had crawled out of our bunks just as a hint of dawn began to creep into the eastern horizon. We had each pulled our two-hour radio watch during the night, and I had been awakened on two other occasions for decisions about one thing or another. Getting up yet again was a painful struggle, but Abney and I were to accompany a patrol leaving the village at sunrise.

Abney lit the kerosene camp stove and started warming a pot of his "hobo" coffee. Abney's hobo coffee was made by just dumping coffee grounds directly into the pot and bringing the concoction to a boil. You could drink it or eat it, depending on whether you got one of the first cups or one of the last. I pulled on my "tiger stripes"—the native camouflage fatigues with a characteristic striped pattern—and laced up my jungle boots. While Abney was getting dressed, I spattered a little cooking oil in a pan and lit the other eye of the kerosene stove. I fried two pieces of the local bread in the hot grease and handed one to Abney along with a little packet of jelly from an old C-ration box. We tossed down the brackish coffee and gnawed on our field-expedient substitute for morning toast. We finished eating in silence and began the routine of checking and strapping on our field harnesses.

The clutter of canvas suspenders, web belts, canteens, wound packets, ammunition pouches, combat knife and scabbard, compass, and other assorted junk was referred to as "web gear." Fully charged with water, ammunition, and other sundries, the lot could weigh thirty pounds. All equipment was clipped onto a thick web belt and the belt was slung from a set of shoulder harnesses. The idea was to adjust things so the weight of the gear was evenly distributed between hips and shoulders. That would supposedly make the load more comfortable and help avoid blisters and chafing. I don't think I ever got it right. Either my hips were rubbed raw by the constant pressure and friction, or my shoulders felt as if I had just been hit across the trapezius muscles with a series of karate chops.

We wore neither flack vests nor steel helmets when operating with the Vietnamese troops. Our local soldiers didn't have flack vests, so we didn't wear them either. Instead of helmets we wore the blue berets of the Vietnamese militia units. Our use of their uniform was an expression of our solidarity with them, but it was also a simple act of prudence to look as Vietnamese as possible, at least from a distance. Men who dressed in uniforms that were obviously American, who were fully turned out in helmet, flack vest, standard-issue jungle fatigues, and so forth, were prime targets for the Viet Cong. In a fight a getup like that would draw fire like honey draws flies. Being inconspicuous was hard enough for a one-hundred-seventy-pound, six-foot, one-inch American when he went walking around with the lightweight, five-foot-tall Vietnamese. We didn't want more trouble than absolutely necessary, so un-American uniforms were *de rigueur*.

Abney and I grabbed our M-16's and our PRC-25 radio as we left the team house and walked out into the compound. The eastern sky was turning gray, and from the flickering lights of the fires and lanterns in the compound we could tell that our troops were already up and about, preparing for the day's operation. Looking out through the gate, I could see the waking village as it prepared to meet the new day. Small cooking fires were already lit. Thin trails of white smoke rose into the dark blue-gray haze of morning. The women and children were already going about their morning chores as they moved slowly in and out of the bamboo and palm thatch hooches. Like the soldiers in the compound, the farmers and fishermen of the village were about to leave—for them it would be another hot day of work in the rice fields and on the canals. Sergeant Abney and I walked out toward the village to the assembly area for the unit we would accompany that day. An ugly old swaybacked Asian sow was rooting in the mud alongside the path. Chickens and ducks so lice-ridden they didn't have any feathers were scrounging for their morning rations. Several of the sow's pigs were squealing and fighting over some morsel one of them had found. The aroma of the primitive village rose to meet us in the morning air. It was a pleasant blend of wood smoke, spices, fish, *nu'ố'c mắm,* and the pungent aroma of Vietnamese smoking tobacco.

We arrived at the assembly area as the men from the compound and the village straggled in with their curious collection of weapons and uniforms. This particular morning I was most taken with a fellow who wore black pajama pants, an army fatigue shirt, an old American helmet liner that almost swallowed his entire head, and a .38 caliber service revolver slung on his shoulder with a piece of string. That was it—no rifle, no ammo, no canteen, no boots, no nothin'! Just a helmet liner and a .38 on a string.

The operation promised to be an arduous one. We were to march to our eastern border and patrol an area thick with jungle and the potential for trouble. All told, it would require a march of about thirty kilometers. We had to get back to the village by nightfall so some of the men could make their security patrols that night. The fact that the rainy season had already begun added a significant problem to the operation. Floodwaters were already rising. Out on the plains, the marsh weeds and elephant grass lay over a land that was in many places already ankle- to shin-deep in water. Slogging through that in waterlogged combat boots was like walking with lead weights around your ankles. I tried not to think about having to do it all day long.

After the militia platoon leader got things semi-organized, we started off. Our little column marched toward the rose-colored sky that announced the rising sun. The platoon strung itself out in single file and settled into the steady pace of men used to walking long distances. I tried to remind the platoon leader about the utility of combat formations, but he wasn't terribly impressed. I did finally get him to put out some flank security for the column, but not without a lot of resistance and several excuses for not doing it. He got a little irritated and probably felt I was too insistent about telling him what to do, but I'd be damned if I was going to just walk out of the village and romp happily into the first ambush that came along.

We walked for some time across fields and paddy dikes, and most of the time we were able to stay on dry ground. Later on we moved out into the uncultivated areas beyond the paddies. The low-lying land was almost completely flooded by a six- to twelve-inch layer of water. We slogged on toward our assigned patrol area, occasionally stopping at a dry elevation of land or on an abandoned housing mound to rest for a few minutes. By late morning the glaring sun was emitting a fierce tropical heat. My fatigues were soaked below the knees by the floodwaters and above the knees by sweat. Sergeant Abney and I both had lost so much body salt that it formed white deposits on our fatigue shirts.

We had made no contacts, sighted no enemy. I was hot, tired, and thirsty. The Vietnamese platoon leader didn't know what in the hell he was doing and he wouldn't listen to my advice. He was more interested in getting from dry spot to dry spot for the rest breaks than he was in completing the operation.

We were walking over a rare stretch of dry ground when suddenly we heard an explosion toward the head of the column. Everyone dropped in his tracks, eyes scanning the flanks, waiting for something else to happen. For a few moments we lay there in the quiet. Nothing happened. Sergeant Abney, the platoon leader, and I moved toward the head of the column, running in a crouch. Up ahead a group of men were huddled around a figure lying on the ground. We parted the men and told them to get back to their positions. The man on the ground had stepped on a small land mine, probably homemade, and it had blown his foot off. His leg ended in a bloody stump at the ankle. Blood was squirting in pulses from a large artery. We stopped most of the bleeding by using a shoestring tourniquet around the stump. The man lay still, immersed in shock from the blast and the sight of his footless leg. He sat up quietly and stared blankly at the Vietnamese medic as the medic tried to offer encouragement.

I called back to the team house on our PRC-25 and told them to request a medevac chopper from province headquarters. I knew that we might not be able to raise the province team on our radio during the day and even if we did, province would have to send the request for a chopper on back to Can Tho. I expected a long delay in getting any help. I was wrong. I got a call back in a few minutes that said we had a "dust-off" coming in.

In about a half an hour I got a call on the radio. "Greedy Petrel Whiskey three-niner, White Knight two-five. Do you read me, over?" I was glad to get the call. I was nervous about sitting still out in the middle of nowhere, and the wounded man was looking worse and worse all the time. His color had turned a pasty yellow-green and his breathing was quick and shallow. I wanted him off my hands fast.

I grabbed the hand mike from the side of the radio, squeezed the push-to-talk button, and said, "White Knight two-five, Whiskey three-niner, I read you five-by-five. Do you have our location, over?"

"Three-niner, this is two-five, negative on your location. Do you hear me coming, over?"

I put the mike down and stood up to listen for the sound of helicopter blades. I could hear him somewhere off to the east but I couldn't tell exactly where.

"Two-five, Three-niner. I can hear you. Do you want smoke, over?"

"This is Two-five. Affirmative, Three-niner. Pop smoke."

"Three-niner, roger."

I pulled a smoke grenade from the webbing on the radio pack, pulled the pin, and heaved it off into the weeds several yards away. I picked up the hand mike again. "This is Three-niner. Smoke out, over." The purple smoke began to drift up from the grass and within a matter of a few seconds, a great purple cloud was billowing from the small canister. The protocol required the chopper pilot to now call me back and identify the color of the smoke. We all wanted to make sure he came to the right place and to the right people. In about a minute the pilot called back and identified the purple smoke. I told him to come on in.

The red cross–marked medevac ship came racing in from over the trees. We signaled him down in a clearing nearby and carried the wounded man over to the chopper. The crew chief helped us get him aboard, then we all ran back out from under the whirling blades. I turned back into the beating wind and flying grass and gave the thumbs-up sign to the pilot.

Immediately the rotating blades picked up speed. I went over to our radio and took the mike. "Knight two-five, Whiskey three-niner. Thanks for the help. Have a safe ride, over."

"Roger, three-niner. Glad we could help. Two-five, out." The Huey pulled up into the air, turned as it lifted, and disappeared back over the trees.

We got the troops up and moving again, but now Sergeant Abney and I stayed near the front of the column. We were looking for other signs of booby traps or mines. It was clear we had entered Cong country. Abney called me over and silently pointed off to our left. The tall grass only partially hid the sharpened tips of bamboo punji stakes. Looking around more intently, we could see the punji stakes scattered around everywhere. The obvious ones stuck out of the water and grass. The barbs I was more concerned about were the ones we couldn't see. Small punji stakes made of sharpened, fire-hardened slivers of bamboo or of barbed nails could pierce the sole of a boot and go right on through the foot. Our jungle boots had a special nylon mesh insole that was supposed to protect against penetration by punji stakes, but I didn't have much faith in it.

Sometimes the tips of the stakes were smeared with human feces or just plain old buffalo shit. Just a scratch could lead to a serious infection or even to blood poisoning. Areas heavily infested with punji stakes and other types of homemade booby traps really slowed movement since we had to pick our way through them very carefully. If we came under attack, it was difficult to move to cover or go into the counterattack. It was not uncommon for a man to be impaled on a punji stake as he dove to the ground or ran through the brush during a firefight.

We had just gotten past the major infestation of booby traps when we began to receive fire from a tree line in front of us. Water spouted up around us, bullets whined overhead, and we heard the stuttered popping of the light arms fire. The men reacted well now, not like the early days when getting any reaction from them under fire was next to impossible. Sergeant Abney took the rear of the column and swung to the right, using it as a maneuver element while those of us in front returned fire. When Abney's troops got to a good protected position they stopped and began firing themselves. Under the cover of their fire we moved ahead to yet another position. In this back-and-forth, stepwise manner Abney's and my groups finally got to the tree line and into the direct assault. Three men in the element I was with had been hit, I didn't know how badly, but everybody had kept moving up. We had done well.

As we entered the wood line, the going slowed down to a crawl. We kept firing, but we couldn't see through the jungle entanglements. Just inside the tree line we passed a few abandoned foxholes. Several of them had piles of empty brass cartridges littering their rims. A considerable quantity of blood was smeared on the walls of at least two and on the grass leading back to the jungle.

We kept the men spread out even after the firing had stopped. We didn't know what would happen next. With the men settled into a loose perimeter, we had a conference—Abney, the platoon leader, and myself. We decided to push on through the wooded area to see if we could hunt down the escaping Cong or find some cache or hideout they might have tucked away in the area. After we had gone only thirty or forty meters into the woods, we came upon just what we were looking for, a small collection of bamboo huts with plenty of evidence that it was a Viet Cong hideaway. A cooking fire was still smoking in front of one of the huts, and a dead man was sprawled awkwardly on the floor of one of the lean-tos. He had been shot twice in the chest. We presumed he had been dragged back to the huts from the foxholes.

The camp bore all the signs of a hasty retreat. Scattered boxes contained papers and documents. A large metal canister contained medicines and drugs. With the exception of one case of small arms ammunition, all military hardware was gone. One of the bunkers had two crocks packed full of dried fish and dried rats. These meager stores were all that was left. Apparently not impressed with his food and lodging, one Viet Cong wag had left a penciled sign stuck in the bamboo thatch of one of the huts. It was in English: "The Mekong Hilton." Sergeant Abney and I got a chuckle out of the sign but it had no meaning to our militiamen. Apparently only the Cong shared our familiarity with big-time Western hotels.

We burned the huts down and broke open the crocks before we moved back to our original line of march. A little later on we pulled up to eat our midday meal and to let the Vietnamese platoon leader report via radio about the morning's actions. It wasn't long before a couple of small campfires were going and men were out collecting the large snails that grew so prolifically in the Delta. The snails were dumped on the coals to cook, and men pulled their dried fish or rats from their pockets. The fish and rats were like jerky in a sense. They were dry, hard, and tough, but you could gnaw on them for a while and at least get the impression you had had something to eat. I noticed I was feeling a little out of sorts, but passed it off as being overtired and still pumped up from the firefight. I decided I had better not try the snails.

Eventually we received instructions to continue our sweep of the area for another couple of hours before returning home by a separate route. We struck out, slogging through the water again, but to no avail. We didn't see another sign of the Viet Cong. As the afternoon wore on, I began to feel a little nauseous, but I ignored it. We continued to slosh through the shin-deep water. Dry ground seemed harder and harder to find. My shoulders hurt under the harness straps of my web gear. My feet and legs hurt from the constant strain of walking in the mud and water. The heat from the sun seemed to be aimed specifically at me. I was hot, itchy, and incredibly tired. At each rest I collapsed on whatever semi-dry spot I could find. When we finally turned for home, I felt like singing the doxology.

The return march was awful. I was feeling weaker and weaker. The troops were becoming more and more lackadaisical. I sent Abney to the rear of the column to try and keep the men from straggling too far behind. I don't remember seeing him again that day. The platoon leader and I kept urging the men to stay together and to keep up the pace of the march. Despite our efforts the tired men walked more and more slowly. Short halts to tie a shoe or to fix a belt tended to turn into excuses to sit down and rest the aching muscles. I knew the problem, too. I felt as if I couldn't take another step. I was weakening fast, and by now my whole body was one big ache. I realized I must really be sick from something.

The closer we got to the village the deeper the water seemed to get, and mud sticking on my boots seemed to gain more and more weight. At last I could see the tin roofs of Tram

Chim glinting in the late afternoon sun. We splashed on for another hour or so, but the roofs didn't seem to be getting any closer. Each step was painful. I tried to put my mind in neutral. I told myself not to think about anything. Just keep walking.

Finally, I got down to commanding myself to simply put one foot down, then move the other foot in front; one foot down, then the other in front; one foot down, then the other in front. Step by step, I made myself keep on going. I was afraid to stop or to sit down. I was afraid I wouldn't be able to move again. As we neared the village the men peeled off to go to their homes. I angled off from the main body to head for the team compound at the end of the village. I was alone. Sagging forward, shoulders slumped, barely making any progress, I continued to slosh through the ankle-deep water. My stomach was rumbling and contorting. My thighs and calves were knots of throbbing pain, and they were so weak my knees were quivering. I thought each step would be my last. The walls of the fort were now only a hundred meters away, but I thought I would collapse before I made it to them.

Suddenly I noticed Cô Ha on the road coming out of the compound gate. She waved to me and watched me moving toward the compound. I waved back, but I couldn't raise my arm over my head. The pain in my shoulders was too great. Cô Ha hesitated, then came out across the field toward me. With a look of concern, she asked, *"Trung úy, are you all right?"*

"I don't think so," I said without elaboration. I was singlemindedly intent on reaching the compound gate.

"Give me your belt and canteens," she said. I didn't complain as she unbuckled my web gear and hauled it off my shoulders. I could hardly move my arms enough to get out of the harness, but she dragged the heavy equipment off me and slung it over her own back. I still thought I would fall over any moment. I put my hand on her shoulder for support and we walked toward the compound. Cô Ha's sister saw us from the village, thought something was wrong, and came out to help. She took my rifle in one hand and held me around the waist with the other. Clinging to the two of them, I limped into the compound.

Actually, Cô Ha and her sister half dragged me over to the

team house and deposited me on the steps. Cô Ha hung my
gear up while her sister started unlacing my boots. I was so
weak I just sat there slumped over, wondering what was going
to happen to me. When the boots came off, I felt a great sense
of relief. I had covered over thirty kilometers since leaving
the village that morning, most of it with my feet underwater.
They desperately needed a moment out in the air and sunshine. The skin tingled to the touch of the air. I managed the
energy to twitch my toes, just to check if there was any communication to the areas below my throbbing calves.

I thanked the girls for their help and crawled over to my
bunk. I don't recall seeing any of my teammates, but they
must have been around somewhere. I do recall that Cô Ha and
her sister helped me out of my wet jungle fatigues. With their
help, I went through the grisly ritual of removing the blood-
sucking leeches from my legs. Rather than pulling them off,
we always burned them off with the lit end of a cigarette or
sprayed them with insect repellent. The spray contained a sol-
vent that worked handily to dissolve the leeches' soft bodies.
Soon after a brief squirt of repellent, the creatures would fall
from their attachment. The spray reduced them to sticky blobs
of black, rubbery mucus. After I got all the slimy little para-
sites off me, I took a towel and dried my feet, legs, waist,
and back. I finally lay back in my bunk. I ached, I was nauseous, I was so weak I could hardly move. I wasn't sure I
could get up if I had to. I was embarrassed by my misery and
told the girls to go on back to the village.

I was drained both physically and emotionally. My guard
was down and I was overwhelmed by a wave of self-pity. I
lay there on the musty, mildew-ridden bunk, feeling totally
helpless and alone. I felt a deep sense of abandonment, a
lonely gloom which came from feeling that despite all my
effort and agony, no one really cared about me or gave a damn
about what I was doing. I was weak, sick, and in pain. I
couldn't even swat the flies crawling on my face and chest.

How could I expect help, I thought. I was thousands of
miles from my family, and they were the only ones who cared.
My goddamned country sure as hell didn't care! "No sir," I
thought. "Those smug bastards are the ones that dropped me
out here in this God-forsaken bog of filth and disease in the
first place. Where are they now when I need them?"

Most of them, I supposed, were in their comfortable living rooms watching their color televisions and eating their double portions of meat and potatoes. I figured they didn't give a damn about me because they didn't have the foggiest idea what was going on over here. Wracked with fever, I lay there in a grim depression, hating those of my fellow-citizens who were so bloody insane that they willfully encouraged the very enemy I had been sent to fight. My own countrymen! Only a cruel people, I thought, would send me out from home when I had done no one any harm, and then whip up the very dogs that were tearing at my heels. What was it, I asked myself, that made my countrymen believe that my life was so cheap or my sacrifice so frivolous that I should be abandoned in such a distant place?

I came out of my black depression long enough to realize I was about to throw up. I flopped over the edge of the bunk and crawled on my hands and knees to the door. I vomited all over the steps of the team house and kept on gagging until I was convulsed by the dry heaves. With quaking hands and arms I dragged myself back to my bunk. I could only wipe the vomit from my face. I didn't have any water to rinse out my mouth. I couldn't think where there was any. I rolled back over into my bunk and felt the damp, sticky mattress cling to my skin. I raised a trembling hand to wipe my eyes. Tears had begun to roll down my face. The emotional cycle had reached its nadir. Pain and exhaustion begat anger and frustration. Anger and frustration begat sorrow and regret. Sorrow and regret begat self-pity. Self-pity consumed me.

I cried like a baby. I know it sounds dramatic, but I called quietly for my mother as I lay shaking in my bunk. I wanted so much to be a child again, not a man beset by the dogs of war. I wanted to hear some comforting word from my mother's lips, to feel the reassurance of her arms. I wanted someone else to be the authority figure, someone else to be the healer, the doer-of-all-miracles, the vanguard of freedom. I was too sick and tired to care anymore. Somewhere along the way as I was listening to my own miseries, I slipped into unconsciousness.

It was the afternoon of the next day before I woke up. Sergeant Fitz said I had had a raging fever during the night and had slept fitfully. The fever had broken during the morning, though, so he had decided to wait before calling in a chopper to take me to the field hospital. I got up and drank some water to get the rancid taste out of my mouth and to cure the parched burning in my throat. Lieutenant Cantrell said that he and Sergeant Fitz had been in the team bunker working on a sump in the floor when I had come in with Cô Ha. Not seeing me and not realizing that anything was wrong, they had just kept at their task. It was only sometime later when Sergeants Abney and Robertson came back up from the village and almost walked up the vomit-covered steps that anyone realized something was wrong. Fitz apparently began cramming aspirins down me to try to break the fever. I guess his ministrations helped. I felt weak but otherwise all right. The only thing I still had to cure was a ravenous hunger. The world always appears to be a better place to a man with a full stomach.

Chapter 10

I was mad. I was mad at the stupefying heat and the constant buzzing of the flies and mosquitoes. I was mad at having to sit shirtless in that human oven called the Mekong Delta with the sweat from my arms smearing the print of the goddamned computer printout sheets I was working on. I was mad because the guys who would take that report and feed it back into a computer would have an air-conditioned office in Saigon. They would be doing the paper-pushing for some staff officer who would have his own air-conditioned office. That officer would file his report to the air-conditioned Pentagon. Reporters would hear condensations of staff reports in air-conditioned lounges, and the reporters would send their information straight to the American public who would be sitting in their air-conditioned living rooms. It was obvious to me that I was the only one in the entire chain without an air-conditioner, and I sat there thinking that I was also the only one who had even the vaguest idea of what the hell was going on! I was convinced that I was the one who deserved the damned air-conditioner, and all those other jackasses should be having to swelter and mold instead of me!

Well, there I was, sitting hunched over a stack of paperwork and cursing the job, the heat, and the insects. Sergeant Fitz and I had pulled the day's stay-behind duty and I was suffering the consequences. Lieutenant Cantrell and Sergeant Abney had gone out to one of the hamlets to work with a local PF platoon, and Sergeant Robertson had been sent to the province town to pick up some provisions. I was way behind on my paperwork as usual, and I was spending the morning filling out forms and required reports. *Bác-sĩ* Fitz called from outside the team house, "*Trung úy,* it looks like something's up out in the canal."

His comment broke my smoldering train of thought. I frowned at the interruption and snapped back, "Well, what is it? What do you mean, something's up?"

I heard Fitz's footfalls thumping up to the door of the house. He leaned in to look at me and said, "There are several big sampans coming down the canal, *Trung úy.* They look pretty full up with people, and they are all hollering at our guys on the wall. Seems like something must be wrong."

I was actually thankful for the excuse to get away from the stacks of computer paper, so I picked up my faded jungle fatigue shirt and went out to see what was the matter. The lead boats had already docked outside the walls and people were coming ashore. Adults and children were getting off the boats, but as they made their way to the gate and came into the compound, I noticed that most of the children were being helped or carried by the adults. There was a lot of yelling, crying, and just noise, mostly made by the adults. Fitz had been right; something was decidedly wrong. I rushed across the compound, wondering what in the hell was the matter, never even imagining the awful truth.

When I reached the first woman carrying a child, I stopped in my tracks. The child was covered with puncture wounds and deep lacerations. He was a pasty gray color and his breathing came in shallow gasps. The bleeding from the deep holes in his arms and legs had reduced to a slow leak, and he had apparently slipped into unconsciousness. I felt my jaw drop and my eyes widen. For a second or two my heart seemed to stop beating, and my brain refused to process what I was seeing. Behind the first came another with another wounded child, and behind her another. It slowly broke through to me that the boats were loaded with badly hurt children and that they had been brought in to my team for help.

The women were crying and babbling about their children as they pressed in around me. More and more people in blood-spattered garments were climbing off the boats; I couldn't tell how many were wounded and how many were just bloody from holding the injured kids. I pointed the women to the team house and yelled to Sergeant Fitz to break out his medic supplies. Then I ran into the house and began to push everything movable over to the walls. I had the adults lay their children down on the floor so we could get a look at each of them in some kind of organized manner. Mothers were pleading and crying; everyone wanted Fitz's and my attention. We put all the jabber out of our minds and started at one end of the room and quickly worked our way through the lineup of wounded children.

We went from child to child, trying to establish a treatment triage. In the background the comments of the mothers and fathers began to come together into an explanation for this mayhem. The Cong had booby-trapped the school in one of the neighboring villages. The survivors had been brought in to us in hopes of medicine, first aid, or even medevac choppers for the seriously wounded. There were several of the latter, already comatose and practically exsanguinated. I thought two were already dead. We put in a call for a helicopter, but we were told to wait for word on availability and priority. We went back to the kids.

It wasn't long before the floor, the bunks, and all the sitting space in the team house were filled with kids and parents. The floor was a carpet of children's bodies. Some were dead, some were dying, some were just mangled and hurting. Some of the conscious children were whimpering quietly, but most were stoically silent. The mothers and the few toddlers around were not quiet; their cries and wailings joined in a cacophony of anguished sound.

Blood was everywhere. With our limited medical supplies there was little we could do except to try to stanch the bleeding where we could. We had two bottles of IV infusion fluid, so we started a drip in two kids we had triaged as being severely-injured-but-might-make-its. The won't-make-its received only courtesy attention and the probably-will-make-its got first aid and bandaging after we had done what we could for the more seriously injured. I cannot possibly describe the sense of desperation and frustration as I went from child to child and from parent to parent and realized how much hope they placed in Fitz and me. The problem was that I knew there was no hope in me to hope for; I was no healer, no miracle man, no savior of their children. Yet the stoic kids looked up at me with agony in their eyes and expected me to ease their pain. I knew I couldn't do it. I was up to my knees in dying children and I felt so hopelessly impotent.

The feeling of frustration was gradually transformed to one of anger. I felt it crawling up my throat, tightening my chest, clenching my jaws, and narrowing my eyes. I stewed in my hatred for the Cong for this stupid butchery. I was angry at the medevac choppers for not getting to us more quickly, and I was mad at God for letting this whole thing happen in the first place. I was mad at myself for not being what the people hoped I would be.

Fitz and I worked our way through the triage and were down to those we really didn't think would make it no matter what we did. The young boy I was working on had two holes in his head, each about the size of a penny, maybe even a nickel. His breathing had almost stopped; I couldn't feel a pulse. With blood-stained hands, I tried to stuff a swatch of cotton into the largest hole in the side of his head. His brains were protruding and I didn't want them to mix with the pools of blood on the floor. My hands were shaking, my breath came in deep gasps as the humiliation and anger overcame me. Hot tears began to trickle down my face. I stopped trying to plug the hole in the boy's head because I couldn't see what I was doing. I just knelt there on the floor, hands braced on my knees, and tried to squeeze back the tears. God, I felt so helpless!

I eventually got over to Sergeant Fitz and the walking wounded. We probed surface lacerations and shallow puncture wounds for shrapnel, dusted the wounds with antibacterial powder, and sewed them up. Some of the kids who had been out of the way of the blast had a lot of these small cuts and shallow gouges. It took us quite a while to clean them all up so we could inspect each wound and probe where necessary for possible shrapnel. We were still digging and patching when the medevac choppers finally arrived. By that time two of the most seriously wounded kids had died. The boy and girl getting the IV drip were still alive and were taken aboard one of the choppers. Four other seriously wounded children and all their mothers were put aboard the other. The helicopters took off and Fitz and I went back to the wounded we still had left. When we finished cleaning them all up the best we could and patching up what we could find that needed mending, we told the parents that it was important to keep the wounds clean and not to allow the kids in the canals for several days. I felt bad that we didn't even have aspirin to give them to help ease the pain. We tried to explain to the mothers that they should resist the temptation to go to the local Chinese medicine man and buy some sticky, smelly ointment to put on the wounds. I told them to keep the wounds clean and dry and hope for the best.

The whole episode was over within a couple of hours. It didn't take long for Fitz and me to wash up the bloody floor and the spatters of blood on the bunks. In a few minutes the whole place was back to normal. I cleaned the blood from beneath my fingernails and threw my blood-soaked shirt and pants in the pile to be washed by Cô Ha. When the other team members came back in, they didn't even know anything had happened until we told them. I wish there was some way to clean my mind of the incident as well as we cleaned the team house.

On two later occasions the local Cong unit booby-trapped schools in my district. There was no question but that it was done intentionally. The Cong had purposely elected to attack and kill children. On each occasion, the suffering of the children, the depravity of the Viet Cong, and my apparent inability to stop the murderous bastards filled me with resentment, dejection, and frustration.

It was a hard thing to deal with. I was psychologically prepared for war as a demonstration of man's inhumanity to man, but I was not prepared for the shock of war as an example of man's inhumanity to children. I felt a deep sense of cultural outrage when I saw for myself that our enemy had absolutely no qualms about victimizing innocent children in their campaigns of terror. Oh, I had read about the strategies of terrorism, and I knew how it had been used by the Viet Cong and by other groups before them, but I never really appreciated the shallowness, the meanness, the incredible inhumanity of intentionally slaughtering children until I had to deal with it firsthand. More than in the exchange of shot and shell, more than in the paroxysms of close combat, more than in any battle line, it was in watching over the agonized death of mutilated children that I met war in all its vile and vulgar glory, and it was there I grew to truly know my enemy.

Chapter 11

Sergeant Abney and I were in the team house one morning, trying to get our kerosene-burning camp oven to work. Suddenly I heard the rushing whine of low-flying jets. They sounded like big ones, too. I cocked my ear because it was unusual to hear jets flying by so close, especially when I knew there were no clearances for local air strikes. I wondered what the jets were up to, so I left Abney with the stove for a moment and went to the doorway of the team house. I looked toward the sound of the passing planes, and not far off to the west I could see two low-flying aircraft. They were headed toward the border regions north of us. Both planes were quite large and appeared to be painted black. I could not see any numbers or national markings on either their fuselages or their wings.

That struck me as odd, but even more odd was the realization that I could not recognize the aircraft as any of those being used by the American services. I didn't think of myself as an expert on aircraft identification, but I did think I was familiar with most current types of American combat aircraft. After a few seconds of flipping through my mental card file on jet aircraft, I became convinced the two planes were British-made Canberra bombers.

That didn't make sense, though. The British weren't helping us in Vietnam. The Australians were involved and their air force probably did have Canberra bombers, but I didn't think the Australian Air Force was involved in the border bombings. I never could figure out why those big jets were flying so low, why they were unmarked, why they were painted black, and why they didn't appear to be in the American inventory. I've always wondered if the Australians were involved in the border air war but just not telling anybody.

It could be I was just wrong about the identification of those aircraft. I certainly was not under the impression that the U.S. Air Force needed any help with their bombing! They used to drop a lot of powder along our border with Cambodia and they sure tore up a lot of real estate. Just hearing a B-52 bombing run is an awesome experience, let alone ever seeing one.

We were only a few kilometers from the Cambodian border and the bomb runs set for the NVA sanctuary areas just on the other side of the border would sometimes really rattle our can. We never saw or even heard the planes themselves. The B-52 raids, called "Arc-Lite's," usually came at night. Without any warning the ground would begin to vibrate. It was similar to an earthquake of the variety that shakes plates from the shelves and pictures off the wall. You could hear the dull mutter of the distant explosions. The sound of an Arc-Lite going in was like the continuous percussion of a large but distant summer thunderstorm. The shaking and the muted groaning of the earth would go on for several minutes. The air would be thick with a heavy, ominous sense of an incredible violation of nature. My teammates and I would just look at one another without speaking, staring out across the yellow glow of our kerosene lamp. Words seemed trivial and inappropriate in the presence of such destructive power.

After an Arc-Lite mission, the gouged and wounded earth released its grip on shattered trees and other pulverized vegetation. It was difficult to find any evidence of the enemy units that had been caught in such barrages. Victims were sometimes practically atomized by the constant cover of explosives.

I remember once standing on the rim of a huge bomb crater among a vast expanse of other craters. I was looking out across what could pass for a moonscape spattered with partially digested tossed salad. As I looked in wonder at the completeness of the destruction, I said a silent prayer of thanks that our own air superiority was unchallenged. No matter what else hap-

pened, I wasn't going to have to try to live through this kind
of hell.

It was common knowledge in Kien Phong province that
two NVA regiments were perched just across the border in
Cambodia. The two units had been in place for several months,
but they had mostly limited their activity to bullying the Cambodians, rocketing the Special Forces outpost at Cai-Cai, and
supplying and encouraging the Viet Cong units in our area.
Our province's Main Force Viet Cong battalion was constantly using the NVA-dominated area across in Cambodia as
a rest and resupply area. The NVA in Cambodia were supplying the Cong with money, medicine, ammunition, and other
necessities of war. The Cong supply units had special routes
and checkpoints set up so they could travel unmolested from
the NVA areas inside Cambodia to the VC sanctuary areas
inside our province. The resupply convoys, usually boats,
could be well into my district and on into the VC sanctuaries
after only one night's travel. We made a concerted effort to
break up these supply routes, and we became pretty proficient
at it—a fact that pleased neither the Cong nor the NVA.

We had been hearing for some weeks that the NVA were
getting ready to make a move into Vietnam. For a long time,
nobody had known whether the communist units would come
into the country on our side of the Mekong and try to attack
Cao Lanh or Vinh Long or whether they would cross to the
southern bank of the Mekong and come up to attack Long
Xuyen. The last intelligence estimate we had heard was that
the NVA were going to come in north of the river and move
against Cao Lanh. That meant they were going to have to
come through my district. Specifically, it meant they were
going to roll right over my little mud fort. Believe me, I did
not want to have to face two regiments of NVA with four
other Americans and a platoon of local militia. We could never
hope to stop them with a band of villagers. I figured if the
two regiments did start to move on our side of the river, it
was going to be time to order the roses. We couldn't stop 'em
and we couldn't just waltz out of the way. We would have to
stand and fight, slow them down as much as we could, and
hope for the best.

Late one night, Sergeant Robertson woke me during his

radio watch and whispered urgently that I should get to the commo bunker right away. I stumbled over to the bunker, struggling all the way to get into my shirt and to slide my feet into a pair of rubber sandals. Robertson was already hunched over the PRC-25. The yellow flicker from the single kerosene lamp cast dark shadows on his worried face. I listened as I entered the bunker. Dark Delta, a code name for what was apparently a border reconnaisance plane, was talking to Green Flagon, the current code name for our province team back in Cao Lanh. The tone sounded urgent. Robertson quickly explained: "Air recon sees a lot of lights moving around on the ground just upstream from Hong Ngu, but on the Camboat side of the border. They seem to be coming out of that NVA area up there. I'll bet those damned regiments have decided it's time to come over here and kick some ass."

A voice squawked on the radio. "Dark Delta, this is Green Flagon. Can you give us coordinates for those lights and give us a general direction of movement, over?"

"This is Dark Delta. Roger, Green Flagon. Coordinates whiskey sierra six-two-four-niner-three-three. General direction of movement appears to be southeast, over."

Neither Robertson nor I had to look at the map over our radio to know that the coordinates put the location of the lights on the border just above us. Their direction of movement was toward Cao Lanh, with us directly in the way. I grabbed our hand mike and broke in. "Dark Delta, this is Green Flagon Foxtrot [my team was the F station on the Green Flagon net]. Can you estimate the number of lights, over?"

"Foxtrot, this is Dark Delta," the radio sputtered. "There must be a thousand of them. I've never seen anything like it, over."

A thousand! My knees turned weak. Sergeant Robertson put his head in his hands and closed his eyes. I hoped he was praying.

"Delta, Foxtrot," I quickly returned, "how are the lights moving? Do they appear to be on vehicles, over?"

"Foxtrot, this is Delta. Negative, they look pretty dim to me and each one looks like just a single light. They are moving along sort of in a row. . . . Over."

It was common for sampans to travel at night with a single little lamp lit in the bow of the boat. From the air a convoy of them looked like a string of ornamental electric lights. I guessed that the NVA had decided to make their move by sampan. I couldn't figure why the boats would have their lamps lit, though. It was a dead giveaway.

It was pitch black night out and the NVA commanders knew they had to move rapidly over what would be an unfamiliar canal system to most of their men. They might have thought lights were necessary to avoid losing time and people in the labyrinthine canal network. Without some sort of beacon to follow, the people would never have been able to end up in the right place at the right time. For whatever reason, there they were, strung out for all to see, and sure enough, they appeared to be coming my way. I wanted some help! When I called the province team, I tried to keep the desperation out of my voice.

"Green Flagon, this is Green Flagon Foxtrot, over."

"Foxtrot, this is Green Flagon, go."

"This is Foxtrot. Those lights must be from small sampans. They seem to be coming my way. They can be at my location well before dawn. I could be in real trouble. Can you get me a Blackhawk, over?" Blackhawk was the code term for a nighttime air strike by air force fighter-bombers. A good strike by a flight of F-4's would turn that boatyard to sawdust.

"Foxtrot, Green Flagon. Negative on the Blackhawk. We have already inquired. All available Blackhawks have been committed by IV Corps. Something might come available later, but we can't tell, over."

"This is Foxtrot, Green Flagon. Roger the negative Blackhawk. Can we get a Raven, over?" A Raven was a group of army helicopter gunships. I figured they could do almost as much damage as the F-4's if they caught the boat convoy out in the clear. They would be army guys, too, not air force. Maybe they would be a little more responsive to our request.

"Foxtrot, this is Flagon. Negative Raven, over."

"Now what," I thought. No air support, no artillery, and no reserves. How were we to stand off two regiments of NVA with just a motley band of native militia and a mortar tube from World War II? A voice came back over the radio.

"Green Flagon Foxtrot, Dark Delta, over."

I picked up my handset and spoke into it. "Dark Delta, Foxtrot, over."

"This is Dark Delta. I can probably get an Arc-Lite diverted for these people, over."

I could hardly believe my ears. An Arc-Lite! A B-52 raid on a sampan convoy! Would that ever upset the NVA's day! I was desperate; it sounded like a great idea to me.

"Dark Delta, this is Foxtrot. Request the Arc-Lite. Will they be able to get here soon, over?"

"This is Dark Delta. Wait, out."

A few minutes went by before a call came back. "Green Flagon Foxtrot, Dark Delta, over."

"This is Foxtrot, over."

"Foxtrot, Dark Delta, I've just received confirmation on that Arc-Lite. There is a mission inbound about thirty minutes out. They are being diverted to me. I'll be leaving the net to talk to them on another freq. I'll give them the information they need to put the strike on target. Anything else, over?"

"This is Foxtrot, roger your last. Thanks much. Warn the big birds about our western hamlets. Be sure to keep those people out of your strike pattern, over." Before Dark Delta could sign off, province headquarters broke in.

"Dark Delta, this is Green Flagon, over."

"Green Flagon, Dark Delta, go."

"This is Flagon. Be reminded that bombing within one mile of the international border without a statement of emergency from the ground is a violation of international agreements. You will need to get the name of any person making such a statement and requesting a border bombing, over."

Sergeant Robertson stared at me in disbelief at what he had heard. I just gaped back at him with my mouth open. I raised my hands and shouted, "What!? What the hell do those bastards think they are doing? Here we are about to be eaten alive by the NVA and those assholes are talking politics!" I felt like calling Green Flagon and saying, "O.k., guys, a joke is a joke, but gimme a break, will ya? I mean, you people are supposed to be on my side!"

Apparently the message from Green Flagon had caused some concern to Dark Delta, too. There was a long pause before he came back on the net.

"Green Flagon Foxtrot, Dark Delta, over."

"Dark Delta, this is Foxtrot, over."

"This is Dark Delta. You heard the man. I need the full

code name for the person making the request for the Arc-Lite. I want his initials, too. Over.''

I looked at Robertson and shook my head in disgust. We didn't send stuff like names, initials, and all that in the clear. I was going to do it now, though. I didn't feel I had any room for argument. ''Dark Delta, this is Green Flagon Foxtrot six-niner. I say again, Green Flagon Foxtrot six-niner. Initials are Delta, November, Delta. I request a limited strike on the target you have identified. I don't want my entire western border bombed to oblivion.''

''Foxtrot six-niner, this is Dark Delta. Roger, you got it. Dark Delta, out.''

Robertson went to awaken Lieutenant Cantrell and the rest of the team. I notified the Vietnamese district chief that I had approved the bomb run without asking him first. He mumbled his approval and went on back to his hooch to sleep. I had one of the chief's lieutenants call the western hamlets on the Vietnamese radio frequency and notify them of the coming raid. After the administrative garbage was taken care of, we all went to the wall of the fort and looked out toward the western sky. The gentle breeze blowing across the Delta was pleasant—the cool, quiet darkness was such a change from the muggy heat of the day. I lit a cigarette despite all the rules against it and leaned against the mud wall. Everything seemed to be unusually still, as if even the mosquitoes and crickets knew something was about to break loose. Minutes ticked by slowly. I felt like going back to the bunker and trying to contact Dark Delta. Was the strike coming in or not?

We never heard a thing, no roar of engines, no jet whine, nothing, until the light show began on the horizon. The sky was suddenly lit by the bluish-yellow flicker of exploding sticks of bombs. The noise was louder than from the Arc-Lites we were used to. This had more of the punch and slap of real explosions than the distant rumblings we had experienced before. Suddenly, in less than thirty seconds, it was over. No sound of jets, no nothing—just the pensive quiet as if nature was waiting for some responsive scream.

The strike had certainly been limited. I wondered if they had only used one or two of the planes in a normal Arc-Lite mission. If they had, it was fine with me; I wanted the extent of the strike limited anyway. I just hoped they had put in enough bombs to do the job.

As we walked back to the team house, Cantrell and I discussed our next move. He and Abney were sent to check our barbed wire perimeter and to check the Claymores and "fu gas" canisters scattered in our wire barriers. I went to the bunker again to try to contact Dark Delta. I had no sooner dropped the blackout curtain on the bunker door than the radio sputtered out a transmission. "Green Flagon Foxtrot, Dark Delta, over." The voice was flat, professional, even bored sounding.

"Dark Delta, this is Green Flagon Foxtrot," I said into my hand mike. "Was the strike on target, over?"

"Roger, Foxtrot, we nailed 'em." Now I could hear the satisfaction in his voice. "As per your request, we used a limited strike and we put it right down their backs. I can't tell from here the actual extent of the damage, but under a flare it looks to be a real mess, over."

"Delta, this is Foxtrot. Roger. We'll send out a patrol to check things out. Thanks for your help and pass that on to your friends in the big birds, over."

"This is Dark Delta. Roger, Foxtrot. Glad to be of help. I'll be leaving now; I've got to check some things out farther up the country. Dark Delta, out."

I looked at my watch. The whole episode had taken only forty-five to fifty minutes, but it seemed as if I had been working on the problem all night. We sent out an alert warning to all our outposts in case the strike hadn't worked all that well and the NVA decided to come on down. Next we began our preparations for the patrol to check out the damage.

Sergeant Robertson and I were going to take two squads of our militia in the small motorized *ghes* and go up to the strike zone. We wanted to be there at first light, so we had to leave the fort without much delay. I caught a quick catnap while we waited for the Vietnamese platoon leader to get his men and boats together. It wasn't long before everything was ready and Sergeant Abney was shaking me out of my sleep. We struck out through the night, en route to what we hoped was a shattered enemy convoy.

It was before sunrise but well after first light when we approached the impact zone. We had been very cautious in our movements since we never knew what the next bend in the canal would bring. On several occasions we had put men ashore to go ahead and act as our flank security. We didn't want to go putt-putting right into the middle of a regiment of live NVA. When we got to the impact area, we knew it. The results of the strike were evident; it had hit home.

The whole area looked like an ant's view of chopped steak. Nothing was really recognizable—a piece of this and that, but nothing of consequence. The most tell-tale sign of success was the abundance of splintered boat planking. The place looked like the remains of a lumberyard. I figured the troops not caught in the bomb run had probably collected the dead and all the salvageable equipment they could find before making tracks back toward the border. That entirely imaginary line was about three kilometers, or "klicks," away.

We found only two intact bodies, four AK-47's, and a couple of mangled and sodden packets of papers. Nothing else was worth holding on to. We got back in our boats with the AK's and the papers, but we left the bodies where they were. The party was over; I just wanted to get back to the team house and get some sleep.

By the time we made our way back to the fort it was almost noon. After squatting in one of those little boats all morning, my joints complained violently at being straightened again. I dragged myself into the compound and told Lieutenant Cantrell to process the captured equipment and documents and prepare the after-action report—I was going to bed. I went to my bunk and peeled off my muddy boots and soggy fatigues. My aching frame stretched out on the bunk and immediately began sliding into sleep. On the way down I said a brief prayer of thanks for the bomber command, United States Air Force.

Chapter 12

I HEARD through the grapevine one day that Benjamin Howard had been killed. He had been a classmate at the Special Warfare School and had been assigned to a MAT team up in the central highlands of II Corps. Ben got killed by being stupid. Ben wasn't a stupid person, mind you, but he made one stupid move, and he got killed for it. Word was that he took a patrol out one afternoon and made the mistake of going on the operation dressed up just like most of his troops, in black pajamas, a colored scarf, and a green bush hat. His unit got into a heavy contact and he called in air support. The communists were apparently at the point of crawling all over them, so Ben called the helicopter gunships in really tight for pinpoint support. To the pilots the battle on the ground looked like a melee, and they couldn't tell the good guys from the bad guys. Ben and a few of his men were trying to make a run for the cover of a tree line when a chopper pilot saw them making their move. He thought the blackclad men were Cong, so he poured everything he had into them. He must have been a good shot because they say he got 'em all.

Ben was killed by Americans because he made the stupid decision to go out on a combat operation dressed like a common Viet Cong. I heard the news with a combination of anger and sorrow. "Dammit, Ben," I thought in frustration, "how dumb can you get? We were warned a hundred times about pulling stunts like that." The more I thought about it, though, the more I realized we all pulled stunts like that at one time or another. Some of us were just luckier than others and managed to live in spite of ourselves.

Most people do not start out as heedless adventurers hell-bent on the road to destruction. It's just that danger is like most things in life: you can get used to it. After a while you stop paying quite so much attention to it, then you ignore it, and finally you are contemptuous of it. You might even be so audacious as to taunt it on occasion, just to see if it can be pricked to a response. But the worst thing of all is to think that it is no longer worthy of your attention. That's when you start doing stupid things and making stupid decisions. I am as guilty as anyone on all counts.

Like most everyone else entering a combat zone, I spent my first weeks nervous and scared. I swore to myself that I would obey all the rules, that I was never going to be caught without my helmet and flack vest, and that I would never, absolutely never, take an unnecessary risk. Well, it is hard to be always disciplined and constantly on the alert when danger surrounds you twenty-four hours a day. It grinds at you and wears you down, and you start to lose that edge—units are allowed to move without flank security, night positions are taken without going to the trouble of digging in, commanders ignore commonsense precautions, and the troops are allowed to be inattentive to common dangers. God knows how many men were killed in Vietnam not by some inevitable act of war, but by some act of carelessness by men practically inviting death.

I've done some pretty dumb things on military operations myself, things that would make the referees at the Infantry School choke—and I wouldn't blame them—but I was always lucky, and I managed to get out of rough spots one way or another. I was lucky in combat and I was lucky in other places, too. I know, because for solid gold, diamond inlaid, real McCoy stupidity, nothing beats my voluntary mission of mercy to help a friend out on a visit to a whorehouse.

This particular whorehouse was nothing but a grass and bamboo hooch with a row of thatch partitions separating the cots. It was in a part of Cao Lanh that was not patrolled by government troops after dark, so it was a dangerous place to be after sundown, especially if the Viet Cong bandit gangs were out "tax collecting." One might ask why a portion of town was unprotected from the Viet Cong. A good question.

In the border areas of any of the Indo-Chinese countries, there are always minority groups made up of the people whose native country is on the *other* side of the border. In our case, the Cambodians were the unfortunate minority. Over in Cambodia the Vietnamese were the minority. In both cases, the minority were second-class citizens and were treated as such by the local majority. In Cao Lanh, the Cambodian section of town was not given the benefit of government protection after dark. The Vietnamese, frankly, didn't give a damn about the Cambodians and didn't care if the Cong went in there and killed a few people or looted some of the businesses. I also suspect that the Vietnamese authorities figured that such a tempting and open target on the outskirts might keep the Cong from bothering the more "uptown"—Vietnamese—parts of the city. Any reasonable person can see the shortsightedness of such neglect, but the Vietnamese government never was guilty of looking ahead.

Well, the whorehouse was down in the Cambodian section, and Clinton Crews, a friend of mine, wanted to go there. Clinton was the team leader of another MAT team and we had both been called back to the province town for a conference with the PSA. We were to spend the night in the province team compound before returning to our teams the next day. The promise of a good night's sleep was too much for Clinton. His first reaction to a night without stress or a radio watch to pull was to be horny. He was determined to vent his pent-up passions on one of the young ladies in the aforementioned establishment, and he wanted me to go with him, if not as a participant, then as a bodyguard.

Well, hell, I had absolutely no interest in going to a fleabag whorehouse on some canal bank, especially one that was liable to be overrun by a Viet Cong bandit squad at any minute. Besides, it was contrary to standing orders to leave the compound after dark unless on official business. Clinton insisted; he said he was going with me or without me, but he could sure use a bodyguard. After making several attempts to dissuade him, I saw it was hopeless. I agreed to go as his cover, to protect his young ass while he drilled away at the local oil wells. Clinton told me he had already paid the Vietnamese gate guards, and they would let us out of the province compound without noting the fact in their log. One of the NCO's on Clinton's team was back in the province town with him, and he had talked the sergeant into driving us out in a jeep that Clinton had also managed to procure from somewhere. A real wheeler-dealer, that Clinton.

As we walked out to the jeep, I strapped on my .45 service automatic and Clinton buckled his on. I was too dumb to grab my M-I6. I had lulled myself into a sort of spectator's attitude and viewed the whole thing with a sense of bemused derring-do. After all, what is a friend for if not to act as your body-guard while you screw the eyeballs out of a young beauty in a bamboo shack on the banks of the Mekong River? As we climbed into the back of the jeep, Clinton was telling me not to worry, he had A-class information that the Cong "tax collectors" would not be out tonight. It was going to be perfectly safe; he just wanted me to watch his wallet. Right.

Clinton told his sergeant to drop us off in the Cambodian section of town and to pick us up in the same spot forty-five minutes later. The driver had a big smile plastered across his face as he nodded, dropped the jeep into gear, and drove us out the compound gate. It was already past sundown and the tropical night was fast approaching. We went careering down the dirt avenue, swerving past the pigs and chickens and billowing dust and exhaust behind us. At the appointed place the jeep screeched to an abrupt halt, and we leaped out and squatted in the ditch. Clinton's sergeant reapplied the gas and roared away into the darkness. After everything had quieted down and no one had shot at us, we got up into a crouch and ran over to a dark alley that ran between the tin and bamboo thatch hooches.

I figured Clinton knew his way since he moved quickly through the alley and made all the turns without hesitation. Men and women moved quietly along the dark passageway. They looked up with surprise at seeing two Americans walking about practically unarmed at that time of night and in their part of town. Groups of men were squatting by the doorways of many of the hooches, chatting quietly and smoking their pungent cigarettes. Other people were gathered on the pallets inside the houses, eating their evening meal under the dim glow of a kerosene lantern. The smells of cooking fires, dried fish, and other Oriental aromas were thick in the air. Having developed quite a liking for village life and cooking, I was getting hungry. My mind was drifting off to the various foods I could identify when Clinton disappeared through the doorway of one of the small thatch hooches. I followed him in.

When I stepped inside, Clinton was already discussing terms with the old peasant woman who kept the place. The woman sat behind a table just inside the door and calmly chewed on her betel nut leaves. She was alert, though. She kept her eyes on the room in front of her and her hands on the cash box. She was all business. It was evident that the old woman sold dope as well as sex. A group of Cambodian and Vietnamese men were sitting on a platform in the main room, chatting and smoking bulky marijuana cigarettes or pipes of opium. They were clearly not interested in the girls.

There must have been four or five girls in the place and with no other customers in sight, they were crawling all over Clinton and me before we could take a breath. Smiling, calling for our attention, rubbing up against us like pet kittens, stuffing their hands down our pants or our hands down their blouses, they wanted our business. Clinton negotiated quickly for his choice, an unusually tall Vietnamese girl without much else to recommend her. I figured that Clinton, who was pretty short, must have gotten a kick out of screwing tall girls, or else he knew something about her talents that were not evident at first glance. The other girls began to concentrate on selling their wares to me. I told them several times that I wasn't interested, that I was just there to protect the other *shĭ quan Mỹ*. The more times I told them, the less I meant it.

One of the girls came over to the chair I had taken by the door and saucily took a seat in my lap. She ground her fanny around, and with a wicked grin on her lips she reached across and took my hand, placed it on her breast, and rolled it around and around. Her sales technique was very persuasive. My no's were not very enthusiastic and I liked the sales pitch, so it took a while to convince her that I really wasn't buying. Finally the girls wandered off and left me to sit by the old woman and keep watch out the doorway.

Clinton took his girl to one of the stalls in the rear of the hut. The partitions between the little booths were nothing but thatch and army ponchos hung up on bamboo poles, and the beds were just the conventional wooden platforms with a bamboo mat rolled out as a cover over the planks. Once the couple were engaged in their contractual obligations, the ponchos began to flap about and the planks began to creak. The girls out front gestured toward the enclosure and made lewd remarks and called jokes back and forth to each other. The men smoking on the platform joined in the banter and laughter, and even the girl humping away with Crews would occasionally throw out a one-liner that left everyone in stitches.

Clinton's stall was beginning to creak and sway like a Conestoga wagon when a shot went off down the alley. A green tracer zinged by in the night. Green tracers meant communist bullets. The alley erupted in a sudden flurry of people running by, scooping up children, darting into houses, putting out lamps, and shutting doors. I called to Clinton, but having heard the shot he needed no urging. I could tell from the bumping and thumping and cussing that he was already struggling into his pants and boots.

A young man came into the hooch and in a panting whisper told the old woman that a Viet Cong tax collection team was coming up the alley. They were stopping at each house and, with their usual collection methods, just taking whatever they wanted. The old woman curled her lips around her betel-blackened teeth. She slammed the cash box shut and in a shrill voice demanded that everyone leave instantly. She got instant obedience. Men, women, and cash box disappeared into thin air. When I looked around, the whorehouse was empty except for me standing there with a .45 in my hand. I turned and called again for Clinton just as he came stumbling out into the dim light, cursing as he tried to stuff one foot into a boot, put his shirt on with a sleeve wrong side out, button up his pants, and buckle on his pistol belt all at the same time. I was viewing this whole scene with total disbelief.

While I was telling Clinton to hurry up, I was cursing my own stupidity. "Of all the dumb-assed things to pull," I thought, "to come out here alone in the dead of night and run a chance of getting shot just so Clinton can get a piece of ass!" I could already imagine the obituary in my hometown newspaper: "Lieutenant Donovan killed in a whorehouse while standing guard for a friend." Sure, everybody was going to believe that!

By the time Clinton was ready to run, the alley was completely deserted. We could hear the Cong moving up the path, arguing with the residents over their cash and valuables and threatening them loudly. We could occasionally hear the thud and grunt of a well-delivered blow. That usually terminated any discussion until the guerrillas got to the next house, where the protests would start over again.

Clinton and I went to the rear of the hooch and tore a hole in the thatch wall. We crawled through and crouched in the darkness at the rear of the building. Furtive figures slinked by in the night, all trying to avoid the Cong goon squad. We moved away from the house and crept from the rear of one hooch to the rear of the next. We were moving away from the trouble spot, but we never knew if the people we bumped into were friend or foe. I figured that sooner or later the Cong would get the word that two Americans were in the area, and then they would be after us.

We were hoping to find our way back to our pick-up point. We figured the jeep should be coming back pretty soon now, so we wanted to be in place. We moved on through the dark, trying to avoid the occasional dog or person we saw coming. Suddenly a shout went up behind us, and a spray of green tracers made a fan across the night sky. Other shouts followed. Somehow Clinton and I both knew the Cong had found our trail. I guess the fox must know as well as the houndsman the sound of the pack on a scent. It was clear to us that the hounds were coming. We didn't know if they had our direction or if they only knew we were in the area. My heart was in my throat; I could feel my pulse pounding behind my eyeballs. I was one scared son of a bitch.

As we moved quietly behind one of the hooches, the back door cracked open and a spear of light slashed across the dark shadows. An old man hung back inside the doorway and waved us in with his arm. Inside the lantern-lit room, he told us that his son had seen us coming up behind the line of houses. He said the Cong unit was making its way in our direction, but he would hide us if we wanted. We thanked him but said no; we were trying to make a rendezvous with our pick-up. We asked him if we were going in the right direction to get back to the main road. He confirmed the direction and said we were almost there, so we thanked him for his help and crept out the rear of the house. Sure enough, after going about another fifty yards and sneaking past several more houses, we came to the roadway. The place where we had been dropped out was only another fifty or so yards up the street.

As we looked up and down the deserted dirt road, we could hear the occasional calls and shouts of the Cong as they closed in behind us. We crouched down and ran across to the ditch on the other side. We instinctively moved a few meters apart, and lay in the ditch to await the arrival of the jeep or the Viet Cong, whichever came first.

I had never before considered the more intimate aspects of life in the ditches of a primitive village. The ooze and stench were incredible. The combination of heat, humidity, garbage, urine, feces, and other residue of village life made an elixir that would gag a maggot. The pigs loved it, though; big old sows kept trying to root Clinton and me out of our places. Wandering ducks and chickens were also plundering the muck for an occasional delight. It wasn't long before I was hoping that even the Viet Cong would hurry up and get there.

Clinton crawled over and tapped my foot with a stick to get my attention. I looked at him, and he cupped his hand to his ear. I listened and heard the faint sound of an approaching vehicle. I strained to look down the street without elevating my head too much, but I could see nothing. Soon I could hear clearly the whine and grind of a jeep coming on hard. The Viet Cong must have heard it too. A burst of tracers came out at us from somewhere back in the housing area. The shots were high but were certainly in our direction.

The sound of the jeep was very loud now. Suddenly I saw two specks of light bouncing in the dark. The lights and the noise announced the arrival of our jeep, running with its blackout lights on. We leaped up from the ditch and frantically waved it down. More shots, and this time the tracers were lower and closer; we heard shouts that sounded as if they were coming from just behind an adjacent house. Clinton's sergeant slowed the jeep but never stopped it, and as we ran, it went right on past us. I almost croaked right there. We both cussed like sailors and turned to run after the sergeant while he tried to slow down and let us catch up without stopping the jeep entirely. We ran up like dogs after bacon, Clinton on one side and I on the other, and both made diving leaps into the back of the moving vehicle, landing in a heap behind the driver's seat. I pounded on the sergeant's back, yelling, "Go, go, go!" At the same time, I was trying to get untangled from Clinton and get my .45 out of my holster.

The driver put the accelerator to the floor and the jeep lurched off, the wheels digging into the already rutted street. Clinton and I bounced around on top of each other in the rear. We finally pulled our heads over the rim of the back seat and looked back. A group of men ran out into the road and mingled there in a confused group. For a second, they just stood there yelling and pointing. Then one of the more thoughtful ones put up his rifle and began to let the lead fly. An AK-47 let out a stream of tracers that raced out and over us into the night. The Cong on the trigger held it down until his magazine was empty. First he shot way high, then he overadjusted and put all his shots into the road behind us. The tracers were going over us, then under us, and the ricochets flying all around us, but so far as I know, the man never landed a shot anywhere on the jeep. Clinton and I both had gotten our service automatics out, and we began to shoot back, barely sticking our heads over the back end of the jeep. The .45's were absolutely useless at that range, but the more we shot the better I felt. The flashes from my pistol muzzle blinded me, so I couldn't tell if our firing was causing the Cong to go to cover or not. I did know that the shots coming our way quickly died off to a sporadic round or two. I was feeling better and better as we left the Cong behind us in the dark and dust. By the time we turned the corner and pulled away to safety, I was positively elated.

Courage is a fickle friend. One minute Clinton and I were scared shitless—we couldn't find enough courage to take a deep breath. The next minute we were positively cocky, waving our pistols in the air and shouting jocular derision at the Cong we had left in our dust. Firing off a final round or two into the night air, we collapsed into the back of the jeep and whooped with laughter. I remember even saying to myself that this really wasn't all that funny, but I couldn't stop laughing. Clinton and I were still chuckling and trading licks on the shoulder as we pulled into the compound. We boasted to the sergeant about his part in the "great escape" and promised him free beers from here to eternity. His grinning was more introspective, and he just shook his head and muttered some comment about how army lieutenants were always a threat to public safety.

Clinton and I went back to our billet for the night, cleaned up, and climbed into the rack. I lay on the top bunk and stared at the ceiling. In the darkness I could barely make out the slowly rotating blade of the ceiling fan as it tried to cut the warm, humid air. From out in the compound, I heard the faint strains of "Good Night, Irene," the traditional closing anthem for the men at the province team club. I ran the whole night's episode through my mind again and realized that I really had just about managed to get myself killed, and to make matters worse, it was all on the account of pure stupidity. There wasn't a thing we did that didn't violate law, orders, or common sense. My stomach turned queasy with the knowledge of just how lucky we both were to be alive. I tell you what: that episode plain turned me against whorehouses.

OUT ON THE DISTRICT TEAMS AND MAT TEAMS, IT WAS IM-possible to relieve the psychological pressures that build up in men under constant stress and danger. There were no whore-houses to visit in madcap dashes of bravado, no bars to raise hell in, no movies, no PX's, no Bob Hope shows, no nothing. Every day it was ambush, patrol, administrate, train, teach, eat, and sleep if you could. On top of all that, it was frustrat-ing to live with the feeling that we had been left out there all alone to do our job. We felt that no one really gave a damn about us or what we were doing.

On occasion, the pressures of living that kind of life would get to even the best of men. My team medic, Sergeant Fitz, was a master sergeant with fourteen years of service. He was a good man, a good medic, and a hard worker. Fitz's problem was that he had difficulty getting along with the Vietnamese. Down deep inside he felt superior to them, didn't trust them, and resented having to bust his ass for them. One day the accumulated irritations of our way of life finally chipped through his armor and snapped the discipline of years of train-ing.

On that day, Sergeant Fitz and I were the only Americans keeping the fort. Lieutenant Cantrell and Sergeants Abney and Robertson were out on a combat operation. Sergeant Fitz and

I were staying back because we had been out on an ambush patrol the previous night. I had used the morning to catch a little shut-eye and was doing some paperwork in the early afternoon. Sergeant Fitz decided to go out in the compound and work on an old gasoline-powered electricity generator we had had for several months, but which had never run well enough to provide us with any current.

As Fitz struggled with the cranky engine, a few of the Vietnamese militiamen in the fort squatted around in a semicircle to see what he was doing. Their occasional jokes and chuckles began to get on Fitz's nerves, but he just gritted his teeth and tried to ignore his group of watchers. Finally he began to try to start the engine. The generator had a starter rope like the pull rope on a lawn-mower engine. At each pull on the rope, Fitz would heave with all his might. Each time he stumbled back a few steps as the short length of rope uncoiled and released from the crankshaft spool. The young locals laughed to see the big American lurch about with each false start. I suspect they were pleased at Fitz's obviously growing anger.

As the joking and laughter increased and as Fitz's cursing got louder, I walked out to see if I could cool things down a bit. Fitz had been irritable all day, and I sensed that something might get out of hand unless he was calmed down or the Vietnamese were sent off to work. Just as I approached the group, Fitz yanked back on the pull rope again. The engine coughed and wheezed, but it didn't start. Tran, one of the Vietnamese militiamen that Fitz especially disliked, made an obviously sarcastic remark to the men squatting beside him. The jibe made all the men howl with laughter. That was all Sergeant Fitz could stand. He threw down the rope and headed for Tran with rage flashing in his eyes. Now, Fitz was a big fellow and Tran was barely five feet tall. I thought Fitz might even kill the little man if he got hold of him. Not only did I not want anyone to get killed, I knew that a violent confrontation of any kind between an American and a Vietnamese could cause a lot of damage to our team's relations with both the local villagers and the soldiers. If a confrontation made someone mad enough, it might start them thinking about collecting those bounties the Viet Cong had on our heads. I knew that I had to stop Fitz before he got us all in big trouble.

I got to Fitz just as he was lifting Tran off the ground. I

jerked Tran from Fitz's grasp and shoved Fitz backward. Fitz outweighed me by about twenty pounds at the time, and I don't think I could have budged him at all except that I caught him by surprise. I had hoped Tran would take the opportunity to remove himself, but no, now *he* was insulted. He didn't want to back off after being treated so roughly in front of his friends. Also, I'll bet American money that he figured I was going to be able to stop Fitz myself, leaving him nothing to fear. After one look at Fitz, I wasn't sure of that at all.

Fitz was standing a few steps away, hunched over, taking in great gasps of air. Sweat glistened on his bare chest and shoulders. He glared at the little man behind my shoulder, pointed at him threateningly, and said in a harsh voice, "That little bastard has been asking for an ass-whipping for months, sir, and I'm going to give it to him."

With that, Fitz rushed at Tran as if I were not even there, standing between them. I braced myself to take the impact of his charge and our chests smacked together with a resounding thud. I grabbed him around his shoulders as I tried to restrain him and to recover my own balance. *"Bác-sĩ!"* I yelled. It was the Vietnamese word for doctor, but was commonly applied to American army medics. "No! Stop it!" I said as we stumbled around in each other's grip. Fitz dragged me backward a few feet before I finally set my feet and rammed my shoulder hard into his chest. The blow stopped him and stood him up, but he didn't move back an inch.

Fitz glared at me and said between clenched teeth, "Get outta my way, sir; I'm gonna bust that little runt like an egg."

"I'm not going anywhere, *Bác-sĩ*," I said grimly. "You calm down and get back to your work or go in the team house. This kind of stupid tantrum could get us all killed!"

I don't think he even heard me; he was moving forward again, and this time he was looking directly at me. He put his shoulder down and slammed me in the chest. It felt as if I had just caught a shotput. As I sagged backward, I grabbed around his arms. Our feet tangled and we both fell, groping and grunting in the dirt. He tried to get up, but I held on and tried to keep his arms pinned to his sides. We pushed and pulled and grabbed and grappled and mainly just rolled around in the dirt. I was fighting for time and desperately trying to figure out what to do. I knew I couldn't let the fight continue. Aside from the fact that Fitz could probably beat the hell out of me, I knew that this spectacle was making us look like fools in front of the Vietnamese.

The sight of an American officer and an American sergeant fighting each other was going to undermine the whole team's position and authority. If word of this sort of thing got around, the village chiefs would think I was some kind of lightweight, not able to handle my own men and low enough to participate in a common brawl. Such a lack of propriety was unheard of!

Of more immediate concern was the fact that Sergeant Fitz was out of control. He was already guilty of insubordination, striking an officer, mutiny, and "conduct to the prejudice of good order and discipline in the United States Army." Unless I could bring him in check, he was on a roll for a twenty-year hitch at Fort Leavenworth. I wished like hell that the other team members were around to get me out of this, but I knew I was in it all alone.

I thought about drawing my service .45 and threatening to shoot him, but it seemed to me that the last time an American officer got away with shooting one of his own men was like never. Back at the Infantry School, we had talked about how far an officer could go to get men to obey orders, but shooting them was not on the list of "school solutions." A school solution did come to mind, however, and as silly as it sounded at the moment, I figured I was bound to try it.

I shoved *Bác-sĩ* off me and we rolled away from each other. I got to my feet before he did, and I watched him as he turned to face me again. Anger was storming in his eyes, the afternoon sun had turned the compound into a dusty oven, and the sweat from our bodies streaked the grime on our faces and chests. The compound was completely quiet; I could hear only the sound of our ragged breathing. Blood rolled down my arm from a cut elbow and somehow Fitz had managed to cut his lip; blood streaked the corner of his mouth. I was really pissed. Sweat, dirt, and blood all over the place and all of it from two Americans fighting each other as if they had nothing better to do with their time. The Vietnamese troops just watched. I could see the nervous confusion on their faces. All the laughter was over now and even the soldiers realized that nothing good was going to come of this.

I drew myself up to full height and put my right hand on

the flap of my holster. I popped the flap and drew the pistol. I held it out a little way from my side, but with the barrel pointed to the ground. I raised my left arm up to eye level, and pointed directly at Fitz. Glaring down the length of my arm, I bellowed at the raging soldier, "Sergeant Fitz, I remind you I am an officer in the United States Army! I am your commanding officer and you are sworn to obey my lawful orders! I am giving you a *direct* order to go straight to the team house and wait for me. That is a direct order, Sergeant! If you do not obey, I will have you court-martialed for insubordination and disobedience in the face of a hostile force. I'll see you busted, dishonorably discharged, and chipping bricks in Leavenworth!"

I didn't know about the exact accuracy of any of those charges, and I never said anything about using the pistol, but I had to say and do something that would get the attention of an old army sergeant. I had to find the right formula to make the threat convincing. Something had to ring a bell that would bring Fitz back to his senses. I stood there in the heat and the dust, with my finger still pointing at him. He glared at me and I at him. I could feel the trickles of sweat running down my back and chest.

Bác-sĩ's wild glare never faltered; he leaned forward as if to come at me again. Now my heart was really in my throat; I was down to my last card. I kept my finger pointed at him, trying to use it as a baton of authority. Still glaring but speaking in a lower voice, I said, "Don't do it, *Bác-sĩ*. I'll shoot you if I have to. I am giving you a direct order to stop acting like a goddamned private and go to the team house."

Fitz clenched his teeth, pursed his lips, and slowly shifted his gaze back to Tran. After another pause, he let out a big breath of air and rasped angrily, "That little bastard is a thief and a liar. He is probably a Charlie and would love to see us both dead. You wanna kill somebody, kill that little shit!"

"I don't want to kill anybody," I said calmly, "and I'm not going to kill anybody because you're going to do as I say and go inside. You let me take care of Tran in my own way."

Fitz's rage was fading and his eyes began to take on a more rational look. His arms relaxed and his posture lost its tenseness; I could tell the crisis was over. I just hoped that Tran and his buddies had enough sense to keep their mouths shut.

One little peep from any of them could send Fitz off again. He stood there in the silence for a breath or two, then spat in the dust at his feet. Scowling at Tran, he growled a disgusted and emphatic "Yes, sir," and marched off to the team house.

Tran let out a chuckle and turned to say something to his friends. I grabbed his collar and pulled him to me in an obvious attempt at feigned gentleness. I said in Vietnamese loud enough for the others to hear: "It is not worthy of a man like you to have such bad manners, Tran. American soldiers obey their officers, even when they have cause to be angry. Be more courteous and careful in the future. I will not always be around to protect you!"

I laughed at the thin joke and pounded him on the back with enough force to send him staggering. The other men began to move off and get back to their jobs. I hoped the incident was closed, though I knew the Vietnamese villagers would hear about it, and I figured the rumors would be pretty thick for the next several days. I hoped that Tran would avoid confrontation with Fitz in the future; I was pretty sure that he was glad to get out of this particular tangle with his head still on his shoulders.

As I walked back to the team house, I formulated my speech to Sergeant Fitz. I knew I would make all sorts of threats to him and give him hell for his conduct, but in the end I would tell the medic to forget the whole incident so far as the official record was concerned. No charges would be brought against him; his wasn't the first case of lunacy I had seen. Tales were fairly common of men out on isolated MAT teams who had been doing fine until a small incident just set them off. Some little irritation would send them into a rage that would consume all their normal sensibilities. The rages usually seemed to be acute. They were the boiling up of the animosity and frustrations that develop when men are stuck out all by themselves in a dangerous, deprived, and foreign environment.

The lack of privacy we all experienced didn't help things, either. The five of us on my team were forced to live together in confining, primitive quarters. Whether we actually liked each other or not, we had to get along in order to survive. We all had a lot of suppressed miffs, indignations, and petty resentments. Such vexations, as small as each one was, could become like psychological nettles, stinging, stinging, stinging until even a good man finally needed just one more prick before he lashed out in an absolute fury. In this case, Tran had provided the final sting and Fitz had become the raging demon.

When I walked into the team house, Sergeant Fitz had already calmed down. He was too embarrassed to speak or even to look at me. He was nervous as he sat there waiting for me to light into him. I did; I went through my prescribed litany of threats; I pontificated about military law, discipline in the ranks, and the indispensability of a professional noncommissioned officer's corps. In the end, though, I told him to keep the whole thing to himself: there would be no record of the incident in the team log. Fitz, of course, was more than glad to let the whole thing drop. With a look of relief he came over and we shook hands. He walked out of the team house and I went back to my ever-present paperwork. I never could get *Bác-sī* Fitz interested in that generator again. It just sat out there and rusted in the tropical sun.

Chapter 13

CAN Tho, the principal city of the Mekong Delta, was about fifty miles southeast of my village. The old city had been designed by the French, and I used to walk down the streets trying to imagine how it must have looked before the war. The parks were now covered with grime and dust, concertina wire blocked off the public lawns, and the broad thoroughfares were clogged with vehicles, debris, and the intrusions of squatter housing.

There were a lot of Americans in Can Tho. The city was the headquarters area for the IV Corps military region, so a lot of staff and support personnel were assigned there. There was a large American airfield just outside of town too, so there were a lot of transients hanging around for one reason or another. For the men on the MAT teams, the district teams, and even the province teams, Can Tho was the place you had to go to get personnel or administrative problems solved when they couldn't be handled locally. In fact I used to try and make sure every month that one member of my team had a "problem" that required a trip to Can Tho. It was a way of sending a man to the rear for a couple of days so he could relax and enjoy a well-deserved, brief reprieve from the war.

Can Tho was also a place to get some good scrounging done. A pair of Vietnamese tiger-stripe camouflage fatigues or a piece of captured Viet Cong hardware would do wonders in prying loose some plywood, or sandbags, or even portable field kitchens from the usually tightfisted Amercian supply sergeants and property book officers. I got back to Can Tho several times myself just to scrounge supplies from the Americans.

When I was in town, I would stay in a transient officers billet right in the middle of the city. Each little room had a red tile floor, white plaster walls, a door of expanded steel, and four double bunks. The expanded steel doors were designed to be sturdy while still allowing some air movement. For that matter, the room walls did not extend to the ceiling; a foot or two of open space was left at the top to allow for better air circulation. Chicken wire was stretched across the ventilation spaces to prevent hand-grenades from being tossed over the walls into the rooms. There were toilets and running water in a room on every floor. Whores were available just outside in the street, twenty dollars a night. Security was important, so the front door of the officer ''hotel'' was protected by a sandbagged wall and a twenty-four-hour armed guard.

In the evening one could go to the roof of the hotel, where there was an open-air bar with a few tables and chairs. It could be quite pleasant up there at the end of the day when the sun had gone down. The breezes blowing off the Ba Sac river offered some natural cooling, and one could sip a drink with actual ice in it while watching the city tucking in for the night. As dusk advanced, kerosene lanterns were lit in the small shops and shanties. The lights cast their dark yellow glow and filled the surrounding walls or curtains with faint and flickering shadows. The electric lights of the more prosperous shops and the government buildings added their pale blue shimmer to the developing darkness. I always enjoyed the scene: it looked so peaceful and settled from where I was, up on the roof of our building.

After dark, the barman would set up a small screen and movie projector. Everyone would sit down and watch whatever film had been made available from the army's selection. We never got a *Ben Hur* or a *Gone With The Wind*, or even an *Easy Rider*. We always got the B-grade movies with titles like *Honky Tonk Heaven* or *Savage Monsters of Mars*.

I was up on the roof late one afternoon, waiting for the bar to open, when a flight of old propeller-driven A1E Skyraiders came roaring over the city at a low altitude. The old war birds had once had shiny silver skins, but now they were a dull gray, grime-streaked with the black exhaust of thousands of engine hours and smeared with the powder burns of hundreds of rocket blasts. Each plane was so loaded with ordnance that it seemed about ready to fall out of the sky. The planes flew right over our hotel and headed in the direction of the river, which we could see from the roof.

The jungle on the other side of the river came right down to the water's edge. Apparently the Skyraiders had a target over there that we could not see. We watched as the planes gained a little altitude and began to make runs on their quarry. We could see the HE and napalm bombs falling from the planes' bellies and could anticipate the fiery explosions as they hit the ground. Rockets streaked from the planes' wings, and the tracers from the wing machine guns could be seen arcing through the air. The failing light accentuated the pyrotechnics of the assault.

Three old landing craft suddenly appeared around a bend in the river. The gray boats lined up and headed into the far bank, where the air attack had been concentrated. Some hundred yards or so from the bank, a lone machine gun from one of the landing craft entered the fray. We could see its reddish-orange tracers flying into the thick jungle at the water's edge. As the boats hit the bank and their square front doors dropped down, the A1E's came roaring in again, spouting flame and lead. In the gathering darkness the tracers could be seen pouring out from the planes in deadly streams. Fans of green tracer bullets rose from the jungle-covered riverbank, reaching up to the planes overhead. The green tracers were from Chinese or Soviet weapons. Enemy bullets could also be seen flying out past the landing craft and dousing themselves in the river. Ricocheting rounds, both green and yellow, spattered an erratic pattern across the sky.

The Skyraiders seemed to have emptied their ordnance, and they pulled lazily away from the battle below. They regrouped out over the river and together flew slowly into the approaching darkness. They seemed like a group of fickle birds who simply got tired of looking for worms where they were, so decided to move on to better ground.

The fight on the ground continued for some minutes more. We continued to watch the fanciful light display from the firefight. The rapidly falling tropical night blackened the sky and made the deadly light show even more luminous. Before long, however, the sputter and thump of the distant fighting began to fade away and we all lost interest in the far side of the river. It had been fascinating to watch while it was going on, but now we all got fresh drinks, dragged up our chairs, and settled back to watch another grade-B movie. None of us thought it would be as good as the air strike and ground assault we had just witnessed.

SERGEANT ROBERTSON AND I HAD COME BACK TO CAN THO together for a couple of days. I was trying to run down an army post office unit which had vanished along with about eight hundred dollars' worth of my postal money orders. Robertson was supposed to spend two days scrounging for sandbags and replacement parts for our outboard motor. He was staying at the senior NCO billets near my usual lodgings, so on the morning of the second day we agreed to finish our business by early afternoon and to meet for a drink or two. Robertson said he knew a quiet place that I would find agreeable.

When I finished my rummaging around at IV Corps headquarters, I dropped some papers off in my room and went to the street corner where Robertson and I had agreed to meet. I was leaning against a lamppost, smoking a cigarette, when Robertson came swinging into view. As he approached, I noticed he already had a full bottle of bourbon tucked under his arm. I pushed off the pole, flicked away the cigarette butt, and adjusted my beret to a jaunty angle. "Which way to the watering hole, *Trung sĩ*?"

"Follow me, *Trung úy*," Robertson said with a grin. "I've got just the spot."

We walked down one of the main thoroughfares of the city until we came to Can Tho's so-called Combat Alley. Combat Alleys exist in military towns around the world. They are usually the main avenue through the local red-light district, where drunken troops, disgruntled whores, and the local constabulary give true meaning to the "combat" appellation. This one was indeed an alley. It was wide enough to be a street, but it wasn't one. Two rows of store and bar fronts faced each other across some fifteen yards of mud and garbage. Scrap wood and cardboard provided a patchy bridgework across the more sodden areas. A pair of American MP's was stationed in a bunker at the street entrance to the alley. They glared at Robertson and me with that practiced police look which combines contempt and boredom. Trying to ignore the MP's, I looked up and down the street and alley and noticed that Robertson and I seemed to be the only other Americans in the area.

"Where is everybody?" I asked, squinting over at Robertson. "I thought this place would be hopping with guys off duty."

"Well," said Robertson, "from what I hear, the place has been declared off limits to the guys stationed here. Seems that a few nights ago, some of the local Vietnamese troops got tired of the Americans taking all the whores for themselves. Pushing and shoving turned into fighting, and the fighting damned near turned into a riot. Lucky for everybody the MP battalion came in and broke it up before both sides broke out the machine guns and artillery! Anyway, there is a lot of bad blood around, so the local GI's have been told to stay on post until feelings die down. Nobody is supposed to be down here unless they are just passing through on official business."

While Sergeant Robertson and I were technically not covered by orders given to the local GI's by their commanders, it struck me that perhaps we ought to stay out of the area too.

"Sarge," I said with some exasperation, "if that's all true, then why the hell are we going into this hole? You and I won't stand a chance if trouble starts in there. We'll be sitting ducks for anybody who wants to pick a fight with the Americans!"

"Aw, come on, *Trung úy*," said Robertson. "I've got one place specially picked out. I know the mama-san and most of the girls, I swear! Nobody will bother us and we can drink this bottle of bourbon in peace and quiet."

"How do you know so damned much about this 'special' place?" I asked. "You haven't spent more than three or four days in Can Tho in your life."

"I got lucky," Robertson said with a grin. "The first night I was ever in Can Tho, I happened to walk into this place and who should I see but an old buddy of mine from Fort Benning. Name's Browning. He worked over at IV Corps headquarters and was about to catch his freedom bird back to the States. It seems that he owned the place and he was crying the blues because he knew the old woman who ran it for him would stop sending his share of the profits as soon as he left the country. He must have been taking it philosophically, though, cause he and the old mama-san still seemed to be on friendly terms. We both got pretty sloshed that night, and I remember that he called the old woman over and told her that no matter what she did after he left, she better see to it I got treated right anytime I was in town. I think the mama-san must be afraid that Browning will be back for another tour and will want to re-establish his account. She's always been extra nice to me every time I've been back in. I guess she doesn't want to risk pissing old Browning off, just in case. Anyway, if we go in there they'll look after us. We won't get into any trouble, come on.''

I caved in and went along with him. The bar he took me to was down the alley a bit, but it was a nice enough place on the inside. It was a small room with a red bar and bar stools going down one wall and a line of red and white booths along the opposite wall. The real workshop was the upstairs area, where the girls could take their paying customers. It was convenient, the in-and-out customer lost no time, and all the cash flow was kept in-house.

It was only about three in the afternoon when we got there, and the old, blackened ceiling fans were having to work hard to keep the place ventilated. A couple of Vietnamese men were talking to girls at the bar, and they didn't look any too happy when they saw us two Americans coming into the place. But it turned out that Robertson's story was true, and the old woman behind the bar came out and greeted him warmly. Several of the girls called to him and made some remarks that set them all to giggling. Robertson acknowledged them with a big grin and waved to everyone around, acting like a small-town mayor in a parade.

We sat down in a booth and asked for some ice and a couple of glasses. The old woman and a couple of girls came over and sat with us for a while. We chatted about nothing in particular for a while, just to be polite. The women eventually drifted off and left Robertson and me to sit there and sip our bourbon while we shot the bull about the team, the war, and life in general.

Considerable time must have passed because I suddenly noticed that the bottle of bourbon was half empty, all the other customers had left, and some of the girls had drifted back to our table. I heard the old woman talking rapidly to two of the girls in the front of the bar. She pointed to the folding steel shutters that were pushed back against the side walls of the bar's front porch. The girls ran over and moved some chairs out of the way in order to close the steel lattice. Noticing all the activity up front, I looked around the bar and confirmed that the place was deserted except for Robertson, myself, and the Vietnamese prostitutes. The steel-lattice shutters slammed together, and the old woman went outside to padlock the metal curtain in place.

"What the hell's going on here?" I asked no one in particular.

Robertson craned his neck around to see what was happening. "Hey, what's up?" he called to the old woman.

She came back to our table, stopping to cut off the lights up front, and smiling all the while, assured us everything was all right. It did seem, she said, that a group of drunk Vietnamese Rangers were getting rowdy out in the alley. Word was out that the Rangers would like to run into some American soldiers and show them what was what. The woman explained that she thought it would be prudent just to close the place up until the excitement had died down. It wouldn't be good for her establishment or for us, she said, if the soldiers found out we were in the bar.

I stood up and said that Robertson and I would leave rather than cause trouble, but one of the girls who had been listening to our conversation pulled me back into the booth. The young woman was dressed in black pants and a simple white blouse. Her thick black hair framed an attractive face now marked with concern.

"No, *Trung úy*," she said. "If you go outside now, the soldiers will see you. They are drunk and feeling brave. You will never make it to the MP station at the end of the street. It is best just to wait here until they all get tired and leave."

Robertson just shrugged, handed me the bottle, and waved me down into my seat. I took the bottle from him and poured myself another drink.

The girls had nothing to do since there were no customers around and the place was locked up, so eventually they all drifted over to our table to join the conversation. We ended up talking and joking with all six or eight of them. The bottle continued to drain. Time drifted on. The conversation must have degenerated considerably because somehow or other the girls decided that they would have a pubic hair contest with Robertson and me as judges. That's right, a pubic hair contest, I swear it.

Two of the girls were Eurasian. Their fathers were Frenchmen from the old colonial days. Eurasian girls always seemed to be taller than Vietnamese girls, and they were always strikingly beautiful. As I recall, the barroom conversation had turned to the sexual attributes of various kinds of men—Vietnamese, Cambodian, American whites, American blacks, Chinese, Indians, or what have you. One of the girls complained of the hairiness of a lot of American men. That was when one of the Eurasian girls said it was true, European men were too hairy. She said that European blood had left her more hair than women who were pure Vietnamese. Eurasian girls had lots of pubic hair, she said proudly, but everyone knew that Vietnamese girls had hardly any at all. The other Eurasian girl laughingly agreed and said she was often complimented by her American customers on her abundant pubic hair. She said that it seemed that Americans wanted girls with lots of pubic hair. Was that so, she asked us?

I looked at Robertson and shrugged. One of the Vietnamese girls then rejoined that Vietnamese girls had plenty of pubic hair; they certainly weren't getting any complaints from their customers! Robertson and I were asked again what we thought about the importance of pubic hair, and the good-natured repartee between the girls continued. Finally they came up with the idea of the contest. The girls were going to deposit one hundred piasters each in a kitty and line up in front of the bar. On cue they were to drop their pants or pull up their dresses, as the case required, to display their escutcheons. Robertson and I were to go from girl to girl, inspecting the breadth and thickness of pubic hair, and choose a winner. The girl with the most hair would win the several hundred piasters in the kitty.

Despite having gone through the large part of a fifth of whiskey, Robertson and I both managed to take on an air of grave and studied seriousness. I tell you, every Justice on the

Supreme Court would have been proud of us. With absolute impartiality we studied each specimen, mumbled knowingly over each case, and occasionally pointed to a particularly interesting shape or shading. Hands behind our backs, we bent studiously over each bared groin. It was a close decision. As a matter of fact we had to go back for a second look and include a "fluffiness" factor that Robertson suggested as the deciding trait among the three front-runners. One of the Eurasian girls won. She had been right in the first place: she did have more pubic hair than her colleagues. The other Eurasian girl came in second. The pure Vietnamese girls hooted impiously at their judges and made jokes about our lack of expertise.

While Robertson and the girls were still laughing and kidding around, I made my way to the front of the store and peeked through the steel security lattice. A few Rangers were still prowling around in the alleyway, shouting back and forth to each other and to the girls in the bars that had remained open. I noticed that most of the storefronts were shuttered, just like our place. Everybody seemed to recognize that the Rangers were bad for business. We used to say you could always tell when American Rangers have been in your neighborhood—your house is a mess, your garbage cans are in the street, and your dog is pregnant. I guess that's true for Vietnamese Rangers, too.

The old woman came up and hustled me to the rear again. She didn't want me to be spotted, she said. She didn't want any trouble. I sat back down with Robertson and we polished off the rest of the bottle of bourbon, and it wasn't long before one of the girls came by and told us that the troublemakers had left and the bar was opening up again. Sure enough, two of the girls were sliding back the metal latticework, and others were setting up the chairs on the small front porch. Robertson and I went and glanced up and down the alley to make sure the coast was clear. There were no Rangers in sight, so we figured we had better get out of there while the getting was good.

Sergeant Robertson went back and told the old woman that we were leaving. He and I passed through the bar, saying our good-byes and thanking everyone for hiding us while the Rangers were out looking for trouble. I had not planned to be locked in a whorehouse all afternoon, but what the hell, everybody has to be somewhere.

Robertson and I were both drunk as skunks but somehow we managed to make our way past the MP station without drawing attention to our condition. I led as we threaded our way down the alley and past the small boys who were trying to sell the sexual services of their still smaller sisters. I concentrated on walking without having to lean on buildings or electrical poles. Finally we got to the main street that led back to our billets. The MP's were still hanging around their bunker, but they gave us nothing more than bored glances.

The late afternoon traffic was zooming by. The place was thick with cyclos, buses, bikes, and motorbikes. It wasn't unusual to see a family of four or five all crowded together on a small Honda as it sputtered by in the dust. The motorbikes and cyclos zipped in and out of the traffic. The small two- and three-wheelers challenged the lumbering trucks and buses for road space as if they were there by divine right. There was not even an attempt at traffic control. It was every man for himself, no holds or feints barred.

Robertson had to cross the street to get to his billet. As he disappeared in the swarm of traffic and dust, I heard him shout something about meeting me at the chopper pad the next day for the ride home. I yelled a time to meet and then turned away. I didn't have the nerve to stay and see if a drunken army sergeant could negotiate that hell-for-leather traffic maze. I went on back to my billet to catch what I knew would be the only good night's sleep I would get for months.

Chapter 14

THERE was a Special Forces "A" team stationed back in Cao Lanh. An A team is the basic ten-man group for which the Special Forces are famous, and the team in Cao Lanh appeared to be a good one. The SF troopers were all effective soldiers so far as I could see, and it was good to have those guys back in Cao Lanh to scrounge from and to get help from every now and then. I liked the SF a lot, but they hardly lived up to the "Green Beret" myth that has sprung out of Hollywood movies, popular novels, and good public relations. We used to call the SF guys "snake eaters," partly in good-natured ribbing and partly in derision of their inflated self-image. We all learned to put up with our SF friends being a little like the Marines—deluded enough to believe their own publicity.

I was perfectly willing to let them believe anything they wanted so long as I could get them to come out and help us with our own combat operations every now and then. The A team from Cao Lanh and my MAT team got on well together. They were always helpful and friendly and would bring us supplies we could never hope to receive through our own channels. I got the impression that the SF guys liked to come out to my district for these combat operations, and I think it was because going out on the operations with us made them feel they were actually doing what their publicity said they were doing. I had to warn my guys several times not to bruise tender egos by mentioning to the SF that so far as we were concerned they were our friendly helpers from "the rear."

This particular SF team came from a compound back in the province town which was pretty plush by my team's primitive standards. The walls were thick and high, strengthened with steel-reinforced concrete and bristling with as many machine guns as we had rifles. The fort afforded showers, bunkers, private rooms, a bar, movies, girls, and enough equipment and supplies to make us boonie rats drool. The SF units were well funded, by their own internal funds and by monies crossing over from the Central Intelligence Agency.

My recollection is that the CIA paid a considerable portion, perhaps all, of the costs of maintaining the Civilian Irregular Defense Groups, or CIDG's, that the SF ran. The CIDG troops were mercenaries, paid directly from American funds to fight under the leadership of American soldiers. That was considerably different from the case of MAT teams. MAT teams had to use native villagers, men who made some of their living from farming or fishing at the same time they were fighting for their government.

For some reason CIDG units were often made up of men who were not ethnic Vietnamese. In the Delta the CIDG's were usually Nungs, men of Chinese ethnic background but who were Vietnamese by nationality. Many of these men were recruited from Cholon, the Chinese sector of Saigon, and had little in common with the rural Vietnamese. This social dichotomy was always a problem, but I was willing to put up with it because those Nungs were damned good fighters. They had good leadership from the A team and they had good morale, a quality painfully lacking in the regular Vietnamese forces.

The CIDG units had good morale because they liked working for the Americans; they were highly paid and well supplied. But they knew that if their job performance was not up to par they could be fired, and if they were fired from the CIDG, they became eligible for the Vietnamese draft. The draft would doubtlessly put them in the Vietnamese army, where they would have to do the same fighting for less pay, under worse living conditions, and without the direct American assistance. In short, the Nungs did their jobs well because they knew when they were well off.

The really good thing about the SF A team back at Cao Lanh was that they had airboats. The boats were the flat-bottom, airplane-propeller-driven, rudder-steered craft that are often seen in the Florida Everglades or in the Mississippi delta marshes. The only thing different about these airboats was that they had machine guns mounted in their bows. They operated in units of three boats each, two with a .30 caliber machine gun in the bow and one with a .50 caliber. The "Mike Forces," or that part of the CIDG out on an operation, usually came to us with six boats. That allowed two groups of three boats each which could operate somewhat independently of each other and could be very flexible in tactical operations.

The airboats were a very effective means of moving out to some of the more remote areas of my district, especially during the rainy season. With a Mike Force we could get around quickly, hit the Cong in some of their sanctuary areas when they didn't expect us, and clear out some of the nests that would have been impossible to successfully attack by poling in on sampans.

The social clash between the Nungs and the Vietnamese villagers was not a trivial matter, and when they were resting between operations I always tried to keep the Nungs out of the local villages. The village fathers made it clear to me that they had a severe dislike for the Chinese "*cao*-boys," a term that meant anything from dandy to hood, depending on how one used it. The boisterous, cocky Nungs were usually from urban areas like Cholon because the Chinese form the merchant class throughout Asia and tend to concentrate where business traffic will reward their enterprise. The Nungs' urban background gave them nothing in common with the native villagers. They would often ignore local customs, flirt outrageously with the village girls, be abusive to the local men, sarcastic to the old women, and just plain trouble in general. Sometimes having a group of Nungs around was as disruptive as having a group of American GI's! The young Nung fighters knew that the SF had gotten them better guns, food, money, and billets than anybody else had; they thought they were the cock-of-the-walk. So despite the fact that I was glad to have the Mike Forces to work with, I usually felt a little sense of relief when the force returned to Cao Lanh and the villagers could settle back into their normal routine. Angry complaints from the husbands, fathers, and village elders would cease abruptly;

the old village woman who ran the beer hooch by the market would stop coming in to demand restitution for some unpaid bill or broken piece of furniture. A relative calm would settle in, and it was back to the life with the pigs and chickens.

All said and done, though, I can't really bitch about the Special Forces. They were like rich uncles to my team and were usually glad to help out their underprivileged relatives whenever they could. They were good men in a fight, too, and I guess that was the bottom line. Hell, I've still got my CIDG tiger fatigues and my Mike Force patch. I look at them every now and then and wonder why I ain't dead.

FEAR HAS MANY FACES, SOME OF THEM LIKE THE CONTINU-ous, gnawing fear I experienced to some degree on every combat patrol. Another kind is the instant shock variety, where you are given no chance to think—you just have to act reflexively and hope your animal instincts will get you out alive. Proper reflexive action is a big part of staying alive in a guerrilla war. Sometimes things just happen too quickly for you to have time to think and come up with a rational approach. An episode of the shocked-shitless variety happened to me one day while I was out on patrol with a Mike Force from the Special Forces team back in Cao Lanh.

It was during the rainy season, and we were using the airboats to operate against our local Viet Cong District Mobile Company. The plan called for us to go to the far southeastern corner of my district where there were no settlements and where, according to our intelligence estimates, the Cong were preparing a sanctuary area. We had left our compound at sunrise. As the sun came up on the cloudless horizon, the roar of the small aircraft engines ripped the tranquility of the early hour. The morning light transformed the spray from our bows into a silver veil falling into the water beside us. It was exhilarating to zip along, riding the bounce and slap of the airboats as they skimmed over the surface of the canals and paddy flats.

The airboats carried us swiftly over the broad expanse of flooded plain. We reached our area of operation and began a map-grid-by-map-grid search for any evidence of enemy activity. We had been patrolling about an hour when I spotted several big clay crocks on a large earthen mound off to our left, about one hundred yards away. We got the boats on line and speeded into the area of high ground, keeping our eyes on the thick patch of forest that bordered the mound on three sides.

We had prearranged our landing parties in case we had to beach the airboats like this. When the bows of the boats rode up on the ground, those of us assigned to do so leaped from the boats and hit the beach in the best war-movie fashion. We had received no fire coming in and the landing was quiet. We quickly spread out and checked the area over. The mound of earth was apparently a deserted Viet Cong bunker, hollow on the inside, with firing slits in the sides. The crocks were full of salt and dried fish. We saw nothing else. There were a couple of small canals running by the area, and I noted that one clump of trees reached out from the patch of nearby jungle into an area immediately behind the mound. We gave the whole area a quick once-over before breaking open the crockery. Everyone stuffed a few fish in his pockets and scattered the rest around the mound and in the water. We were about to leave when one of the Special Forces men yelled from over by the trees, "Hey, there are some sampans hidden in the reeds over here!"

Several of us walked over to the trees and looked back into the shadowed reeds that lined the small canal. Sure enough, floating in the black water were three wooden sampans. One of them seemed to be loaded with the makings of a crude homemade hand-grenade factory. There were also several land mines lying carelessly among the grenade shell casings and fuses.

We couldn't reach the boat from our side of the canal and I didn't want the men to just hook it and drag it over. A common Cong trick was to leave some bait like this and booby-trap it. A tug on the boat might spring some trigger mechanism which would in turn explode the whole damned thing right there in our faces. Before moving the sampan someone would have to get into the water and go around the boat, feeling for trip wires. It was not a job I thought highly of, but I wasn't sure enough of my Vietnamese language to think I could give sufficiently detailed, cautious instruction to the Nungs. And since all the other Americans were back at the boats or in the beaching area (the SF sergeant had gone back to his partner), it fell to me to check for the booby traps myself.

I took off my flack vest and handed it to a nearby soldier. I laid my M-16 down on the ground along with my web gear, but I felt too vulnerable without any weapon, so I stuck my .45 automatic into my waistband. As soon as I stepped into the water it was up to my waist; the steep-sided canal was deeper than I had thought. Another step toward the boat and I was up to my chest in the water, surprised and not a little disconcerted at the depth.

Finally I reached the side of the boat and fixed all my attention on it. I looked for wires or nylon line running above the boat or beneath the water. I felt around under the bottom of the boat for anything that seemed suspicious. I worked very slowly. I wanted to be damned sure I didn't blow myself up in the process of giving the boat a safety inspection.

I was standing in chest-high water as I carefully made my way around the boat. The other men crouched on the canal bank, staying out of the way in case I triggered a big surprise. I worked my way completely around the boat and found no evidence of a booby trap. Just to be safe, though, I wanted to get back to the opposite bank and get behind some cover before we pulled the boat over to get a closer look at its contents. I was making my way through some tall reeds that were growing up through the water when I felt something jerk under my right foot. Before I could really react, something struck the side of my right leg, and then suddenly a man burst from underneath the water at my side. His leap from the canal bottom shot him way up over my head. Water spumed up with him and his eyes locked onto mine. I jerked back reflexively and gasped in fright! The man seemed to hang up there in the air, surrounded by a white spray of water. For a split second I thought of a great whale powering up from the ocean's depths.

I was still standing in chest-deep water, momentarily immobilized with fright, but I felt myself leaning back in the water, off balance because of the steep bank and the blow to my leg. I was looking straight up at the Vietnamese man in shocked disbelief. That fleeting pause at the top of his bound allowed me to see two things in the same instant: the wildness in his eyes and the knife clutched in his right hand, raised high over his head. If I could have I think I would have fainted dead away. I couldn't, so I flailed out in a desperate attempt to ward him off. As he fell back down on me, I tried to block his right arm with my own and grab onto anything I could with my left hand. As we tumbled over into the water in a foamy tangle of arms and legs, I waited for the burning pain of his knife in my ribs. My wild attempt at blocking his arm must have been successful because the expected stab never came. We struggled around in the water, both of us either too scared or too inexperienced at this sort of thing to do anything but wallow about and jerk at each other.

I could neither see nor breathe. I had hold of one of the man's wrists with my left hand and I wouldn't let go. I prayed it was the one with the knife! I remember seeing those old Tarzan movies where he would always have an underwater knife fight. I always got the impression those guys could see what was going on when they were fighting underwater—not so! You can't see a damned thing and you have no idea what you are doing or what you ought to be doing. In a situation like that the big thing becomes not so much to hurt your opponent as to keep him from hurting you. You have to do that while making sure you roll to the surface every now and then and suck in another desperate gasp of air.

Eventually I was holding on to the man's arm with both hands. I resorted to kicking wildly with my booted feet, trying to land blows to his body. From the stretch of his arm at one point I figured his chest was about at my knees, so I tried for knee lifts into his head and chest. Something must have landed because I felt his arm go slack for a second, and then after another feeble jerk or two, he went completely limp. I shot my legs downward, trying to find bottom. I was still holding his arm with both hands and was afraid to let go, but I had to get to the surface before I passed out from lack of oxygen! Much to my surprise we were right at the edge of the canal, and as I straightened my legs, I stood up in only waist-deep water. I sucked in a beautiful lungful of air. Still gasping for more, I glanced down at the man I had dragged up with me. I saw that he was also taking in great gasps of air and he didn't appear to be concerned about much of anything else.

As I stood there holding on to the man's arm, two or three of my guys jumped into the water beside me and grabbed the

Vietnamese prisoner. His knife was gone, probably at the bottom of the canal. I released my grip and the men dragged him on the bank. He didn't resist. All the fight was gone out of him, and out of me too for that matter. I was trembling and still trying to catch my breath as I crawled up the canal bank. I couldn't believe this had happened! During the entire fight I never processed a rational, intentional thought. Every move was just a reflex to some stimulation. I never stopped to think; I just moved rapidly from one contortion to the next. My heart and brain were still racing, trying to catch up with all the action. The incident was over, but my fright was just starting to sink in.

One of the SF men helped me up to the top of the bank. I collapsed on my back and flopped my arms out away from my sides. I closed my eyes and tried to slow down my pounding heart and racing nerves. The SF guys and the Nungs pulled the boats over and went through their contents. It turned out that we had captured a small water-borne munitions factory. The boats had materials for making hand-grenades, booby traps, and small land mines. One of the SF guys came over and told me about the captured equipment. He said the Nungs were excited about the find and were certain that we could find more Viet Cong in the area. The man we had just captured had been hiding in the canal and breathing through a bamboo air tube when I had bumped into him; others might be close by, doing the same thing. The fact that there were three sampans implied that more than one guerrilla was hiding nearby. The sergeant said the Nungs were going to question the Cong and make him tell where the other men were hiding and where their arms cache was hidden.

I had had a few minutes to pull myself back together and was now trying to act as if this sort of thing was an everyday exercise for me. I nodded my assent without really thinking about what he had said, and he walked back to the Nungs, who were holding the prisoner over by the airboats. I asked the men emptying the Viet Cong sampans a few questions about the things they were taking off the boats, told them to sink the sampans when they were through, and finally got up to walk back to the airboats myself.

As I approached, I noticed a huddle of men in front of one of the boats. The captured guerrilla was tied down on the bank and the Nung leader was raging at him about something. The other men were also pretty agitated and were occasionally shouting their own interjections. The Nung leader had a combat knife in his hand. I saw him bend over the prisoner and press it into his chest.

"Oh, shit!" I said to myself and began to run over to the group of men. I pushed my way through the line of soldiers that had formed a circle around the Cong and his interrogator. When I got to the inside I saw the Nung leader standing over the Cong with his knife in the man's face. A scarlet streak of blood ran diagonally across the prisoner's chest, obviously the result of a knife blade's heavy travel across bare skin. The Cong's eyes were white with fear. He was denying there were any other VC around besides himself. One of the SF sergeants was already standing there, trying to calm the Nung leader down. The sergeant was squatting and had placed a hand on the prisoner's chest as if to establish a claim. He held his other hand out toward to the agitated Nung and calmly said, "Don't cut him, o.k.? Just don't cut him." The sergeant paused and stared intently into the Nung's angry eyes. He continued, still speaking slowly, "We can't take him back and count him as a prisoner if you cut him up. So just put the knife up and don't cut him again. We can say he got this scratch when we hauled him into the boat, but just calm down and don't cut him again."

The interrogator turned his angry glare from the prisoner, looked at the American sergeant with a sudden nonchalant air, and nodded in agreement. He told the SF sergeant not to worry, he was just trying to scare the prisoner, not to hurt him. He leaned back over the stretched-out guerrilla and asked again where the arms cache was hidden. The frightened Cong denied any knowledge. The Nung flashed his knife back to the other side of the man's chest and pressed the tip of the blade into his skin.

"*Không được!*" I said loudly and grasped his shoulder with my left hand. "*Xin lỗi, ânh, không được,*" I repeated firmly, wanting him to know I didn't approve of his methods either. The Nung looked at me angrily; he didn't like Americans butting in on his method of questioning prisoners. I continued talking to him in Vietnamese. "The sergeant's right. We cannot harm prisoners. We can't cut him and take him back alive.

If we did, we would all be in big trouble. We can't kill him because the people back in Cao Lanh need to question him. So don't cut him again, o.k.? We can explain the cut he already has, but don't do it again.''

The Nung listened without comment. When I finished he looked at me with a flash of disgust. He didn't say anything, but he stepped over to one side of the prisoner and put his knife back into its scabbard. Finally he shrugged his shoulders, said, "O.k.," and turned to walk back to his boat. The American sergeant and I grabbed the Cong and hauled him over to our airboat. We wanted to keep a close eye on him, just to make sure we got him back to home base in one piece.

We continued to search the area for several hours for signs of enemy activity, but found no other traces of recent habitation. Late in the afternoon we headed for home. As we skimmed across the flat, water-covered table of marsh and reeds, the engines snarled loudly, but the breeze whipping by provided relief from the relentless heat. I looked at the guerrilla, sitting in the bow of the boat. His arms were bound behind him at the elbows and his face was awash with fear, discomfort, and worry. I suddenly realized how small the man was. He couldn't have been more than shoulder high to me and he had a slight build. Yet when he and I were thrashing about in the water, I thought he was a giant. I guess it was that image of him rising high above me as I stood there in the canal. He seemed to reach way into the sky, and the glinting knife raised above his head was fixed forever in my mind.

I can't describe the intensity of the terror I felt at that moment. It electrified my whole body. My rational mind was frozen in place. Reflex was the only thing that allowed me to move at all. That chilling image still returns to me on occasion. I can do nothing to stop the nervous tremor that comes over me each time I think of that falling knife and the wet smack of skin on skin as the Cong and I tumbled back into the black waters of the reed-choked canal.

I NEVER COULD GET USED TO FIGHTING WOMEN. JUST RAISED wrong, I reckon. I never got particularly upset if I saw a male prisoner get a push or a shove, or a boot in the backside if he wasn't moving fast enough, but I always felt uneasy, would even get a little mad, when I saw a woman prisoner being treated the same way. When I was a lad I was taught that men did not ill-treat women, period. Nobody ever thought about teaching me that exceptions are to be made in time of war: women weren't supposed to be in a war. Oh, I had read books and seen movies with women fighters in them, but they were always presented as novelties. I had never thought about really having to fight women myself.

I was always disconcerted at finding a woman among a group of prisoners or, even worse, finding the corpse of a woman after a firefight. The knowledge that women had been trying to kill me made me very ill at ease. Threatened male ego there, I suppose, but psychology aside, the plain fact is I just didn't want to kill any women. I know that might sound silly. I didn't hesitate at killing men, did I, so what's the difference? Why such value on the life of females? I don't know the answer to that question. I wonder if monkeys have the same rules? I remember one particular operation that resulted in the capture of two women. My subsequent actions were improper and have left a nagging sense of guilt that reaches across the years and still grabs me in my sleep.

I was out with a Mike Force on a standard airboat operation. We had been sweeping a remote area, looking for evidence of Viet Cong use or habitation. We were cruising along in two columns of three boats each, engines roaring and spray flying. I was in a boat in the right-hand column. The opposite column was passing in front of a tree line off to its left. In the trees we could see the remains of an abandoned settlement. Several old housing mounds were evident amidst the dense vegetation. As the lead boat passed in front of one of the mounds, geysers of water jetted up around it. I didn't hear any shots over the roar of the aircraft engines, but it was clear the boat was taking fire. It wheeled away from the tree line as the following boats in its column came into range of the enemy position and began receiving fire also. The trailing boats did have time to return fire as they turned out, and they were able to provide some cover for the lead boat, which was defenseless with its back to the enemy's guns.

The lead boat called us on the radio with an urgent plea for help. One man had been hit, the boat had taken several rounds through the hull, and some of the boat's control cables were apparently cut or jammed. The pilot was having a hard time controlling the craft's direction. Our column immediately began to wheel about in a big circular pattern. We directed the damaged boat to come straight on out to us and take a position beyond our wheel. The other two boats of that column were sent off to the left of the field as we looked across at the area the firing had come from. It was evident that at least one of the housing mounds had been hollowed out to make a bunker. Most of the firing was coming from a mound that we could see clearly out on the edge of the tree line.

Our attack plan was to use the two boats off to the left as covering fire support while we moved our three-boat wheel in close to the Cong position. In a three-boat wheel, one boat always has the objective under its gun while the other boats are turning away or coming around again for another firing run. The target should be under a relentless barrage of machine-gun fire. As we got our wheel set up, the support boats were to shift their fire and try to take up positions that would cut off any Cong trying to escape back into the trees.

After running our wheel and slamming the bunker with .30 and .50 caliber machine-gun fire for several minutes, we called for the support boats to return their firing to the bunker area. We came out of our wheel and lined up for a direct assault on the bunker area. At a signal from the column leader, all three boats went lunging ahead toward the bunker and the trees. The boats flew across the water with their engines howling. The machine guns in the bows opened up, but the gunners had to control their firing rate, especially with the .50 caliber, to prevent the recoil from slowing the boats down. Continuous fire from the heavy .50 caliber machine gun could stop an airboat dead in the water, so the gunner had to be careful. All boats went in firing short bursts from the bow guns, and everybody else with a rifle was firing as fast as he could. We were terribly exposed in those open boats and we didn't want anyone to be able to get up and take an aimed shot at us.

With all the noise and excitement I couldn't really tell how much return fire we were receiving. The boat about ten yards off to my left pulled ahead a little and I saw a man in it get hit. He was kneeling to one side of the machine gunner and was firing his M-16 at the target when he was suddenly jerked out of the boat as if by some invisible hand. He fell overboard, but we were in the middle of our assault and nobody could stop for him. Nobody could even slow down; he was on his own. In a matter of seconds we were on the beach, out of the boats, and charging toward the bunker area. The SF sergeant and I tried to keep the Nungs spread out as we made it to the bunker and on beyond into the trees. We established a perimeter around the area and went back to take a closer look at the bunker. No one had gone into it, but all firing had ceased.

One of the Nungs was calling out, trying to determine if anyone was inside, and if they were, to get them to come out with their hands up.

Sure enough, there was someone still in there, and after a blunt exchange or two, a man and two women came out with their hands high above their heads. Inside the bunker there were two other men, dead, five AK-47's, two or three packets of documents, several cases of ammunition, and two crocks of rice. We were absolutely sure the prisoners were Viet Cong. They had opened fire on our boats and killed two of our men. They were captured with weapons still hot from firing, and they had Viet Cong documents practically clutched in their hands. No doubt about it, they were Charlie with a capital C.

Everybody was excited and the Nungs were angry to boot. They were hot because they had had two of their men killed and they wanted to pass the favor on to the prisoners. They were all still pumped up from the assault, still enjoying the rush of success, the arrogance of survival. When you have to deal with men like that and men who are mad as hell to boot, it is hard to calm them down. After some pushing and shoving and some heated words, the SF sergeant and I got the Cong loaded into our boats and we began the journey back to my team's compound.

When we got back to the compound the pushing and shoving started all over again. The Nungs bunched up around the prisoners and started yelling jibes and threats at them. Pushes and shoves turned to occasional blows before we could get the Cong into our hooch and away from the angry Chinese soldiers. As I got dried off and dressed to go over to the district chief's house and tell him about the day's work, I could hear Lieutenant Cantrell and one of the SF sergeants begin to question the prisoners. I heard the gist of the conversation and knew that the Cong were making the standard denials. The man claimed to be a fisherman. One of the women claimed to be the man's sister, the other a friend. They said they did not know the dead men in the bunker and had never seen either the weapons or the documents before; they had run into the bunker to escape the machine-gun fire and found the men lying there, already shot dead. I didn't believe a word of it so as I slipped on a dry fatigue shirt and pulled on my beret, I turned to Cantrell and told him to keep probing. It wouldn't be long before the prisoners would be on their way back to the province town for interrogation there. If we wanted current, useful information, we knew we had to get it before we lost the prisoners to the province team.

I left the fort to go find the district chief. He was down in the village, working in the district office building, a two-room palm thatch hut like most of the other buildings around. The chief rose from behind his scruffy wooden desk as I came into his office. He and I always maintained a polite formality, so I took a few steps across the earthen floor, came to attention, saluted, and awaited his opening pleasantry. I had found, as I had been told many times, that business cannot be rushed in the tropics. One has to learn to lollygag and bullshit about all manner of things before getting to the point of any encounter. When I finally turned the conversation toward the day's operation, the chief was pleased to hear that we had found the small redoubt and had been able to bring back some prisoners. He made a note of the three Cong we had captured as well as the two Cong KIA's. He would use those in the figures of his own monthly report to province headquarters; beyond that he had no interest. I finished telling him about the operation in as few words as possible. I mentioned a couple of other unrelated matters that needed his attention and excused myself so I could get on back to the compound.

As I approached the fort I heard a lot of shouting and yelling going on inside. I couldn't tell if the noise was made in anger or in jest, but I expected the worst and hurried on through the gate. The Nungs were gathered over on the other side of the fort. In their center was the SF sergeant standing beside a fifty-five-gallon oil drum with one of the captured women standing on top. The woman had her hands tied behind her and she was crying from either shame or fear or both. I was so damned pissed I could have chewed nails. I ran over to the crowd and pushed my way through to the sergeant.

"What the hell is going on here, Sarge?" I shouted over the noise.

"This little lady don't want to talk, sir. I told her if she didn't loosen her tongue, I would auction her off to the Nungs for a little screwing. We'll see if fucking a few Chinamen will get her talkin'."

The Nungs had quieted down immediately when I had shouted at the sergeant. Now, speaking quietly through clenched teeth, I said to him, "Take her down off that goddamned barrel and bring her back into the team house. Nobody is going to fuck our prisoners, talk or no talk!"

I turned immediately and walked away, paying no attention to the scowling Nungs. I stepped through the crowd without hesitating or looking back. I wanted to give no hint that I expected anything but instant obedience. I was afraid that any sign of weakness or irresolution might give the Nungs just enough fuel to spark a mutiny. They weren't my troops, I didn't know them all that well, and I really didn't know how close they were to telling me to go to hell. I did know that Nungs had mutinied before, and these guys looked hacked off enough to do it again. Officer or no officer, American or no American, if they went on a rampage there would be no way for me to control them. If the Nungs were feeling tough enough and mad enough, they could take the prisoners and do what they wanted.

Once inside the team house I turned and looked behind me. The SF sergeant was coming with the young woman slung over his shoulder. The Nungs didn't try to interfere. They just stood there, glaring at us. The sergeant stepped through the doorway and dumped the prisoner beside her two companions, who were bound and squatting on the floor.

"What the hell do you think you are doing?" I asked angrily. "You know you can't sell women out for gangbangs! Are you nuts?" I stuck out my chin and glared at him. I was getting madder and madder, and I thought, "Doesn't this son of a bitch know anything about the rules of war? How can he treat a woman this way?" I guess that seems silly, given the politics and social attitudes of today, but as I said already, I had always been taught that men were not to ill-treat women. No rough stuff, no harshness, no insults. It just wasn't done. You know, the last flower of chivalry and all that. So what's all this about selling bound and weeping women to raving soldiers? Not on my parade!

I found that the SF sergeant was almost as mad at me as I was at him. He stood with his hands on his hips and glared at me as he said, "I wasn't going to sell that bitch, Lieutenant. Hell, she's scared shitless of those Nungs! I was just trying to shake the goddamned truth out of her. We've been sitting here with all of them lying through their teeth and not one damned piece of info that we can use. It won't be long before we lose them to the S-2 boys back in Cao Lanh!"

Some switch inside me flipped over. I don't know why, I don't know how, but suddenly I knew that the sergeant was right. There was no conscious rationalization process, no struggling with conflicting feelings; it was just that I all of a sudden knew we had to have that information. The qualms I had had a few minutes before simply vanished. I still cannot explain what happened, but suddenly I was a different person. "Don't worry," I said to the sergeant, "I'll get the information."

I walked over to the three prisoners and pulled the man up by the rope tied around his neck. I tried to exude as mean and threatening an aura as I could. I spoke to the man in Vietnamese: "Come with me." As I led him out the back door of the team house, I picked up my rifle and said loudly to him, "You will talk, or you will die." I tried to make it sound convincing, not for him, but for the two women left behind. A couple of Vietnamese soldiers helped me hustle the man out of the house and force him down to his knees.

I felt angry, righteous in a vague sort of way, and nervous. I really didn't know what I was going to do. I hadn't thought anything out, I was flying by the seat of my pants. I was a loose cannon on the deck. I was omnipotent; I knew that nothing would stop me, no matter what I did. I was king. I was riding a surge of absolute power. I think that one part of me knew that another part was ready to go the limit. I was in uncharted territory and my moral navigator was calling out urgent soundings.

The man was kneeling on the ground. He looked up at me with fear illuminating his eyes. We were in the rear of the compound by the latrine. The stench of the shit cans was offensive and made me even madder. I placed the muzzle of my M-16 against the man's head and said in Vietnamese, I know that you are Viet Cong. I know those women with you are Viet Cong. You have killed two of our men. The only way for you to live is to tell me where your unit hides and where your supply caches are hidden. If you don't talk, I will kill you."

The man stuttered out a denial. He repeated that he was just a fisherman. I asked him another question. Nothing. I pushed the muzzle tightly against his head for a second. I pulled the trigger. The man's head snapped back, and a grimace whipped his lips up at the corners. I had moved the barrel off his forehead as I squeezed the trigger and the round had gone off with the muzzle right beside the man's ear. The bullet didn't hit him, but the sound must have at least blown out his eardrum. I thought nothing of it. The Cong slumped forward, shaking his head and clenching his teeth in pain. I had no pity. I thought he should be damned glad I had let him live.

"Quickly, quickly," I said to the men with me, waving them over to help me out. "Gag him and put him in the bunker," I said as I pointed to the nearby door of a small bunker. When the man was out of sight, I sent for the woman who had claimed to be his sister. I pushed her down to her knees and put the rifle muzzle to her forehead.

"Your brother refused to tell the truth," I said. "He lied and I killed him. You heard the shot. Unless you tell the truth I will kill you too. Where are your friends? Where do they keep their weapons?"

The young woman began to sob quietly. She bowed her head, and shaking it from side to side, she said that her brother was not a communist and neither was she. They were all just fishing when our firefight erupted around them. I threatened again, this time pressing the gun barrel into her stomach for emphasis. Still she said no, she was innocent.

I stood over the young woman as she kneeled there in the gray mud. Tears ran from the large black eyes that looked directly into mine. Suddenly, another switch went off inside me. A flicker of doubt entered my mind. Maybe it was only a small doubt, but I was startled by it nevertheless. I had been totally committed to the idea that the prisoners were guilty. We had caught this woman and her friends red-handed. Guilt was written all over them—they had to be guilty! But suddenly

I wasn't so sure. Looking down at her, watching the tears roll down her cheeks, I had a great fear that she was telling the truth.

The angry emotion I had been riding on suddenly collapsed. I stared vacantly at the kneeling woman, trying to find my mental footing. I was shaking as I considered what I had just been doing. "My God," I thought. "One minute I'm yelling at the sergeant about abuse of prisoners and the next I'm acting like Atilla the Hun! Am I cracking up or what?"

A few months before I had thought Captain Jackson was such an s.o.b. for trying to scare prisoners by shooting at them, and now I was doing the same thing. I just stood there, staring blankly through the woman, my M-16 hanging in my slack grip. A rush of guilt hit me. I thought I was really nuts and I wanted out of this situation as quickly as possible. I didn't want to look at the prisoners, I didn't want to think about them, I wanted them out of my sight. In a matter of seconds I went from absolute certainty that they were all guilty, to a smaller flicker of doubt, to certainty that they were all innocent. The whiplash of emotions was almost unmanageable. I couldn't think of what to do or how to act. I was disoriented and was becoming very frightened.

The only way to rescue myself was to get rid of the problem, so I decided to just let the prisoners go. I had the man brought back from the bunker and put with the two women. Over the protests of Lieutenant Cantrell, the SF sergeant, and the Nung leader, I took all three prisoners to the gate, untied them, and told them they were free to go. Without comment or question, without any expression of relief, the three bedraggled peasants simply turned and walked away toward the village. As I watched them I was certain we had all been wrong from the beginning. They were innocent. It was all an awful mistake, and I was guilty of mistreating an innocent man—worse than that, guilty of mistreating an innocent woman. I couldn't begin to cope with the question of how that could be.

I walked back to the team house and confronted the others. The SF sergeant was full of scorn and my teammates were incredulous. Everyone threw questions at once. Just exactly what the hell did I think I was doing? Did a little tear from a native girl mean more than the fact that those people were caught *in flagrante*? Did I think this was just a child's game where the little girls got sent home to mother if they stubbed a toe? Was I nuts or what?

I couldn't really answer their questions, I didn't know what to think, but when I had pushed my rifle barrel into that girl's stomach I suddenly had a flash of how far outside the bounds of custom and law I had wandered. I couldn't believe it! Hell, I was a good ole' boy from down on the farm. Anglo-Saxon, Protestant, member of the 4-H Club and the All-State Chorus, all that sort of stuff. How in God's name does an American farm boy get to the point of blowing the eardrums out of defenseless prisoners? I didn't know. Later, I still couldn't deal with it, so I packaged the whole episode up in a tight mental box and put it back in my memory where it would never be disturbed. It is easy to avoid dealing with a problem if you simply ignore it.

Life isn't simple though, and answers never come in neat little packages. Six weeks later Sergeant Abney and Sergeant Robertson were on a patrol that ran into an ambush. They ran through a successful counter-ambush drill with the loss of one man killed and two wounded. They found two dead Viet Cong at the ambush site. One of them was the fisherman's "sister." Her fingers were still entwined in the shoulder strap of an AK-47 and the rifle's magazine was almost empty. This time there was no question: she was an enemy soldier, playing the part in full.

When Abney told me that they had found the girl again, I was embarrassed and ashamed. The sarcasm in his voice and the look in his eyes made the clear accusation that I had carelessly turned a killer loose on him because I cared more about remote regulations and pampering women prisoners than I did about the safety of my own friends and teammates. I knew that Abney and the other guys thought I had demonstrated an irresponsible disregard for our safety by letting those three prisoners go. In their own minds they were thinking that I should have known that sooner or later she would be shooting at us again. I'm sure that they were bitter and nourished the thought that I was just damned lucky she didn't kill one of us.

For a brief while the report that the young woman had been caught in yet another ambush attempt made me feel better about shoving my gun barrel into her stomach. Since it now appeared that she was guilty in the first place, I could rationalize that she deserved what she got. But then a thought occurred that still approaches from time to time and whispers to me from my dreams: Was she a Viet Cong before we captured her or only afterward?

A FEW WEEKS AFTER THE GIRL WAS KILLED BY ABNEY'S PAtrol, we heard about My Lai and the now infamous Lieutenant William Calley. We began getting secret cables all the way from CINCPAC in Hawaii, reminding us to abide by the rules of war. The message senders and memo writers were having a field day. The PSA came out to all the district and MAT teams to pound on the desktops and demand that we make sure that only enemy soldiers were caught in our operations. We were to take no chance that Vietnamese civilians would be endangered. The colonel knew he was asking the impossible, but I don't think that was even the point. He wanted to cover his ass. The press and the politico-type brass hats back in Saigon and Washington were on the lookout for any more My Lai's or anything that even smacked of wrongful killing. Any commander who was foolish or luckless enough to get caught with some dead civilians on his hands, no matter what the reason, was going to be food for the wolves. I think that was the reason our PSA was willing for us to do nothing rather than run any risk of accidently killing civilians.

The fact of the matter is that wars simply are not run without risk to noncombatants. There is no such thing as war without endangerment of the civilian population. On my team everybody recognized that and we were always very careful about our operations. I was a damned sight more averse to killing innocent villagers than was my PSA—I had to live there in the village! Risking or ruining innocent lives and property worked counter to our pacification and development efforts; it only made a hard job more difficult. Still, in a guerrilla war there is no such thing as being one hundred percent sure about anything. The only way to make certain that a group of men passing by in the dark were really Viet Cong was to go up and ask them. We damned sure weren't going to be doing that.

Out-and-out massacre of women and children is a different item from mistakes of combat, though, no matter how deplorable the latter may be. Maybe I was naive, but I found it unbelievable that an American infantry platoon at My Lai had slaughtered women and children just for the hell of it. It ran counter to all my training and experience. I had not operated more than a few days with American army units, but I couldn't help but think that this My Lai thing was some awful aberration. My reaction was that Lieutenant Calley was clearly at fault for letting his men run wild, and that his commanding officer should have prosecuted him to the full extent of military law. Since he didn't do that, I felt the commander was as guilty as the murderers under him, and so on up the chain of command. Army officers are told over and over again, "You are responsible for *everything* [italics mine] your men do or fail to do." It's a part of the code; it's just the way things are. Calley and all officers over him should have been held to it.

I had seen back in college how cadets with good training records were allowed to select the branch of the army they wanted to serve in. This meant that many of the "good" cadets were allowed to choose the safe-'n-soft corps like Ordnance, Transportation, or Medical Services. Infantry slots were understandably not all that attractive and were sometimes filled with the lower achievers from the cadet ranks and OCS graduates. Well, one of those slots was filled by Lieutenant William Calley, a college dropout and a just-get-by in OCS. He didn't have the "right stuff," whatever that is, and he probably should have never been given an infantry commission in the first place. I hope the army will learn that you don't find the "right stuff" by scraping the bottom of the barrel. You have to skim it off the top.

It may be just infantryman's prejudice on my part, but I imagine that the Lieutenant Calleys of the world would probably be all right in the quartermaster shed or in some signal battalion. That way they would probably never come to any harm or get the chance to harm anyone else. But I say for God's sake keep them out of the infantry; hell is hot enough without the extra devils.

Chapter 15

GUERRILLA warfare is clandestine by nature. It is imperative to establish good intelligence networks to keep track of the local marauders or any other enemy that might drift into one's area. I had learned about setting up information networks and running smalltime agents when I was at the Special Warfare School. Once in-country I received ten thousand piasters a month to pay for the intelligence net I established out in the villages and hamlets in my district. The money was said to be from CIA funds, but we picked it up each month at the office of the army intelligence advisors back in the province capital. Officially, the money was to be used for "village development" projects, but expenditures were purposely unreceipted so the funds could go toward maintaining the local intelligence operation.

In actual practice I paid for information only when I had to. Local civilians usually did not demand money for information, so it was sometimes used to entice turncoat Viet Cong to come by and spill the beans on their buddies.

The shadowy nature of the system made the quality of the information we received difficult to assess. Some tips were accurate but others were not. It was hard to judge any given piece of information, so we worked hard to keep in touch with reliable agents. We would set up secret meetings with our agents, go sneaking around the hamlets at night, and hold whispered conversations in the dimly lit corners of little thatch huts. It was not unusual to have to haggle about price, estab-

lishing the value of the intelligence the informant had. I had
to find out what kind of information was being offered: were
we talking about troop movements, school bombings, arms
caches, or what? I had to assess the source: was this informant
directly knowledgeable, or had he simply overheard something some passerby said after having chugged a few beers?
If I paid for information I wanted it to be relevant to my needs
and I wanted it to be from a high-quality source. Failing the
presence of a perfect world, of course, I often had to do with
lower-quality intelligence than I would have liked. Any time
I went on an operation based on recruited information, I was
very jumpy. I was always afraid we were being set up, that I
had been suckered into some kind of a trap.

One of the minor VCI officials in my district was an occasional source of information. One night the VCI and his local
contact man were passed through our gate guard and presented
themselves at the team house door. They wanted to talk. I was
in the middle of being given a haircut by the village barber,
so I motioned the two men on in and offered them cigarettes
and some hot tea. The barber finished clipping my hair with
his old-fashioned hand shears and began the painful process
of dry-shaving around the back of my neck and around my
ears. Another teammate always stood watch when one of us
got a haircut. The guard always had an M-16 in hand and
watched particularly closely when the razor blade came out.
The barber would whet the razor on the palm of his hand and
begin shaving, *sans* lather, everything from the bottom of the
hairline down to the crest of the shoulder. Shaving the forehead and the edge of the ears was also part of the Oriental haircut treatment, so there was a lot of blade work to be
done. It tended to make the shavee very nervous if he was an
American with a big price on his head. I usually accepted the
entire treatment because I tried to adopt as many of the native
customs as possible, but this time I waved off the final ministrations and made do with just the haircut. Sergeant Fitz had
been standing guard for me so I had him escort the barber
back to the compound gate. That left me alone in the room
with the VCI and the contact man. I made the requisite polite
inquiries to each of them and began the bargaining session.
Never underestimating the real intent of the VCI, I made sure
my hand stayed close to my pistol grip.

The informant said that the next evening his hamlet would be paid a visit by a district-level VCI officer. The officer would be coming in for a visit with his wife, who lived in the hamlet, and he would probably stay overnight. We set up a meeting for the next evening just outside the informant's hamlet. At that time he would verify that the VCI official had actually come in and would lead us to the house where he was staying. A group of us would then move in and make the snatch, and I would pay the informant for the tip. The informant agreed to the scheme, and he and his contact man went out the door and disappeared into the darkness.

The next afternoon Sergeant Abney and I selected ten Hoa Haos for the operation. We wanted good men we knew we could trust. We left our village well after dark, traveling up-canal in small sampans. We quietly poled and paddled our way along in the small wooden boats. It was a clear night, with the stars flashing brightly in the black sky. I glanced up at the sky and knew we had to get the operation completed before the moon came up. A bright moon would reduce the cover of darkness and make us vulnerable to attack ourselves.

We arrived at our assigned spot well after ten p.m. I was already worried about the potential for an ambush, so I sent a small reconnaisance group out to check the perimeter of the village. The men came back and reported finding nothing unusual. The informant showed up as scheduled, verified that the VCI officer was in the hamlet, and said that he could lead us to him. I made a partial payment to the man then and there as a demonstration of good faith.

A path led through the middle of the small hamlet. I spread the men out on either side of the path and whispered a warning about the importance of being alert, silent, and very cautious. Sergeant Abney took five men on the right and I led five men on the left. The hooch we were going to hit was on the right side. Our plan was to have Sergeant Abney's group go behind the targeted hooch and cover the rear. My team would get in front of the house and move in from that direction.

Each team would be responsible for checking out the area around the target on its side of the road. That meant that several of the neighboring hooches on each side would have to be inspected prior to our closing in on our prey. We had to ensure that the hooches did not hide a platoon of Viet Cong just waiting for us to turn our backs. We would use a prearranged flashlight code to tell each other when our checks were complete and all was ready for the snatch. When everything was set, my group would rush across the road, crash into the hooch, grab the VCI and any of his fellows, gag them, and rush back out of the grass house, dragging the prisoners with us. Abney's group was to stay outside and give us cover in case anything went wrong. When we came out of the house and moved off toward our rendezvous point, Abney was to swing his group in and protect our rear as we moved away. All that may be simple to describe, but it ain't easy to do.

The night was very dark despite the clear twinkling of the stars. I could hardly see the ground and the bushes in front of me, let alone any potential enemies waiting on the sidelines. We crept along, passing hooch after hooch, each one practically bordering on the narrow road that passed through the center of the hamlet.

I was worried about the local dogs. If one of those mutts started yapping at us, others would join in and the noise was sure to bring attention. The dogs might think nothing about other Vietnamese walking through the hamlet at night, but if they got wind of an American the howling wouldn't stop until they had run us off. The potential threat from the water buffalo was even worse. If Abney or I got upwind of a water buffalo we were really in trouble. Groups of these beasts would herd up together at night and stand around sleeping in various parts of the hamlet. Vietnamese could walk past them all night long and they would never even flinch. Just let an American come within fifty yards, though, and the snorting, shuffling, and horn waving would begin. If one of us got too close, we were liable to get our butts run over or tossed into the next province.

Sure enough, right in the middle of the hamlet a dog started yapping at us. One of the Vietnamese men was on point for my team and I was right behind him. A scrawny little mutt ran from a hooch and stopped directly in front of the point man. The dog braced his legs shoulder-width apart, lifted his head, and began a staccato, high-pitched barking. The point man tried to shush him by calling quietly to him and stretching his hand out to the dog so he could take a friendly sniff. It didn't work. The young dog was not interested in the proffered hand, and he wasn't going to give way without a good reason.

That damned dog was going to call the whole village down on us. I was desperately trying to figure out what to do when the door cloth of the hooch was pulled back by someone inside. A stern voice muttered something to the dog. The dog didn't budge and just kept arfing away. I was sure the little flea-ridden hound was going to foul up the whole operation. Suddenly a piece of wood came flying out of the doorway of the hooch. It smacked the little mutt right amidships and bowled him over. He yelped when the stick hit him on the ribs, but he was up in an instant and skittered away in the darkness with his tail tucked between his legs.

Quiet returned. No one made a sound. The door flap was still being held back by an unseen hand. I didn't know if the person was looking for the dog or if he had spotted one of us. We all remained frozen in our positions and waited to see what would happen next. Finally the door cloth dropped. We all breathed a sigh of relief and double-checked around us to make sure everything else appeared to be all right. No one noticed anything unusual, so we all crouched low and continued on down the row of hooches.

My team finally got into position in front of the target's house. Two of the men were sent ahead to the closest huts on our side of the road to make sure they did not contain any Cong waiting to ambush us. They came back reporting all clear, so I took my flashlight with its red filter in place and blinked across the way to where Sergeant Abney was supposed to be. After a few seconds the proper series of red flashes came back from Abney's position. The security team was in position and we were ready to make the snatch.

I posted one man off to our left to stay back and provide warning or covering fire if the need arose. Two men were sent on across the village road to the front of the target's house. They crouched over and ran across the hard-packed dirt in front of the small hooch. Each man went to one of the front corners of the house and hugged up against the wall. The other two men and I were to run across to the house and just barge through the door without ever stopping. After about two or three seconds, the two men already over there were to follow us through the door. I saw the top edge of the moon glint from the distant horizon.

I signaled the men with me to get up. We bent over at the

waist and held our rifles loosely before us. I nodded again and we took off running. Getting across the open ground seemed to take forever. The door to the hooch was a piece of thatch framed in split bamboo. I slammed into it at full speed and tore it from its perch. I thrashed about blindly as I struggled to get out of the grip of the splintered door. I could tell a small lantern was burning over by the bed pallets, and I had a vague vision of an astonished, naked woman rising from her reed mattress as an equally naked man rolled away from her side. I finally got loose from the broken door, but my partners, who had come in right behind me, already had the prisoners covered.

The naked woman got about two exclamatory words out before a cloth was stuffed into her face and a gag was tied around her head. She tried to squirm away from the man holding her, but a cuff on the neck made her go slack in his arms. The naked man never offered any resistance. He was thrown a pair of black peasant pants that had been lying beside the reed mattresses and was told to put them on. The girl was jerked up and told to put on shirt and pants. Both the woman and the man got into their clothes with dispatch. Any slowness brought a jab with a rifle butt. We bound them by simply tying their elbows together behind their backs. The man was gagged like the woman and we were ready to go. I was now paranoid about there being a Cong unit out there just waiting for us to make our break.

I stepped back outside. Standing in the darkness under the eaves of the thatch roof, I looked and listened. I muttered curses at seeing the moon rising above the distant tree line. The clear but previously dark night was being lit up by the glow of the pale yellow sphere. I looked across to where my security man was supposed to be hiding, but I could see nothing in the dark shadows of the bushes. I motioned to those still in the hooch and they came out, practically dragging the man and woman with them. Muffled complaints were answered with muttered threats. We now had to sprint back across the open roadway and make our way out of the hamlet and back to the boats. Abney's team was to cover our withdrawal and follow us out.

I was afraid to take off across the opening to the other side of the narrow road. Shadows hid everything around us, but the area we had to cross was now bathed in moonlight. I felt like a duck in a shooting gallery. I just didn't know if there were any customers around to take shots at me. I knew I couldn't stay there against the house, so I gritted my teeth and prepared to go. I gripped my M-16 tightly against me, flipped the safety switch off, and curled my finger loosely around the trigger. I looked at the other men kneeling or standing by the house. They were all looking at me and waiting for my signal. I jerked my head in the direction we were to go and whispered loudly, *"Đi đi mau!"*—"Let's get the hell out of here!"

The two men in charge of the prisoners jumped up and took off across the roadway, dragging their charges with them. They were about halfway across the moonlit space when the other two men and I took off behind them. I was about two steps into my run when off to the left a dark figure came into my peripheral vision. The crouching, moving specter was approaching the house from my left; somehow, without taking the time to really look at him, I could tell he was armed. I leaped back to the corner of the house and in the same motion brought my M-16 up to my shoulder. As the rifle butt snugged into my shoulder and as I pulled the gun barrel over to its target, I was already squeezing down on the trigger. I was looking over my gun sight and anticipating the kick of gun's firing when I realized the man I was going to kill was Sergeant Abney. The next second seemed to last an hour.

First, I was shocked by the realization that it was Abney out there on the end of my gun barrel. My God, it's Abney! In that same millisecond I sensed the growing tension in my trigger finger. I knew the rifle was about to fire. In my memory everything seems to have proceeded in slow motion. Now I recognized Abney, but I couldn't stop my finger from still tightening down on the trigger. It was as if the finger was responding to old neural impulses and had not received the information that I was about to shoot a friend. I felt as if I had to frantically send another communication to my finger, telling it to ease off the trigger. I also tried to move the gun barrel off target, desperate to do something before the firing pin was released. All this took place in the blink of an eye, but it seemed as if I were a spectator watching a slow-motion film, waiting to see if I could relax my finger before the rifle started firing.

The rifle didn't fire, thank God! It was a near thing. I sagged weak-kneed against the wall of the hooch. Abney had realized that I had a bead on him about the same second I realized it was he in my gun sight. While I was trying to stop myself, he was trying to get out a sound of protest. Abney's whispered "Don't shoot!" came out just as I was able to relax my grip on the trigger.

Abney came hustling on over to me, his eyes casting about him in the dark. "Jesus Christ," I whispered as he squatted beside me, "I almost killed you!" I leaned back against the wall of the hooch, my rifle slack in my arms and my hands shaking like leaves. It is hard to explain the bonds that develop between men who live and fight together in a world of isolated desperation, but suffice it to say that I loved Abney like a brother. I was numb.

"Get out of here," Abney said urgently. "My men are coming in! You guys should already be ahead of us!"

I shoved off the wall without making a reply and loped out across the road to the darkness on the other side. I caught up with my group and we began making our way back to the boats. I cautioned them to keep spread out, to keep an eye to our front and sides, and to keep quiet. I tried to pay attention to what we were doing, but I kept flashing back to the chilling freeze-frame in my memory where I was squeezing down on my trigger as I realized it was Abney in my rifle sights. Holy God, I had almost shot one of my own men! I couldn't believe it.

We got back to our boats without incident, and Abney's group came in behind us as we were getting the prisoners stowed into one of the sampans. We loaded up and set off for home. Moving down a canal at night was a tricky business, especially during the dry season when the water fell far below the canal banks. It was impossible to see over the banks while sitting in one of the boats, and we could never be sure the enemy wasn't up there waiting for us to come under their guns. Being ambushed in the open boats was sure death, so we treated any movement up on the banks with great paranoia. We were constantly stopping and putting someone up there just to have a look in the moonlight and check things out.

We got back to our compound just as the pre-dawn light began to give a gray tint to the eastern sky. We called back to province headquarters and requested that a chopper be sent out to pick up the prisoners. It turned out later that we had made a good haul: the man we had captured was the assistant VCI district chief. He and his wife provided the boys in S-2 with lots of information, or so they said; but as usual, none of it got back down to us until it was too old to be any good.

The incident with Abney still provides me with some of my most chilling dreams. In them I am always leaning up against a tree or house, and some sound or motion off to my left gets my attention. I throw up my rifle and bring the sights onto the target. I am already squeezing the trigger when I recognize Sergeant Abney. Then the frightening part begins. My finger continues to squeeze the trigger as if it has a will of its own. I try to relax the finger, to stop the trigger pull, but I can't. Abney watches helplessly, forced in my dream to stand frozen and stare at me with terror in his eyes. He is a captive spectator as I struggle to keep from killing him. In every dream I have the same terrifying fight with my finger. One message to it is saying, "Pull, pull," the other screaming, "Stop, stop! It's Abney!" I never do pull the trigger, but I think it is because the dream is never allowed to end. I come awake with my heart pounding and my right hand practically cramped from the tension.

I wish the dream would stop coming. I am always afraid that one night my trigger finger will not stop, that somehow my willpower will not be sufficient to the task, and that I will kill Sergeant Abney. What screams or reaction that might bring I do not know. I guess that is part of the fear.

THE WATER-TAXI FROM TRAM CHIM GLIDED UP TO THE DOCK at An Long and deposited its passengers on the rickety contrivance that substituted for a pier. Sergeant Fitz and I, along with District Chief Thu and two of his staff, had come to An Long to inspect the local militia platoon and to pow-wow with the village chief. An Long was built on the banks where the Dong Tien Canal and the Mekong River met. From where we stood on the pier, I could see out across the broad Mekong and watch it flow by the mouth of the canal only a few hundred yards away. High up over the banks of the river and canal, and right at their juncture, was the old French fort.

It was a fascinating structure to come across out there in the middle of nowhere: a large, clearly European fortification of quarried stone, bordered on one side by the river and on the adjacent side by the canal. It was hemmed in the rest of the way around by the village huts and shops that had grown up in its shadow over the years. It was a large fort with perfectly preserved walls and a tall, crenellated central watchtower over the main gate. It was like something out of a film about the French Foreign Legion. Each time I saw it, I half expected to see a tricolor flying from the flagpole over the main gate and men in white kepis walking the ramparts. I never found out how old the fort was, but I was told that the French had built it there as a way-station between the coast and Phnom Penh in the early days when they had ruled all of Indo-China.

Our small party made its way up to the lichen-covered walls of the fort along an avenue bordered by overhanging banana trees. A series of small shops lined the way, and the street was noisy with activity. The huge wooden doors, apparently original, swung open as we approached. I marveled as we walked through the gate and into a large cool cloister which completely surrounded the courtyard. The local militia commander presented himself to the district chief and escorted us around the fort, which was clearly his pride and joy. The cloister served as the barracks for his troops. Hammocks were strung in the breezeway, and blackened walls were evidence of the use of open cooking fires without benefit of chimney.

Despite its grimy state, I was amazed at the good physical condition of the place. The walls were all sound, and the parapets and towers were as strong as the day they were built. A small headquarters building sat in the center of the courtyard. Louvered French shutters and doors still hung in place, paint chipped and weatherworn, but keeping out the rain for the natives just as they had once done for the colonial masters.

The district chief and I inspected the militia troops and discussed some problems with the platoon commander, and finally passed back outside the walls to go to our meeting with the village chief.

"Well, *Trung úy*," asked Thụ, "what do you think of the old fort?"

"I think it's fascinating," I said. "I'm glad you are able to keep it in such good repair."

"It was made well. Fortunately, it stays in good repair by

itself,'' said Thụ with a grin. "I'm glad you liked it; maybe we can spend some more time here in the future." I didn't know what he meant by that, so I just smiled and nodded my head.

We walked on down into the village and found the village office in a busy, alley-like street next to the canal. It was just another grass and thatch hut, but it had the quasi-official symbol of office proudly posted on the lone table in the main room: an old manual typewriter used for making out reports. We greeted the village chief, whom I had met on several previous occasions, and were introduced to several hangers-on who were standing around trying to look helpful.

We all sat around the single table and discussed village problems as we sipped hot tea from the little handleless cups. The chief was noting the need for repairs on the schoolhouse roof and on a bridge north of town, before it collapsed entirely. I thought it was strange when the district chief nodded without comment. He usually was the first to respond to requests for assistance—with reasons why none was to be forthcoming. The village chief then pointed out that An Long was the largest and busiest village in Dong Tien district, even larger than Tram Chim, and said that he felt that the district's Regional Forces company ought to be stationed in An Long to make sure the people and commerce were protected. I expected Thụ to explain that the RF company was stationed in Tram Chim, as were the district offices and military headquarters, because it was central to the entire district. An Long was on one border of the district, literally hours away from villages on the opposite border. The district simply could not be administered effectively from An Long. But Thụ made no comment. The village chief looked over at me with a questioning smile. I just blinked back at him with no expression other than one of pleasant attention. Inside I wondered what exactly was going on here.

After the meeting broke up, we were all given a meal at the village chief's hooch. The food was good, the beer was plentiful, and at midafternoon I was sorry to have to go back down to the dock to catch the water-taxi for our return to Tram Chim. I wasn't in the mood to sit for an hour on a tiny wooden seat that was guaranteed to give me a backache and leg cramps. Fitz was groaning all the way back to the dock about the coming torture, and there wasn't a damned thing I could say to him except to shut up and take it like a man.

The small water-taxi was filled to capacity with our group plus a young man and woman with several trussed-up ducks and an old farmer with a pig, two hoes, and what looked like a bundle of miscellaneous clothing all tied up in a ball. As the boat got under way I tried to pack my carcass into as comfortable a position as I could find, and I started watching the canal bank on my side of the boat. Fitz had automatically placed himself so he could do the same thing on the other side, and I couldn't help but grin at noticing that he was having to fight the pig for legroom.

The drone of the small boat's engine, the hot breeze, and the aftereffects of the meal and beer would have put me to sleep if it had not been for the cramped position I was stuck in. My knees and back were really beginning to give me the devil when Thụ leaned back and began to talk with me. I was almost grateful for the distraction.

"Do you like An Long, *Trung úy*?" he asked with a smile. He spoke loudly to be heard over the sound of the engine.

"Sure, it's a nice place. All the river traffic and business make it a little more active than Tram Chim, don't they?"

"Yes, much more happens in An Long than in Tram Chim. It is a much nicer place to live, too. There are more shops, there are businesses, and the old fort! An excellent place for a military headquarters! I'll tell you, *Trung úy*, I am thinking about moving the district headquarters to An Long."

I frowned at that news and tried to think of something to say that wouldn't be offensive. "Are you joking with me, *Dại úy*? You know the province headquarters won't allow that. If we moved to An Long we would never see the other side of the district. Tram Chim is in the middle of Dong Tien; it's equally accessible to everyone. In An Long most of the people in the district would never be able to reach us."

"Fewer problems from them, fewer problems for us, *Trung úy*," said Thụ, smiling blandly. "But you are right, province will never agree. That is, they won't agree unless you recommend it too. There are good reasons that could be given, *Trung úy*."

"I'm sorry, *Dại úy*," I said, shaking my head, "there are no good reasons I can think of."

"*Trung úy,* there are small businesses in An Long and Hong Ngu that do a lot of traffic in items from China, Thailand, and Cambodia. They want a secure place to do their work. They can make it profitable to everyone if we provide that security."

"You mean with the RF company," I said, remembering the discussion with the village chief. So that was it, I thought. The village chief and Thụ were in cahoots to try to get the district headquarters moved to An Long.

"Yes, with the RF's and with our presence, too. The village businessmen feel sure that we will protect where we are living. These people will pay well, *Trung úy.*" I knew what kind of businesses Thụ was talking about. The Mekong was the major waterway for all of Southeast Asia. Contraband jade, gold, dope, and even some of the more exotic ingredients for Oriental medicines were traded up and down the river, especially in the border areas between countries. Hong Ngu and An Long were the first two major Mekong villages on our side of the border, so I wasn't surprised that local businesses were engaged in bootleg enterprises of one kind or another. Now, it seemed, they wanted protection and were willing to pay for it. The district chief was willing to sell.

"I'm sorry, I don't think province headquarters will let us move. I cannot give recommendations that are sure to get me in trouble with my colonel." I leaned back in my seat and looked sympathetically at the district chief. "My hands are tied," I said with a shrug and a smile. "They know I would be crazy to recommend a move to An Long." I leaned farther back and half turned to stare back out at the canal bank. I wanted to end the conversation. I was no saint, but my general dislike for Thụ and his incompetence made me quick to think double ill of him for his corruption. Thụ looked at me for a moment with a smile that meant nothing, then turned and stared straight ahead without saying another word.

I sat there and stewed. It wasn't just the incident itself that made me mad, it was this whole thing about corruption in the government. I needed a distraction from my backache, so I sat there and fumed about the incidences of corruption that I had run into again and again. Vietnam was a veritable cesspool of government obliquity.

I already knew my district chief was corrupt: he had tried

to get me to buy him an American outboard motorboat with money set aside for repairing the roof of a maternity clinic in one of our other villages. The National Police were corrupt: the "White Mice," so called because of their white shirts and hats, were known to be pliable to a little cash pressure on the palm. Anything that had to be processed through the government paper mill went better if the right hands got some cash to grease the skids of a barely functioning bureaucracy.

The company commander of our district's Regional Forces company was corrupt: he was always stealing funds from his company's payroll. It wasn't that hard to do since the Vietnamese pay system was very complicated and many of the militia soldiers were basically illiterate. The men often didn't know how to calculate their own pay, so they were used to just accepting whatever money their pay officer gave them. A couple hundred piasters a month lifted from each man's pay mounted up to a tidy supplement for the company commander.

When we turned in the company commander for this corruption, the province chief pretended great indignation at him. The officer was snatched away in a great hurry and sent back to Can Tho for appropriate action. In four weeks he was back. Promoted.

I knew our province chief could be bought, too. A friend of mine who ran a MAT team in another district hit paydirt one night on a VCI roundup operation. His patrol captured the Viet Cong's province treasurer, the VCI local district chief, and a VCI village chief. The patrol captured guns, documents, and a considerable stash of money along with the captured men. There was no question that these guys were real plums of the local Viet Cong organization.

The VCI were put in the province town jail, supposedly awaiting trial. A couple of weeks went by, but no proceedings got started. Then the word began to circulate that the three prisoners had been released on the orders of the province chief. The word was that the chief had been paid the equivalent of about five thousand dollars to let the men go. The VCI disappeared instantly. My friend who captured those guys was disgusted, and the PSA was livid. I heard he sent blistering complaints all the way back to Saigon. When I heard the news I was pissed off too, but in the long run I was just saddened. It was pitiful to see all that hard work and honest effort go to waste because some corrupt son of a bitch was willing to sell his country down the drain.

It appeared to me that corruption was the clear enemy from within. It was a cancer eating away at the Vietnamese government. Corruption violated the people's hope for fair treatment under their laws and made them cynical about the legitimate needs of government. Corruption helped create a necrotic culture for the germs of revolution, and the major inoculation of honesty required from the Saigon government was never administered.

Chapter 16

At least two men on my team were out on a combat operation practically every night and day. The wear and tear on everyone was considerable, and we were left with little time or stamina to perform the nonmilitary part of our mission. We did what we could, but I never felt it was enough.

I was always behind on my HES and TFES reports. There were hamlets or villages waiting to be visited again, leaders I was supposed to meet, or some special project that needed tending to. But the Cong were always just outside our door, some bandit gang was robbing the fishermen, or some outpost was being attacked. It has been said before: it's hard to remember you came to reclaim the swampland when you're up to your ass in alligators.

I believed very strongly that the first thing the villagers needed was a sense of security. The first right any human has is the right to life, so I set about trying to provide that right with the help of the villagers themselves. That was why I committed myself and my team so strongly to counterguerrilla and counterinsurgency operations.

My team was constantly trying to show the people that they didn't have to just assume that the Viet Cong would come into the village and kill or rob whomever they wished. We wanted to convince the villagers that they could protect themselves, that they could run the Cong off if they would just organize to do it. The five of us on my team were continually out with patrols of one kind or another, and we became known as a group of Americans willing to fight right alongside the villagers we were training.

The old Hoa Hao warriors had a bitter hatred for the Cong and they really liked to see my teammates and me in the village. They would always invite us into their small thatch houses for a cigarette, a cup of tea, or a small glass of *ba si dê,* a potent homemade firewater. We got along well with most of the young militiamen, too. They were not so much pro-government as they were anti–Viet Cong. They wanted their villages to be safe for their families, and they saw that we Americans were there to help them obtain that safety.

One day I was working in our mortar pit, trying to repair our 1944-vintage 81mm mortar. It had collapsed in the mud the previous night while we were in the process of firing it, and I had just discovered that the yoke holding the legs to the barrel had cracked in two. My old friend Trần Trong Tái came into the compound and walked up to me with a big grin plastered on his face. The ex-district chief paid no attention to what I was doing, but simply asked if I could come to his house that evening for a meeting with some of the other Hoa Hao men in the village. He said we would talk, eat, drink, and really make an evening of it. I reminded Tái that it was against my rules for members of the team to be in the village after dark, and I tried to explain that I couldn't very well do myself what I had not allowed my men to do. That logic didn't hold with Tái, though, and he continued to insist that I accept his invitation. When I politely refused again, he looked exasperated and leaned over as if to tell me a secret.

He whispered that the men he wanted me to meet all belonged to a Hoa Hao warrior society, as some would call the primitive-style men's club. Membership was predicated on having fought for Hoa Hao causes, against the Viet Minh, the Viet Cong, or even the central government. Tái told me that I was invited to become an honorary member of the group, that my acceptance by the key men of the village was a great sign of respect, and that I really must find a way to come to his house that evening!

Well, I couldn't refuse after all that, so later in the day I explained to the rest of the guys, and that night I pulled on my best pair of tiger fatigues, donned my blue beret, and walked down to Tái's house in the village. The house looked dark as I approached and I wondered where Tái was. The children were still playing in the darkening village street and the smell of cooking fires and *nước mắm* was heavy in the air. I nodded to the women who were quietly talking in the dark shadows and went on up to Tái's house. I called to Tái through the palm thatch door, and a hand slid it open and waved me in.

A single kerosene lantern was burning in the main room of the house. In the flickering yellow light I could see that a group of about a dozen men, all dressed in black peasant attire, were squatting silently around the walls of the room. The lantern was on a small table in the middle of the room; Tái was sitting on one side of the table and he motioned that I was to take the chair on the other side. I took off my beret and sat down. I didn't know what to expect next; all the faces around me were somber and, to my cautious mind, even angry looking. I began to wonder what I had let myself in for.

Tái began by telling me that he was honored I had been able to come to his house. He motioned to the glum figures around us and said that the men of the village were honored that I had accepted their invitation to become a part of their group. My willingness to join them showed that we were all brothers in the same cause, he said. My slow translation of Tái's speech soon left me so far behind that I completely lost the thread of his monologue. I just nodded from time to time and tried to smile where I thought a smile was appropriate. I wasn't going to venture a comment about anything.

Tái finally motioned to one of the gray-bearded men in the corner of the room. The old man came up and began a kind of droning chant as he moved around the table, facing in, then facing out. Finally he grasped my arm and said something to the others in the room. I couldn't follow what he was saying, but one or two other men stepped out of the shadows and spoke briefly to the group. When they finished, they nodded politely in my direction and moved back to their places. I didn't know what was going on anymore, so I just sat there with my mouth shut.

Next, a man brought a duck from the rear of the house. Ducks were everywhere in the village, as were chickens and pigs. The birds were allowed into the houses so they could help the pigs clean the scraps and bits of food from the earthen floors. This particular duck looked to be a healthy specimen, not all that common a phenomenon among the ducks I usually saw. The man with the duck brought it over to the table and held the bird firmly while Tái cut its throat. Blood gushed out into a small bowl. I wondered what the hell this was all about. The blood flow slowed to a gentle stream and finally to a slow drip. The duck quivered in the man's arms, and that seemed to signal the end of the exsanguination. He took the bird back to the kitchen part of the house and left it for the women to cook. Tái smiled and told me that his wife would prepare the duck for the meal we would eat later.

Tái then picked up the bowl full of duck blood and looked at it as he talked to the men around us. Finally he stuck his finger in the blood and drew it away. The thick strand that followed his finger showed that the blood was almost completely clotted. In a few more minutes the blood thoroughly congealed, and I began to suspect that I wasn't going to like whatever was coming next. I didn't.

Tái told me that protocol required that I take a chopstick and cut a wedge of the clot off from the rest. Then I was to pick up the bowl, tilt it toward my mouth, and direct the clump of clot into my mouth with my chopsticks. I guess he could tell from my expression that eating raw duck blood was not my idea of a good time, so he said he would demonstrate first, then I would take my plug, and then I was to pass the bowl on to the other men in the room. That way we would all share in the same bowl of blood, a gesture signifying our bond or something like that. I wasn't translating too well again; I was trying to convince myself that I was actually going to go through with my part of this blood-eating business.

Tái picked up the bowl and deftly rolled a big dollop of blood into his mouth. Mouth full, eyes sparkling, blood dripping from his lips, he passed me the bowl. I thought I would have to treat this like the man who first ate an oyster: just tilt my head back, flip a mucousy orb into my mouth, keep the throat open, and let it slide right on down. Do not stop at go, do not collect two hundred dollars, just slide, slide, slide. If I did it right, I figured I might not even taste it.

I sliced off a chunk of the coagulated blood, lifted the bowl to my lips, and slid the clot over to my mouth with my chopsticks. I flipped my head back, ready to let the blood slide right on down the tube, but the sensation of the still-warm blood in my mouth almost made me retch. I had to stretch my neck upward again, trying to get the slime to go down. This time I was successful, and with great relief I passed the bowl to the man behind me. I forced a smile as I gave it to him and hoped I had blood dribbling down my chin like Tái did. After such a gut-wrenching experience, I wanted everyone to know that I had done it, by God!

As the bowl went around the room, the atmosphere began to lighten. I even heard a few chuckles from the men in the shadows. Tái was beaming and was giving everyone a sort of I-told-you-so speech on what a good guy I was. I was relieved that most of the men seemed to be smiling and nodding in agreement. Tái started into another speech and pulled out a small package from his pocket. It was wrapped in a piece of yellow paper and tied with a string. Tái tore open the package and shook out its contents. He handed it across the table to me and I took the gift in my hand. It was the claw of a tiger, with a silver cap on one end which had an undulating dragon carved into it. Tái smiled and fished inside his shirt to pull a similar claw out into the dim light of the kerosene lantern. He held it out for me to see and told me that all the men in the group wore them as an amulet against bad luck and bad nerves. He said the men wanted me to have one as a gift from them. By wearing it I would be one with them, and if others saw it around my neck they would know that the group had accepted me. It would be presumptive evidence that I was a man to be trusted, among the Hoa Hao at least.

I was terribly pleased and excited. One of our major day-to-day efforts was to get on with the local native population. It was very difficult for a different-looking, different-acting, different-speaking, different-thinking person to be accepted in that conservative, highly traditional culture. There were just too many slips to be made, too many oversights to be mis-construed, and too many attitudes to be changed for real acceptance to come easily. I felt that this gesture from some of the older men of the village was a signal that my team's efforts to get along and be helpful were really being appreciated.

I accepted the gift by clasping it between both my hands and holding it out between Tái and me. I bowed my head deeply and thanked him for the gift and the honor of membership in their group, speaking loudly enough in my halting Vietnamese for all the men to hear. I thanked them for their confidence in me. I said that I was pleased to be a representative of my people to their village and district. I said that I would continue to do the best I could to help them improve their lives and fight their enemies. The men standing around the shadowed walls all nodded and smiled as I spoke. I hoped they understood me, because I really meant it.

Soon after I finished speaking, the women brought out the evening meal. The duck was brought back, all chopped up and cooked. With some rice and one of the local green leafy vegetables, it was a very good meal. When we were about halfway done with the food before us, a turtle was brought into the room. It was whole and had been cooked in its shell, simply laid on its back in the coals of a fire and left there for a few hours. The turtle had stewed in its own pot.

One of the men cut the bottom plate of the turtle and pulled it away from the rest of the upturned shell. The steaming entrails were pulled out and the head was cut off. The head was politely placed on my bowl of rice. I knew it was given to me as a gesture of respect, so I picked up the cigar-shaped head and began to gnaw on the tough, dry turtle skin. After the duck blood it didn't seem so bad.

Later in the evening, after I had been laden with food and laced with beer, I began making my apologies and slowly got ready to leave. Tái came over to the door to see me off, and as I stopped in front of him he grabbed me by the shoulders. He leaned forward as if to kiss me on one cheek, but instead of kissing he brought his cheek close to mine and made an audible sniff, first on one side, then on the other. It was a very old and traditional way for a Vietnamese man to express affection for another. I was surprised and moved by Tái's expression of care. It made the duck blood seem not so bad after all.

Chapter 17

Two Americans assigned to another MAT team in our province were killed in an action to the south of Tram Chim. I didn't know either man very well, but for some reason I was called in and assigned to escort their records and personal property back to Saigon. I had been out for three months without a break, so I guess province thought I needed a trip to the rear.

I reported in at Cao Lanh, where I picked up all the necessary paperwork and personal property of the KIA's. One of the sergeants in the compound gave me a jeep ride out to the single-runway airstrip that served the province town, where I caught a ride to Saigon on an Air America plane. The planes normally stopped in once a day, just to bring in or pick up the occasional traveler or special cargo. The plane was usually a Swiss-made PC-6 Pilatus Porter, one of those overpowered single-prop aircraft that are especially designed for getting into and out of tight little airstrips. It was common knowledge that Air America was a front organization for the CIA; it was a so-called proprietary company, and it was presumed that these planes fit the agencies' peculiar needs. Everyone knew not to ask where the planes were coming from or what the load was. We just accepted our free rides and kept our mouths shut.

Going from my village back to Saigon, a hundred miles to the rear, was an amazing experience. I remember being awed by the power lines, paved roads, and television antennas. It was almost as if I had never seen such things before. As I walked along a busy street en route from the airfield to my billet, I thought how neat it was to have an asphalt road for the trucks and pedicabs to travel on. It seemed like such an ingenious idea! I stooped over and touched the hard, black surface of the road. I guess I wanted to make sure it was real, and to get a feel of what it was like to have something under me besides the pasty ooze of Delta mud.

The electric power lines were astonishing, too. I just stood on a corner by the big MACV headquarters complex and stared at the lines, trying to imagine where they all went. There wasn't a single power line in my entire district, and I guess I had sort of forgotten about electricity. Yet, here in Saigon every pole, tree, or building corner seemed to support an entwined jumble of thick electrical cables. It was like the time I saw my first escalator, when I was twelve years old. I was filled with a sense of amazement combined with a somewhat disparaging sense of amusement.

After the quiet pace of my village, where there wasn't a single four-wheeled vehicle within twenty miles, the bedlam of Saigon's traffic seemed incredible. Army trucks full of boxes and crates, civilian buses laden with people and chickens, old automobiles that looked like rejects from American junkyards, gaudily painted cyclos, and thousands of motorbikes crammed every street. At every intersection the traffic solidified into a mass of people and steel that bellowed, tooted, honked, ding-a-linged, and cursed in at least five languages. The cacophony of sound and the heady smell of blue diesel smoke laced with a whiff of Vietnamese cooking are what I think of as the true essence of Saigon.

I was always astonished by Saigon or any other place where there were a lot of Americans around. I was uneasy there because I never felt that I was a part of those other Americans. They seemed so different from my teammates or the other men I knew who lived out by themselves in the villages. The guys in Saigon or Can Tho were "civilized" Americans. Some even seemed to have a source of laundered uniforms. They appeared to worry about different things, like "Will the club be open tonight?" or "Will the pizza chopper make its run tonight?" They used jargon I wasn't used to. Vietnam was referred to simply as "Nam," an abbreviation that somehow always seemed tinged with discourtesy. The United States was "the world," implying that this backward little country with its backward little problems wasn't really part of the globe we nice Americans ride around on day after day. Killing people was referred to as "wasting" them, a macho transmogrification that somehow implied a similarity between people and condiments from the quartermaster. The country's natives were referred to as "gooks" or "slopes," racial epithets that seemed particularly ironic when coming from white or black servicemen who would have been enraged at hearing the word "nigger."

I was also always taken aback by the degree of racial tension evident in the big American camps. Black Power seemed to be the only theme of many black servicemen I saw around the big cities and American camps. I never questioned the fact that black GI's could point to many acts of prejudice against blacks in general, and probably against themselves individually, but the black soldier's almost monolithic prejudice against whites seemed to me to be terribly destructive and only served to increase the targets available to white racists. I was only an outsider looking in, mind you, and maybe the fact that overt racial animosity was allowed at all caused me to take more notice of it than it deserved. Out on the small teams I was familiar with, it was unthinkable to allow racism or prejudice to show their faces without a sharp challenge. We were all smart enough to realize that our mutual survival required the full cooperation of every man. Our attitude was that of cover your buddy and he will cover you. Skin color be damned.

I remember thinking that it seemed as if we had two different armies back in Saigon, one white and one black. I wondered how many men were dying on combat patrols because black men wouldn't talk with white men or vice versa. It seemed to me that black racism and white racism were equal crimes—both should have been punished to the full extent of the law. War allows no room for racism. Rules that sanction it are unconscionable violations of the rights of every soldier.

THERE WERE A NUMBER OF OFFICER BILLET "HOTELS" IN SAI-gon. Several were located just outside Tan Son Nhut airbase, where many army and air force officers worked and where many transient officers stayed when they needed a temporary billet. At least one of the hotels, the Ohio I think, had an air-conditioned restaurant on top. The restaurant had plate-glass picture windows all around so one could dine in comfort while looking out on the bustling Orient down below. I had heard of the place, so on the second and last evening of my trip to the rear a friend of mine, Lieutenant James Parton, and I went over to the Ohio Hotel to have an early dinner. The steaks were $1.50 with potato and tossed salad. The mixed drinks were 50¢ each. Parton and I went double on the steaks and at least quadruple on the drinks. We were both stationed on MAT teams, so we wanted to take full advantage of the opportunity to sample the amenities of service in the rear echelons.

Parton and I took a table right next to a big picture window, and it wasn't long before I noticed that the adjacent building was a large American army hospital. We had been sitting there for a good while, slowly eating our meal and carrying on a lazy conversation, when I noticed a flurry of activity on the hospital landing pad directly below our window. Suddenly a helicopter appeared over the rooftops. It was followed by another, then another. The choppers landed one at a time on the pad down below. They were met by scrambling teams of medics and nurses, who helped unload the bloody cargo. Wounded Americans covered with mud and blood were helped or carried off the choppers. The men were already patched up in various ways: big combat bandages were tied to the side of the head or across the belly, arms were slung, legs were bandaged, and some were already plugged into IV infusion bottles. Some men had no recognizable bandages; they just seemed to be wrapped in the tattered remnants of their jungle fatigues. From our air-conditioned, convivial environment we stared out at the gory scene being played out below. The men who were stumbling off the choppers on their own or who were being helped away by the nurses had agony and shock written all over them. The dead were unceremoniously tumbled off and out of the way to allow each chopper to take off quickly and make room for the next one. Right outside my window American soldiers were dying from shot and shell, nurses and physicians were working frantically to save the wounded, and chaplains were praying over the dead. It was like watching television.

As I watched all this, I absentmindedly continued to eat my

steak and drink my bourbon and water. The plate-glass windows kept out all sound except the muted whop-whop of the helicopters' rotor blades. It was easy to have the sensation of not really being there, not participating in the same life as those bloody men being rushed into the hospital next door. The situation outside the window seemed remote and unrelated to the situation inside. Inside there was music, dancing, good steak, and the jingle of ice in the whiskey glasses. Outside there was war, agony, and death. Later I thought of that experience as a capsule of the American problem in Vietnam. Many of the Americans in Vietnam and all the Americans in the States were on the inside of the glass looking out, living in cool, sanitized comfort while outside in the heat and bog men were dying before their eyes. The outside seemed so remote and unreal to those on the inside that they never even stopped eating their steak long enough to consider what the hell it was they were doing. The men outside kept dying, and the men inside just kept eating and shaking their heads at the suffering going on all around them.

As we walked back to our billets later in the evening, Parton suggested we stop in a local Vietnamese bar he knew about. He had been there before, he said, and it was a clean, quiet place. I agreed, and so we turned into a small courtyard down the street. No sooner had we walked into the enclave than we were surrounded by a horde of leaping, laughing, grabbing Vietnamese women. They were all calling to us or pulling on us, trying to convince us to select one of them as a partner for the evening. Some grabbed our hands, others pulled at our watches, and still others stuffed their hands into our pants pockets and clutched for a handful of penis or testicle. One young lady got my cap and went dancing away to a corner of the room, hoping I would follow. I couldn't do that since one of her colleagues had my scrotal contents in her hands and was pulling in the opposite direction. Parton and I both played along for a while just so we could get to a booth and sit down. Once there we ordered some drinks and after many refusals finally convinced the girls we weren't interested in their wares. They all pouted and simpered and called us ''cheap charlies,'' but they finally left us alone with our drinks.

Parton and I both were going back to our teams the next morning, so we knew this was the last of our relaxation for quite a while. We nursed our drinks and made rambling small talk for a long time before moving on back to our billets. I kept thinking about the restaurant and the hospital landing pad, thinking about the people on the "inside" and those on the "outside." I was about to go back to being an outsider again and the thought of it filled me with despair.

LIEUTENANT CANTRELL STUCK HIS HEAD THROUGH THE TEAM house doorway and said, "Hey, Dave, the chaplain's here." His head of red hair quickly disappeared again.

I looked up from the well-worn paperback novel I was reading and called to him, "I'll be there in a minute. I've got to get on my boots." No rest for the weary, I thought. I had been back from Saigon for almost a month now, with never a day off. This was a Sunday, if my calendar was right, so I had kept everyone in for the day to get some much needed rest. I hadn't expected visitors.

I put my book down on the mattress beside me and bent over to stuff my feet into my boots. I laced up rapidly, and as I stood to pull on my shirt I remembered that I had taken an unusual liberty that morning: I had not shaved. I almost always insisted that everyone shave daily. It was just a ploy to make the men remember that we did have some rules and customs and that not all of them were destroyed by being stuck out in the middle of nowhere. It was an anchor point that helped keep us civilized.

As I walked out of the team house I shouted "Chaplain's Call!" back toward the bunker, and I headed on down to the canal dock. I knew that the chaplain Cantrell was talking about was a navy chaplain; he had been out a time or two before. The navy would send him out every so often to visit the men in the PBR units on the USS *Benewa*. The sailors must have told the chaplain about us five grunts living alone up the Dong Tien canal. I guess he felt sorry for us or needed a challenge, because this was the third time he had caught a ride up the Mekong and then down our canal on one of the PBR's. I liked the little man. I thought he was gutsy as chaplains go, and I was always glad to see him.

I couldn't help but smile every time I did see him. He always remained encased in his flack vest and steel helmet, no matter what. It was as if he expected to be attacked at any second. He stood out in comic contrast to the brown-water sailors, who padded about their boat in cut-off fatigue shorts and a variety of faded shirts, with no helmets or flack vests. I could tell by his face and even the way he moved that he was nervous about being out here. He was sitting on the edge of real fright, yet here he was to see if some army guys needed his help. We all respected him for that and always tried to give him a hearty welcome for his efforts.

Cantrell, the chaplain, and three of the sailors from the PBR came through the canal-side gate, and I met them in the middle of the compound. We exchanged a few pleasantries, and after Abney and Robertson came over to join the group, the chaplain as usual offered to hold a service. We knew he was the only chaplain we would ever see, and we never knew what tomorrow would bring, so we took him up on his offer.

The sweating little man went back to the boat to get his gear and all of us, sailors included, went to assemble in the only place that could pass for a worship area—in front of that statue of the Virgin Mary that stood in the middle of the compound. The statue had a rail in front, so it was a handy place to lay out the communion gear, and the statue lent the aura of "church" to the proceedings. The chaplain came up from the boat, doffed his helmet, and draped a purple sash around his neck. One of the sailors passed out hymnals while the chaplain laid out his other gear on the rail.

The padre stood behind the rail in front of the statue, and we all stood on the other side. He began with a prayer, and then we sang a hymn. We must have made a strange sight to the Vietnamese looking on. Six or seven of us gaunt Americans in faded, nondescript uniforms were lined up side by side and standing hatless in the sun while a little guy in a flack vest led us through a communion service. The natives must have thought our toneless renditions of "Amazing Grace" and "Faith of our Fathers" were odd indeed.

After the brief homily we took communion, each of us kneeling in the dust to take the bread and wine. After that we all stood for a closing prayer, and that was it. The primitive services were always short and without adornment, but I remember them for the solace they gave us. The familiar service, the religious significance, and even the sight of a fresh American face made us feel less lonely and forgotten.

Outside of those services my own religious life was pretty limited. Religion was a hard thing for me to hold on to in the army, especially an army at war, but I can say it was the only time in my life that I developed the consistent practice of saying a prayer twice a day. The prayers were brief and to the point. Every morning at daybreak I thanked God for letting me see the morning sun. I prayed that I would live to see it go down again. In the evening when the sun sank from sight on the western rim, I thanked God that I had lived to see the sun go down and I asked that I might live to see it come up again. That was about it—maybe a brief mention of my wife and family if I wasn't too distracted—but about two sentences each morning and evening was all I was good for. Nothing fancy, mostly selfish, but boy, did I mean it!

Chapter 18

I<small>T</small> was Christmas Eve, 1969. Saigon and the NLF had declared a mutual twenty-four-hour truce, so we had called off all operations until the morning of December twenty-sixth. We had beefed up the defensive watch around each village with some of the men who would otherwise have been out on patrol. We didn't trust the Viet Cong to stay out of our hair, and I was afraid they might try to take advantage of us during the Christmas celebration.

It was hard to believe this was the day before Christmas. The weather was hot; I hadn't heard, let alone thought of, a single Christmas carol; and there were no Christmas trees or Christmas lights. It just didn't feel like Christmas. I was even a little irritated. Hell, the guys in the rear at least got to go to a Bob Hope show or something. Out here, if it weren't for the truce, I would have never known the season was upon us.

I sloughed off my ill temper and determined to make the best of the easy day I hoped was coming up. My men were glad to get the rest, and as I hung around the team house I could feel that they were picking up a little bit of the Christmas spirit. We had all gotten a few packages and letters in the last run of the mail chopper, so I guessed everyone was looking forward to opening them on Christmas Day. If I had taken time to think about it, I guess I could have gotten into it too, but I was worried about the Cong. I didn't trust the little bastards any farther than I could spit them.

Walking in the village on that day I had seen several pale,

sullen young men who drew back into the shadows when they saw me coming. I was sure they were part of the local Cong force who had come into the village for the truce period. I was also afraid that one of them might want to take the easy opportunity to collect the price on my head, so I had a tense trigger finger all day long. I was glad we had planned precautions and had already posted guard details all around the village.

Just after sundown I pulled on my tiger stripes and my driest pair of jungle boots, strapped on my .45, grabbed my M-16 and a bandolier of ammunition, perched my beret on my head, and went out to check the guard. I walked to each outpost, chatted with the men, and tried to get a sense from the dogs and water buffalo whether or not anything was developing out there in the dark beyond our vision. All seemed well, so I started making my way back across the village toward the fort.

As I walked past the hooches and stepped around the pigs in the path, I began to think about the fact that it really was Christmas Eve and here I was halfway around the world from my family, totally remote from the season we had always enjoyed together. I began to think of home and our favorite Christmas traditions. I could see the fire in the big fireplace at home and could smell the Christmas wreaths. I could use my mind's eye to see the lights on the big Christmas tree that always stood by the front door. I could hear the voices and laughter of relatives. I could imagine my father popping with pleasure at treating his new granddaughter to her first Christmas morning. I knew that this night would be a special night back home in Georgia. And here I was, guarding a village in the middle of nowhere on the other side of the world. It was just another hot day in Vietnam.

Suddenly I heard behind me the faint sound of distant music. I turned and looked back down the village street. There at the far end I saw a small light appear in the darkness. It was quickly followed by another, then another, and another, and another. A whole line of flickering lights was coming around the corner of a house and out into the street. The line turned and came in my direction; it was a group of children from the Catholic church, all marching in a line and carrying candles. They formed a string of lights which sparkled through the gloom of the village night. The faint sound of the children's singing became louder as they approached. I gradually realized that they were singing a familiar tune. The words were Vietnamese, but I could not fail to recognize the melody of "Silent Night." How achingly beautiful it was!

The children filed past and stopped in the street not far from the walls of the fort. At the rear of the line four boys had been carrying a manger scene made of bamboo, chicken wire, and colored tissue paper. I watched as the children held their candles and gathered around the crèche, their faces lit by the glow of the flames. The parents came up behind them and formed a semicircle around the children and the little manger scene. At a signal from the young priest with them, they all began singing the Vietnamese version of "O Come, All Ye Faithful." The poignant beauty of the ageless hymn was made even more special by hearing it in such a distant place, sung by such a different people.

I stood alone outside the crowd and watched the celebration of the Nativity. I gradually became aware of the pressure of the pistol on my hip, the tug of the bandolier on my shoulder, and the weight of the rifle in my hand. Armed to the teeth, I watched the celebration of the birth of the Prince of Peace. I was not only separated from my family and a world away from my own country, but now I felt estranged from my God. I struggled to control the lump in my throat and fought back the tears that were threatening to roll down my cheeks. A black depression settled upon me, and I felt abandoned and alone.

The small ceremony was soon over, and the recessional began. With the faint strains of another "Silent Night" filtering up toward the clear Christmas stars, I turned and quietly walked on into our compound. I felt like a fragile hollow shell, ready to collapse inward at the slightest pressure.

Many Christmases have come and gone since that distant night, but every year when Christmas rolls around again and I hear the first rendition of "Silent Night," I relive that village scene. I always have to stop and fight back the tears that come with the memory. Once again I stand face to face with my own inadequacy, that of my country, even that of mankind, and I wonder that after these thousands of years God still has compassion on us all.

* * *

SOMETIME DURING CHRISTMAS EVE DAY SERGEANT FITZ HAD gotten hold of a small green bush and he and Sergeant Robertson had potted it in a kitchen bowl. When I came in from seeing the children's Nativity scene, they brought the bush into the team house and with big grins announced they had fixed us up a Christmas tree. Sergeant Robertson had acquired a fistful of flashlight bulbs from one of his buddies back in the province town and had painted them red, green, and yellow. He had wired them all together with cellophane tape and a strand of commo wire, and presto, a strand of Christmas lights! Robertson draped the concoction around Fitz's green plant and stuck the ends of the wire into a radio battery. The colored lights lit at the first contact, and, boy, what a beautiful tree! It wasn't more than two feet tall, and wasn't even an evergreen, but the red and green and yellow lights gave it the warm glow of the real McCoy. One of the bulbs had been left unpainted and its white light gleamed from the top of the little bush. The five of us just stood in a circle around the wonderful little tree and stared at it, each one immersed in his own memories and his own emotions.

Lieutenant Cantrell suggested that since we all had Christmas boxes, cards, and letters we had not opened, we should put them all around the base of the bush and open them first thing in the morning. We all seconded the idea, so Sergeant Fitz went to the desk and cleared off a place to put the shrub— I call it a shrub, but in all our minds it was now a bona fide Christmas tree!

We each went to our bunks and dug around in our packs or under our beds to find our Christmas boxes. One by one we placed our gifts and cards beneath the little tree. Sergeant Robertson plugged the wire into the radio battery again, and one of the other guys turned down the kerosene lamp. The light from the tree cast a glow over the whole end of the hut. It shined down on the gaily wrapped packages and put some magic in the mangled ribbons and ripped wrapping papers. Everything was beautiful in the orange glow of our field-expedient Christmas tree. We were all standing there congratulating ourselves when a call came squawking in over the radio. The call was from "Astronol Zulu," a navy reconnaissance pilot flying over on a night border recon mission. He had some see-in-the-night electronic devices and had spotted a boat con-

voy moving in our direction. Since the convoy was in Indian
Territory it appeared suspicious to him. I agreed.

According to the pilot's description, the string of boats had
all the hallmarks of a supply convoy coming over from Cambodia. I guessed it was trying to get to the Cong units in the
interior before the truce expired. Such movements were contrary to the terms of the truce, so I wasn't surprised when the
pilot requested permission to fire. I had him stand by while I
tried to round up the district chief or a duty officer he had left
in charge. This was a truce day, and I wasn't going to take
the risk of making the decision alone. I finally found the duty
officer in the compound and got the proper clearance. I called
the pilot back on his own radio frequency and issued the clearance to fire. I also told him that when he had finished his
patrol and was returning home, I would appreciate it if he
would fly back our way and check the area out again. I told
him that if he saw anything suspicious when he returned, his
permission to fire would still stand. The pilot signed off with
a "Roger, out," and the net went silent.

We waited pensively, and within a few minutes we heard
the crump of rockets in the distance and a few brief barrages
of machine-gun fire; then all was quiet. The navy pilot called
back to say he had engaged the convoy and that several of the
boats appeared to be severely damaged. He also said he knew
several boats had escaped. He had lost them as they scattered
in the darkness. I thanked him for his help and signed off.
The incident was closed as far as I was concerned. "Let 'em
go," I thought. "It's Christmas Eve."

I crawled into my bunk, hoping for a few minutes' sleep
before it came my turn for radio watch. Just as I was dozing
off, the district chief came charging up to the team house. He
was obviously agitated, so I got up to see him. He had heard
the gunfire and rockets while at a friend's house in the village,
he said, and one of his assistants had come and filled him in
on the Cong convoy. How many boats in the convoy, he
wanted to know? How far away were they? How many boats
got away from the navy pilot? Shouldn't we go check out the
site to make sure the Cong didn't return and salvage their
supplies? To the latter question I answered with an unreserved
"No." I wasn't going to go trekking out there during the
middle of Christmas Eve just to find a bunch of busted-up

Viet Cong boats. I especially wasn't interested in running up on an unknown number of live Viet Cong all mad at me because the navy messed up their Christmas!

Well, the district chief was obsessed with the idea that the Cong were violating the truce. He was certain they were en route to attack one of the hamlets in the district, and he was especially afraid that they were coming in after the district town. He damned sure didn't want that to happen, so he wanted to send out a squad of militiamen to locate the wrecked convoy and assess the situation. There was an implicit demand that since we Americans were already involved in this thing, I should provide a couple of men to accompany the native troops. All of us knew that with Americans along not only would there be more guns on the ground, but we could more likely get some air support in case it was needed.

The district chief also wanted us to use the *Proud Mary* to take the recon group out to the area where the convoy had been reported. It appeared from the maps that a small canal near our compound led all the way back to the area where the shot-up convoy was supposedly located. In fact, the reason the district chief was so concerned about the presence of the convoy was that it was located on that particular canal. It was a straight shot, a long canal running directly from Indian Territory right into the back of our compound. The chief figured that the only reason the Cong would be on that particular canal would be that they were coming in to get us. I thought he was crazy myself. This convoy had all the earmarks of a transient boat group, probably supplies for the interior, I told him. No threat to us, I said.

No, he wanted someone to go check it out. He kept insisting, so I grudgingly agreed; but since I figured the whole exercise was going to be a wasted effort anyway, and since it was Christmas Eve, I didn't want to send out two of the other guys while I stayed back myself. I decided that if anybody was going to go, it should be me and the senior NCO. I told Sergeant Robertson to get his gear together. We would leave Lieutenant Cantrell and the more junior NCO's at the fort so they could get some rest on what was supposed to be a holiday night. Robertson and I got our weapons and web gear together, gassed up the *Proud Mary*, and loaded four Vietnamese men plus ourselves into the little boat.

The engine caught after a few pulls on the starter rope and we backed the boat away from our small dock. We went up the main canal until we got beyond the walls of the fort and then turned into the branch canal where it entered the main waterway. It was a clear, moonlit night, so we made our way very slowly. We had one of the Vietnamese squat in the bow and crane his neck to keep a lookout over the tall grass on the canal banks. We didn't want to roll into a wounded Viet Cong platoon without at least a little warning.

It wasn't long before our troubles began. We were slowed down by the water vines and reeds that clogged the canal. The narrow waterway was largely unused by boat traffic, so the water plants had grown up even in the deepest part of the canal. The outboard motor was having a hard time pushing the heavily loaded boat through the thick growth of weeds. We had to stop several times to clear the propeller blades. After a couple of hours of this stop-start movement and heavy work in between, the engine quit entirely. It had overheated and the prop was once again encased in a tangle of weeds. I was already kicking myself for stupidly trying to come up the small canal in the *Proud Mary*.

We pushed our way over to the banks with our paddles and put two Vietnamese ashore on either side. We told them to spread out and to be alert; they were going to have to be our perimeter defense while Robertson and I worked on the engine. We were now quite a way from the village, and by my night reckoning we weren't far from where the navy pilot said he had hit the convoy. Robertson and I told the men in no uncertain terms that there was to be no talking, no smoking, no staring at the stars. They were to keep a close watch and let us know of any suspicious movement.

Robertson and I went back to the boat to see if we could get it running again. Robertson got back into the boat and went to the rear so he could tilt the propeller shaft out of the water. I eased myself into the black waters of the canal and made my way to the boat so I could get to the propeller shaft and clean it off. The water wasn't over chest level, but it was so packed with plants that it was difficult to either swim or walk. When I got to the propeller, I took out my knife and began cutting away at the thick mat of weeds surrounding it. The moonlight that I had cursed earlier for making me feel so exposed now made it possible for me to see what I was doing. It wasn't long before I had cut the prop free and I hoped we were ready to go again. I whispered to Robertson to drop the prop and as soon as I was out of the way to try and start the engine. When I had pulled back a few feet through the chest-deep water and Robertson had lowered the engine back into the running position, I saw him grab the starter-rope handle and give a heave. Nothing. He tried again but only got an anemic cough and sputter from the hesitant engine. Robertson pulled several more times, one right after the other, but still nothing happened. I pulled myself out of the canal and climbed back into the boat to have a try at starting her up. I pulled on the starter rope a few times and got the same empty response that Robertson had. We tried jiggling this, adjusting that, and just generally fussing around with the cranky old chunk of metal. Nothing else having worked, we fell to softly cursing the beast. That didn't do anything either, and it became obvious that we were going to get nothing more out of the *Proud Mary* that night.

We had two possibilities. We could stay where we were for the rest of the night and take the chance of being found by the Cong, or we could turn around and begin pulling the boat back to the village in the dark. Robertson and I were discussing the alternatives when one of the Vietnamese soldiers crawled up to us and whispered that he had seen some figures passing in the darkness. He said he didn't know how many people were out there or whether or not they were armed. He could only say that the figures seemed to be moving parallel to the canal and were off to our left about thirty or forty meters.

I presumed that whoever the hell it was out there didn't know we were around, and I had to go on the assumption that anybody out and around this time of night would be Viet Cong. It was possible they could just be fishermen, but this area was off limits after the curfew, and it was unlikely that fishermen would still be out on Christmas Eve. Even the Hoa Hao took Christmas off.

If our neighbors were Viet Cong, I didn't like the idea of letting them get between us and the village, and if by chance they did know we were out there, I didn't want to stay in one place long enough to let them organize an attack. I decided we should start back toward the village, moving quietly along the canal banks and pulling the boat behind us. I had to inform the team what was happening, so I risked making a call on the radio.

I picked up the hand mike from the harness of our PRC-25 and whispered into the mouthpiece, "Greedy Petrel Whiskey, Whiskey Six, over."

The radio blared back, "Whiskey Six, this is Whiskey, go." The metallic tone of the radio blared out into the quiet night.

"Jesus Christ!" I muttered to myself. Some asshole had left the volume control turned up. I dropped down beside the radio and fumbled for the control dial. I found it and turned it down before I transmitted again.

I pressed the push-to-talk button on the hand mike and over-pronounced each word as I spoke softly into the mouthpiece, "Whiskey, Whiskey Six. Our motor quit. We are coming back with the boat. I say again, no motor, we are pulling the boat back in. How copy, over?"

"Good copy, Six. Do you have an echo tango alpha over?"

"This is Six, it may take a couple of hours, over.

"Roger, Six. Do you want us to send out a party, over?"

"Whiskey, this is Six. Negative, but keep alert. We've seen some Victor Charlie activity, over."

"Six, this is Whiskey. Roger, give us a call if you need help, over."

"This is Whiskey Six. Roger. Out."

I hung the mike back on the radio harness and stood up in the boat to have a look around. I could just make out the black humps off to the left and right that were the backs of our four companions. I saw nothing moving; nothing seemed suspicious. I closed my eyes and listened. I breathed in deeply for the faint telltale scent of the pungent Vietnamese tobacco. I searched for that smell, that sound, or even that piece of psychic energy that would give me some hint as to whether or not the Cong were waiting for us out there in the darkness. I used every sensory neuron in my body, but I felt nothing. I would usually take that as a sign that no one was out there, but the report from the lookout made me awfully uneasy. I couldn't see them, or smell them, or hear them, but I still had to assume they were there. We would have to make our way back to the village very carefully.

I knew that if we all got out of the boat and walked back along the canal bank we would make perfect targets in the bright moonlight. If the Cong spotted us before we saw them, we wouldn't have a prayer of getting out alive. The alternative was to make our way back in the water. Since the rainy season was over, the floodwaters had begun to recede, and in this canal the water level had dropped below the banks for most of the distance back to the village. The water was down far enough so that the top of the boat itself rode just below the canal bank. People sitting down low or lying in the boat would be almost undetectable, unless someone was standing right on the edge of the canal. I decided that I would put all four Vietnamese in the boat and that Robertson and I would get in the canal and pull the boat along behind us as best we could.

I crawled back up on the canal bank and motioned Robertson over to me for another conference. We were both pissed off, me especially since I was supposed to be the man in charge. I was cursing myself for ever giving in to a dumb idea like this in the first place. I should have realized there would be problems with the weeds in such a small, unused canal. I should have thought about the difficulty in making headway, and the trouble we would be in if we got stuck out in the dark away from home. I thought of a hundred good reasons why I should have told the district chief to forget about this whole damned operation.

Robertson and I muttered in each other's ear about our disgust at being in such a stupid situation. He couldn't say so directly, but he was mostly mad at me for dragging him out there in the first place. When I told the veteran sergeant that we were going to load the Vietnamese back into the boat and that he and I were going to pull them back home, he was even more disgusted than before. I told him that we would each tie a piece of rope to the bow of the boat, get in the water, and pull the boat along behind us as we made our way back down the canal. Robertson wasn't too pleased about it, but he took off his web gear and prepared to get in the water. We took off our boots and socks but left on our jungle fatigues. If we had to get out of the water without our shirts and pants, the bright moonlight would make us shine like dead fish.

In some places the canal was deeper than chest high and we had to swim for it. I was glad I had learned to do the sidestroke when I was a kid. I did all my stroking with the down-side arm and pulled on the rope with my top-side arm. When my stroke arm felt as if it was about to come off at the socket, I would roll over, switch hands, and keep going. I think Robertson was breaststroking along while he held the rope between his teeth.

It was really hard to swim in water that was semi-solid with weeds. They didn't provide enough resistance to walk on, but they resisted any attempt to swim through them. In places where our feet could touch bottom, the going was still slow since the water was always at least chest deep and it was hard to get a purchase on the bottom. When we tried to pull the boat forward, our feet would just sink into the mud.

After we had been going for a while, we stopped to get a breath of air and to let our arms rest a minute. Still standing in the canal, I leaned back onto the nearly vertical canal bank and rolled my head back on my shoulders. I looked up into the clear night air and was staring blankly at the twinkling stars when suddenly I saw the blinking red light. It made my blood run cold.

I knew instantly from the direction and altitude of the light that it was the same navy pilot who earlier in the evening had started this whole thing off. I figured he was coming by again, homebound this time but following my earlier request to check the area on his way back by. What really frightened me was that I had given him a standing clearance to fire on anything that looked suspicious. The clearance was still in effect. Like a bloody idiot I had neglected to inform the pilot that we were going out to the target area. When we had left the fort, I was so mad at the district chief I had never even thought about calling him. So far, I was batting a thousand for stupidity. Now we were out in the middle of a free-fire zone, and I knew we were going to look very suspicious to our friend the navy flier.

Robertson was leaning against the side of the boat so I whispered urgently to him, "Robertson, quick! Give me the handset. The navy's back!"

Robertson pulled himself up on the side of the boat and grabbed the handset from the radio's harness. As he handed the mike across to me, either a weed or the extension cord jerked it out of his hand and *kerplunk*, it dropped into the water. Instantly I grabbed for the mike in the water. If it hadn't been for the simple reflex, I wouldn't have moved at all; I was stupefied with frustration. I muttered curses to everyone and everything I knew of as I stood in the canal and tried to shake the water from the handset. Since the handset of the PRC-25 is necessary for sending and receiving transmissions, and since it doesn't work well when it is waterlogged, I knew we were really in trouble. I tried calling the team house but got no response. Robertson crawled up on the bank and got over into the boat so he could get to the radio and change the frequency. He switched to the frequency of the USS *Benewa*, the only navy frequency that either of us knew from memory. I didn't have much hope of getting them on the net since the *Benewa* was at least twenty miles away, but I thought the navy pilot might be monitoring the *Benewa*'s frequency. If he was on their freq, I thought, he might be able to pick us up. We made repeated calls but there was no response on the navy channel. My adrenalin titer was climbing rapidly.

I watched the little blinking red light in the sky getting closer and closer as we continued to try to transmit both on our own freq and on the navy's. The plane was following a course that would keep it far off to our right unless it changed direction, and I began to hope he might just pass us by and never see us. We continued to watch the light as we switched back again to our own radio net. I tried to raise the team house again, and was elated to hear some sort of faint reply, apparently from Sergeant Fitz. The transmission was very broken; but through the sputtering garble, we could tell that he was saying he could not understand our transmissions. The tantalizing nearness of getting our message through heightened my sense of desperation. I squeezed the push-to-talk button on the handset and sent a short, to-the-point message. "Whiskey, this is Six. Call Astronol Zulu. Give our position. Cancel fire clearance. How copy, over?"

"This is Whiskey. Roger copy."

Our radio was still cutting out, but I could make out Sergeant Fitz's reply amidst the sputter. I hoped he realized what I was talking about from the other few words I had sent. No sooner had Fitz finished talking to me than he sent out a call to the navy pilot.

"Astronol Zulu, Astronol Zulu, this is Greedy Petrel Whiskey, over." Sergeant Fitz was also thinking the navy aircraft might be on our freq since it was flying over our territory. We could hear Fitz's transmissions more strongly now, but they were still very garbled and broken. His calls to Astronol Zulu received no response. He called us back and told us he was going to switch over to the navy freq to see if he could raise anybody there.

I looked up at the little red light and watched it moving slowly amongst the stars. Gradually it began a ninety-degree turn in our direction. I shook my head in resignation as I lost all hope of getting out of this one. I had heard too many stories of guys getting shot up by their own artillery or aircraft because they were out somewhere they shouldn't be, or because they weren't properly identified by spotters or pilots. As far as this pilot knew, we weren't supposed to be out there, and we damned sure weren't identifiable. I tapped Robertson on the shoulder and pointed out the approaching lights to him. A wry look of disgust came over his face, and he just shook his head in quiet acknowledgment of our helplessness. I could hear the drone of the engines now and knew from the sound that the plane was one of those called an OV-1 Bronco. I remember thinking what an ugly airplane it was.

We didn't know it at the time, but Sergeant Fitz had succeeded in contacting the brown-water navy guys out on the *Benewa*. They had to look through their own code books to find the plane's operational radio frequency, then they called him up and told him to call Greedy Petrel Whiskey for a message.

Robertson and I were standing in water up to our armpits as we watched the plane heading over in our direction. We had continued to make attempts at calling the pilot, both on our frequency and on the navy's, but we weren't having any luck. I didn't know if it was because we weren't transmitting, weren't receiving, or if it was because the pilot was just on some other frequency. The Vietnamese in the boat knew something was wrong, too. They had seen the worry on Robertson's and my faces, and now they saw the plane's lights go through another slight turn out in front of us. As the plane went into the turn and headed directly toward us, it began to rapidly lose altitude. It leveled out at an altitude of several hundred feet and was now rapidly bearing in on us. The threatening growl of the engines was much louder. I could feel the pilot charging his guns; it was fruitless to even duck.

Suddenly our radio came to life with another sputtering transmission, "Greedy Petrel Whiskey, Astronol Zulu. You have a message for me, over?"

Sergeant Fitz, who had been calling, calling, calling, bypassed all RTO preliminaries and simply blurted out, "Cease fire! Cease fire! This is Whiskey, I say again, cease fire! *Do you copy? Over!*"

"Roger," Zulu replied without expression. The plane was so close now that we could see its dark silhouette against the night sky. It lifted ever so slightly and roared directly over us, looking uglier than ever, I thought. I felt as limp as a wet noodle as I watched the plane fade into the distant darkness. In a few seconds it was just a blinking light again, the drone of its engines still loud amidst the quietness of the Delta night. We listened as the pilot radioed back to the team house.

"Greedy Petrel Whiskey, this is Astronol Zulu, over."

"Astronol Zulu, this is Whiskey, go."

"Whiskey, Zulu. What the fuck, over?" Navals almost never transgressed propriety on a radio, so I knew this airedale was not at all happy.

"Zulu, Whiskey. We sent a recon out to the convoy you hit earlier this evening. They had some trouble and couldn't get back out of the fire zone in time. We've been trying to contact you to call you off. We don't want you to shoot them up by mistake, over."

"Whiskey, this is Zulu." A tinge of disparagement had crept into the pilot's voice. "Your guys have just had about as close a call as they're ever likely to want. Ten Hail Marys for each of them when they get back in. I'm going home. Anything further, over?"

Fitz radioed back, "Negative. Thanks for your help. Whiskey out."

Robertson and I looked blankly at each other across the black water. A big grin broke out on both our faces and I wanted to shout with relief. I managed to hold it in because we still didn't know whether or not we were surrounded by the Viet Cong. I slapped Robertson softly on the back and he stuck his fist out at me with the thumb pointed skyward, the old army "up" signal meaning everything is o.k. The village militiamen sitting in our boat also realized the threat was past, and they began smiling and muttering with relief. I told them to settle down and to get ready to start moving. Robertson and I grabbed our ropes and started our semi-swimming through the water and tall grass.

Sergeant Robertson and I settled into a routine of swimming, walking, and resting in the water. As we gradually made our way down the canal, the weeds began to thin out a bit, at least toward the middle, and the towing became a little easier. Our lookout never saw any sign of the Cong, but I was constantly worried that we would just pull our boat up to a squad of them sitting on the canal bank. Sergeant Robertson and I both kept our eyes on the banks, praying we wouldn't see anything.

Finally I felt I could go no farther. We were still a half mile or so from our village outposts, but Robertson and I were both exhausted. Each period of swimming and pulling had gotten shorter than the last. My shoulders felt as if they had been stretched on the rack and my legs felt like rubber. I crawled up on the canal bank and looked at the flickering lights of the village. I knew that if we had to depend on Robertson and me to pull the boat the rest of the way in, we would never make it. The Vietnamese were too small to pull the boat with us in it, so I decided we would just take the chance and walk the rest of the way. If the Cong were coming this way, I just had to hope we had outdistanced them or that they had wandered off in some other direction. We were going to take the chance, even with the increased exposure it entailed.

I called the team house on the radio to let them know what was happening. Sergeant Abney was now on radio watch, so I told him where we were and instructed him to inform the outpost guards that we were coming in. I didn't want them to think we were Viet Cong trying to sneak up on them.

As we started moving over the final distance, the combined effects of exhaustion and relief made Robertson and me both a little giddy. Even though we weren't out of trouble yet, we started chuckling about our hapless handling of the whole operation. He was kind enough not to point out my leading part in the entire mess, and it was hardly a laughing matter since we had almost gotten ourselves killed. Also, we both knew better than to let down our guard just because we were close to home. The Cong always liked to set up an ambush just where everyone figured they had made it in safely. We knew we had to keep our eyes peeled till we were inside the compound walls.

When we got just outside the walls and had checked through the outpost guards, I told the Vietnamese militiamen to go on home. Robertson and I got in the boat and paddled it over to the dock and tied it to its place. As we gathered up our gear, we started laughing again. For some reason it seemed hilariously funny that we had almost been killed by our own stupidity while on a combat operation during a truce period on Christmas Eve. Robertson suggested we sing a Christmas carol, so as we walked through the gate back into the fort, hands and feet bleeding, soaked to the skin, mud and leeches all over us, guns and ammo draped all around, we sang for everyone's benefit a hearty basso version of "O Come, All Ye Faithful."

IT WAS LATE ON CHRISTMAS MORNING WHEN I FINALLY WOKE up. It was painful just to crawl out of my bunk, so I took a couple of aspirin to deaden the throbbing ache in my shoulders and thighs. Robertson got up at about the same time, and we both made our way over to the camp stove to share the last of the morning's coffee. We got about half a cup each of the acrid liquid and went to sit down next to the Christmas tree. We just chatted and waited as one by one the others gathered around for the opening of the Christmas gifts. Soon Sergeants Robertson, Abney, and Fitz and Lieutenant Cantrell and I were all there. We started the ceremony. First Fitz plugged in the Christmas tree lights, and we just sat there looking at the tree and gifts for a while. Then Fitz handed out the gifts one by one. We all wanted the little Christmas to go on as long as possible, so we dragged out the opening process with a lot of diversions and small talk. Each bow, each piece of wrapping paper provided a strange, almost mystical contact with home. When the boxes were opened, each gift was greeted with groans of pleasure, like a bunch of old ladies gloating at a baby shower. It was a very small-time Christmas, mind you, but we made the best of it. Thank God for good relatives.

Christmas Day afternoon, Lieutenant Cantrell and I went

down into the village to give candy to the kids. Every month the army issued the team an SP (Special Purpose) pack which had some candy, cigarettes, razor blades, and pens and paper in it. For several months now we had been saving the candy for the village children. I guess giving candy to kids has been a GI tradition for years. I can see why. For one thing, it is an easy way to make a good impression. Also, there is immediate positive feedback, an instant happy response that is otherwise often difficult for a soldier to come by. You just feel good doing it. Cantrell and I walked down the village street, throwing the pieces of candy to the kids as they leaped and yelled and called after us. Soon we had such a crowd of laughing youngsters around us that we could hardly move. There was joy in all their faces. I tell you, it's a miracle what a piece of chocolate can do!

A little later, I paid a visit to the district chief to wish him a Merry Christmas and to give him a small gift. He and I sat around and had a pleasant chat with some of the village elders. We sipped the chief's tea and smoked my cigarettes while everyone talked about not much of anything. I finally said something about having to get back to the compound to be with my team for the holiday. Actually, I was hungry and wanted to see what was being cooked up for our Christmas meal.

The army press releases used to imply that every American in Vietnam was provided with a hot turkey dinner on Christmas Day. Christmas dinner was a big morale factor that we were all aware of, so I wasn't surprised when a few days before Christmas I received a call from the province team, asking if we wanted to get our hot Christmas dinners on Christmas Day. They said we would get the turkey, mashed potatoes, cranberry sauce, the whole works! They would fly the meals out to us on a helicopter if we wanted them. I replied that that would be great. A solid American meal would do us all good, especially since it was Christmas dinner. Fine, they said, now go and collect $1.50 American money from each man who wants the meal. I couldn't believe it. They were going to make us pay! We were to give them the money for the meals when the chopper dropped them off. No money, no meal.

It is hard to explain exactly why I resented being told to

pay $1.50 for a turkey dinner, especially after it had taken a $500,000 helicopter and at least $100 worth of fuel just to deliver it, but I did resent it. So did the rest of the guys when I asked around, so I told province headquarters to keep their turkey dinners. I guess part of our resentment was because we all felt that here we were, five Americans out in the middle of nowhere, halfway around the world from home, trying to do our best with little or no support from anybody else, and the bastards wouldn't even spring for a Christmas dinner. Well, to hell with them, we thought, from the REMF's (Rear Echelon Mother Fuckers) in Saigon, to the middle Americans in Kalamazoo, to the hippies in California. To hell with all of them. We were a goddamned MAT team and we could fend for ourselves! Sounds juvenile, doesn't it? I guess you had to be there.

When I got back to the compound from my visit with the district chief, I found Lieutenant Cantrell cooking a duck over a bed of campfire coals. Sergeant Abney was inside the team house, cooking up a pot of rice. Dipped in a little *nước mắm*, the duck wasn't half bad. We spread some government margarine on the crusty bread we had bought the day before in the village market and took the cookies out of some C-ration boxes. It was enough to eat, I'll admit, but it sure wasn't a turkey dinner.

Chapter 19

CIVIL operations were an important part of my team's mission. I often thought that the civil operations were more difficult to carry out than the military ones, especially since we didn't have the time to do all the things we wanted. My teammates and I became involved in the development of village schools, health and maternity clinics, agricultural projects, law enforcement programs, and the establishment of hamlet and village offices. We didn't do the actual building of the clinics or offices, but we provided the encouragement, advice, and often the bureaucrat's paperwork know-how to get the projects started. Starting up such projects was hard enough, but seeing them through to a successful completion was even more so. The combined effects of war and poverty made it very difficult to sustain interest, funds, or personnel for many of the programs that were needed in the backward rural villages.

The public schools and public health clinics were good examples of rural development projects that both aided the people and provided a daily government presence in village life. Because the schools and clinics were signs of government influence in a village, and because they were so heavily used by the people, they were prime targets for Viet Cong terrorist attacks. The Cong played on the people's fears. As a consequence, the teachers were afraid to teach in the schools and the nurses were afraid to attend their clinics. Additionally, the schoolteachers and nurses were paid very poor salaries and received almost none of the supplies they needed to do their jobs properly. They faced a dangerous, difficult, and very discouraging job.

While the problems with the public education system were immense, and while we always had trouble keeping our schools repaired and the teacher replacements coming in, the problems with education never seemed so stark or intractable as the problems with public health. Disease was everywhere. It seemed that practically everyone had malaria, and tuberculosis was very common. The deep, mucus-laden cough of tuberculosis victims was a sound one came to expect in a walk through any village. Skin diseases and hepatitis were common health problems, as were the full gamut of parasite diseases that come from using water contaminated with human and animal wastes. The scale of the problem was immense. To control these diseases in a way expected by most Western peoples would have required a fundamental rearrangement of Vietnamese society and a budget that would have beggared the central government. I felt totally incapable of even beginning to address the problem in my district, yet I was so struck by the needs of the people that I felt I had to do something.

We started a program of repairing the clinics that had fallen into disrepair and drilling wells so the clinics and hamlets would have a source of clean water. When the government failed to resupply our midwife clinics, I wrote to my uncle, a veterinarian, and my mother-in-law, a nurse, and got them to send me rubber gloves, plastic aprons, sutures, scissors, bandages, disinfectants, and the like. At one time there was no more soap in our village. We couldn't get it for our clinics and the villagers could not get any for their private use. I wrote to members of my family and got them to send me "care" packages containing nothing but bars of soap. We gave it out in cases of special need, where cleaning an infant or washing a wound was going to be important for proper acute care. I came to view soap as a medicine rather than a toilet article. Soap is so ubiquitous in the West that I had never thought of it in that light before, but seeing the extent of disease that occurs in its absence, I became convinced that soap is indeed a medicine, just as much as penicillin is.

* * *

WHEN I WALKED OUT OF THE TEAM HOUSE ONE MORNING, en route to a meeting down in the village, I found a woman waiting for me inside the compound's main gate. The guard apologized for letting the woman inside the walls of our fort, but he said she had come at sunup and had refused to leave. She had insisted that she needed to see me. I told the guard that it was all right, I would talk with the woman. She was squatting by the wall and was holding some sort of bundle in her arms, so I walked over to her, trying to smile in order to reassure her. She rose as I approached, and I could tell from the look in her eyes that she was deeply troubled. She looked old enough to be married, so I said, *"Chào bà,"* the proper greeting to a married woman.

"Chào Trung úy," she responded. She made the polite inquiries about my health, and I in turn asked about hers. She was fine, she said, but her baby was very sick. As she spoke, she unwrapped the bundle in her arms and held it up for me to see. The child appeared to be less than a year old and was completely covered with what looked like ringworm lesions. Secondary skin infections were already at work in many places, and the baby's face and arms were puffed with edema. The baby was lethargic and did not complain about my untrained examination.

I asked the woman if she washed the baby with soap and water. No, she replied, there was no soap in the village. I asked if she first boiled the water she used when she washed the baby without soap. No, she replied, firewood was expensive and she did not have a husband to help her get her own wood. She said she came to me hoping I would give her some Western medicine for the baby. She had been to the traditional Chinese medicine man in the village, but his treatments had done the baby no good.

I called Sergeant Fitz over to look at the baby. He was the team medic and I thought he might have some idea about what we could do. After Fitz examined the baby he said, "I don't know, *Trung úy,* he looks pretty far gone to me. I could give him a shot of penicillin for the secondary infections but I don't know if it would do any good. Unless he gets cleaned up, the ringworms and God knows what else are going to keep him infected."

"Well, let's give him the shot anyway," I said. "Maybe it

will help a little and the lady here will at least see we're trying.''

As Fitz started back to the team house to get his gear, I said, ''Bring out a bar of soap, too. Maybe we can get her to clean him up a bit.''

While we were waiting for Fitz to come back, I found out that the woman was not from the local village, but from a village several miles away. She had paid for a seat on a water-taxi to come in to our village that morning, but she said she was out of money and would have to walk home that evening. About that time Sergeant Fitz came back with the soap and a syringe of penicillin. He gave the baby the shot and it never flinched or cried. The infant's lack of response to the needle prick made me even more concerned about its condition.

Fitz and I talked and decided to ask the woman if she wanted to stay in the compound for a few days so we could watch the baby. I was afraid that she would not accept our offer since staying away from her village even for a night would have been a very unusual thing. For her to stay several days with the strange Americans in a village different from her own was just unheard of.

My premonition was correct; the woman refused our offer. She said she had to return to her village, but she promised to use the soap and boil the wash water before using it on the baby. Fitz looked at me and just shrugged his shoulders. We had no antihelmentic drugs so there was nothing else we could do. I told the woman that I was sorry that we did not have the proper medicines for her baby, but we had done all we could do with what we had. It was a terrible feeling, knowing that the woman had come such a long way, at an expense she could not afford, and in the end there was little we could do for her child because we ourselves had too little with which to work.

When the woman left the compound, her face was still a knot of worry and fear. I think she knew we had not been able to offer her much help. Three days later I was in the commo bunker, decoding a message from the province town, when Sergeant Fitz came and told me the woman with the baby was outside again. I stepped from the dark, hot bunker into the bright tropical sunshine. The woman was standing out in the middle of the compound with the same bundle of rags in her arms. It was nearly noon, the compound was quiet, and the stillness of the moment was emphasized by the rumpled form of a woman standing out there in the wilting heat.

As I approached, I nodded and asked about her health and that of her child. The anxiety and despair written on her face were answer enough. She told me she had been using the soap and had been boiling her water as directed, but now she had no more firewood to use for cooking or heating the water and the baby was getting worse and worse rather than better and better. She said that she had left her village early that morning and had walked in to see us again. Could the *bác-sĩ* and I try again with our medicine, she wondered? She wouldn't ask, she said, except that only a few months ago her husband had been killed in the army, and now she was afraid she was going to lose her only child, a male, and the hope of her old age. As she handed me the bundle, she fixed me with an imploring gaze. The tears welling up in her eyes were silent evidence of her concern and sorrow.

I pulled back the cloth and looked down. The baby's puffed face was slack-jawed and yellowish gray. I was startled and gave a small gasp at holding so closely and unexpectedly the ugly image of death. The welts and sores from the overwhelming parasitic infections were still raw and purple, as if the skin were still alive with its complaint. I called Sergeant Fitz and unwrapped the baby. Its whole body was just as we had last seen it, puffed and distended with edema, covered with sores, and completely marked with the circular welts from the ringworm infestation. I put the infant's chest to my ear and heard nothing. I handed him over to Fitz and asked if he had his stethoscope. Fitz took one look at the baby boy and shook his head. He knew the child was dead without even listening.

Fitz started to wrap the baby up again, and without looking at me he said, "This little kid is dead, *Trung úy*. There's nothing we can do about it now." He paused for a second, looking down at the small, ugly body. "Shit," he said in disgust. "Nothing we could have done anyway, I reckon. Things being the way they are."

I had slipped into my attitude of resignation, that frame of mind where nothing could reach me. All my circuits were disconnected, all emotions were put on ice. "Yeah, I reckon not," I said softly, "things being the way they are."

At times like this I would tell myself to just keep plodding onward. Put one foot down in front of the other. Don't stop, don't think, just keep things moving. Don't be distracted by emotion and all the things that you can't do a damned thing about.

I couldn't help but think about that child a little bit, though, and I thought a lot about it years later when I could afford the distraction. To think what just a bar of soap would have meant to that child if he had had it in time! What a little elementary sanitation, or even a few rudimentary medicines, could have done to save the life of that child or to reduce the misery of thousands of others in my district alone. It was one of those situations where it seemed the smallest things were what we needed the most.

We needed soap. But you can't talk to Americans about soap. Americans don't understand about soap. It is an item that we take for granted. We have lost the cultural memory of what it means to live without soap. Americans in general tend to be a squeaky clean bunch, and we just expect that everybody else can be too. God, how naive! I wonder how long it had been since the last baby died of ringworm in the United States. I suspect we've lost that memory, too.

So I was terribly frustrated, you see, because I realized that my country would never understand about all the small but very important things that were needed in Vietnam. You can't go on the evening news and tell America about the need for soap! People simply won't understand what you are talking about. We Americans find it easy to believe that some other poor country may need our bombs, our bullets, or even our soldiers—but soap? No sir, don't send 'em soap; hell, everybody's got soap!

THERE WAS NOT A SINGLE PHYSICIAN IN MY ENTIRE DISTRICT. We tried to provide what little medical assistance we could by maintaining the midwife and first-aid clinics out in the various villages, but if someone was critically injured or seriously ill we had no way to help them. It is true that when people with serious medical problems were brought in to the district town, we could sometimes get a medevac chopper to come and take the patient back to a hospital, but failing that sort of help the person had to live or die according to his body's ability to survive.

Late one evening a sampan came putt-putting up the canal. It was well after curfew and the riders were taking quite a risk being out at such an hour. According to the well-known rules, anyone out after curfew was presumed to be Viet Cong and a fair target. The man piloting the sampan hailed the fort and was allowed to approach and dock just below our wall by the canal. An old man and woman, each dressed in the standard garb of black pajamas and a cloth head wrapping, came staggering into the fort supporting between them the weight of a young man.

We got the man to a stretcher and laid him down. He was wrapped in a shroudlike cloth, and when we pulled it aside we saw that he was severely burned on his lower abdomen, groin, and legs. He must have been in terrible pain, but his face was a mask of stoic immobility. Not even a groan passed his lips. The old people were his parents, and they told me their son had had an accident while filling the family lanterns. He had spilled some kerosene on his pants where it had somehow ignited, and he had been badly burned before the fire had been put out. The parents had risked bringing him in from several miles away because they knew his only chance for survival was to get to us and from us to a hospital. They begged me to ask for a helicopter to come pick up their son and take him to a place where he could be healed.

I went over to the commo bunker and called the province town to ask for a night medevac mission. Sergeant Fitz started an IV on the young man, using one of our two bottles of saline infusion fluid. After a considerable delay I got a call back from Cao Lanh, promising a chopper later that night, time uncertain. Now all we could do was wait. The man lay still on the rough canvas stretcher, the IV fluid slowly dripping into his vein. He never uttered a complaint. His mother squatted at his feet and chanted mournfully to herself as she rocked back and forth on her haunches. The father sat silently at the young man's head. He occasionally rolled a cigarette and held it by his son's lips so he could take a puff when he wanted.

Just before dawn we heard the chopper approaching. A few minutes later I saw the running lights up in the night sky, so I grabbed our electric lantern and ran out to the landing pad. I acted as a beacon while Fitz and Cantrell brought the burned man down to our LZ in the stretcher. We transferred him to

the floor of the chopper and his mother crawled in beside him.
Like mothers everywhere, she was concerned about her son,
and she was determined to go and see him well treated. The
old man watched the chopper lift off with a look of sorrow
and confusion on his face. None of us had any idea which
hospital the son would be taken to, how far away it was, or
how the mother and son would ever get home again, even if
the young man survived his burns—a slim possibility in the
first place, it seemed to me. How the old woman would ever
get home again seemed a real problem, since I imagined she
had probably never been out of the province before. She could
not have been equipped to take care of herself in the urban
areas where a Vietnamese hospital was likely to be located.

Despite all his problems, the old man soon regained his
stolid attitude, and as he was about to return to his village he
came over to thank me for helping his son. He had known I
would help, he said, because he had been told that the American *trung úy cô vàn* had great power. I had proven that true,
he said, by the fact that I could call in an American helicopter
to come help an unknown village boy. He thanked me over
and over again, and convinced me that he had indeed been
impressed. I shook his hand and said I was glad to do it. I
didn't tell him that my being powerful had nothing to do with
it, that we had just been lucky. On other occasions we had
come up empty-handed; the availability of choppers had to do
with luck, not the influence of a ragtag infantry lieutenant.

Some months before, another burn victim had come in. A
young girl had been badly burned on both legs from about
mid-thigh down. It had been three days since the burning, and
the girl's mother had been taking her to the local Chinese
medicine man. The traditional medication had apparently been
some sort of herb-laden salve, which was smeared on her legs.
The woman had brought her daughter in for our "experimental" medicine treatment only after seeing her daughter's condition get worse and worse. When we saw her, the legs were
huge expanses of edematous, weeping tissue, violently red
under the thick salve. With our lack of medicines and with
the local sanitation being so poor, I knew there was nothing
we could do. Those legs were a great culture medium for just
about every kind of germ you can imagine. We called for a
chopper. None available, came the reply. We could wait, we

answered. Mission not deemed appropriate, responded our superiors. We were instructed to have the mother bring the girl in to the province town by bus or water-taxi.

To make a long story short, there was no way that woman was going to haul her daughter into the province town. First, she probably couldn't afford it, and second, she was afraid. She was afraid for her daughter and afraid for herself. She would not take the risk of having her daughter die so far away from her home village. So, we did what we could. *Bác-sĩ* Fitz bathed the little girl's legs and cleaned them with hydrogen peroxide. He wrapped her raw limbs in cotton gauze to keep out the dirt and dust, even though cotton gauze is not something to be used on burned tissue. We used it because it was the only thing we had. After cleaning and wrapping the legs as best he could, Fitz told the mother to bring the girl back every other day, and he would rewash the legs with hydrogen peroxide and change the dressings.

The bandage-changing routine went on for some time, the mother and daughter coming in every other day as instructed. Each time they came in the little girl underwent a terribly painful cleansing of her legs, but she always bore her suffering in silence. Only an occasional grimace or spark of pain in her eyes would indicate a response to the agonizing procedure. Each time she came in, the gauze would be embedded in the dried secretions of the child's tortured legs. Fitz would pour the peroxide over the gauze, just to soften the yellowish semiscab that anchored it to the limb. After allowing the peroxide to foam and bubble for a few minutes, we could slowly pull the old gauze out of the raw flesh. Just the sight of it made me wince, yet the little girl never said a word or shed a tear. It was the pain in her eyes and in her mother's eyes that was enough to make me want to cry for her.

Our treatments were far from adequate. After about the fifth visit we ran out of penicillin. Without antibiotics the child was soon down with a raging fever, and the aspirins we gave her were consumed without effect. Somewhere in the second or third week she slipped into a coma. The mother became resigned to the little girl's death, and I think that as much as we all wanted life for her, we wanted a cessation of her pain even more. When she died, I still felt that I had let her down. Her mother had come to me for help and I had not helped. By failing to save the little girl, I had abused her mother's trust. I felt I had failed to do my duty.

I wanted so much for the people to have faith in me, to accept my word and my way as being right and proper. I was *the* American in this district, the` cô-vàn trưởng; I was the warrior king! When I was appealed to for help, I had to be able to deliver! Even now, when that little girl's face drifts into my mind's eye, I still feel the dull pangs of that guilt. I knew that warrior kings really only live in fantasy lands, and only there can they always deliver their people's needs. My failings always proved that I wasn't a warrior king at all, I was just another soldier who fell far short of perfection.

ANY GOOD FAMILY PHYSICIAN KNOWS THAT A MAJOR PART OF his role is not to cure people of common diseases—many of them are simply a part of life—but to help the patient get through a disease with a minimum of discomfort. This is a legitimate part of medicine, and in the rural Vietnamese villages the role of this type of healer was played by the native practitioners of traditional, or "Chinese," medicine. The villagers felt that this was a perfectly legitimate form of the healing arts, and unless they were in extreme duress, they preferred it to the so-called experimental medicine of the Western-style physicians.

The traditional medicine man dispensed a variety of powders, liquids, spices, and other nostrums for all sorts of illnesses of the mind and body. There was a plant root or animal body part for every kind of mental or physical indisposition. With these ointments, salves, and draughts the medicine men claimed to cure a myriad of the small aches and pains that nag the human frame throughout its mortal existence.

It was also common to see the natives treating themselves by "drawing the blood," pinching or pulling at the skin over an area of discomfort, causing a red welt to appear. A person with a headache, for example, would repeatedly pinch the skin between the eyebrows; someone with a sore throat would do the same thing down either side of the neck. This form of self-treatment was very popular, and it was common to see people in the village with crimson spots on their foreheads or stripes down their necks. They were sure they had the cure for the headache or the sore throat, but I never had the nerve to try it myself.

There was a more advanced form of this drawing blood business that I always found fascinating, though I never understood what specific illness it was supposed to cure. The treatment consisted of the application of the mouths of heated glass jars to the patient's skin. The jars were allowed to sit there, and as they cooled, the air in them contracted and sucked the skin up into the mouth of the jar. The suction jars were left on for several minutes, and when they were removed, perfectly circular, large red bruises were left in their place. It wasn't unusual to see men or women in the villages with dozens of these circular red marks on their chest, arms, or back. I suppose having one's "blood drawn" to the surface in such a general pattern was supposed to be a whole-body cure for whatever the problem was.

On one occasion, my district chief was feeling poorly and called in the local medicine man. I didn't know he was under treatment and had gone over to his house to discuss some administrative matters. When I called at the door of his house, his wife came and greeted me kindly. She ushered me through to their bedroom, where I saw the chief lying face down on his wooden sleeping pallet. Three other men were squatting around the periphery of the room and greeted me with solemn nods. Squatting beside the chief was the medicine man, his head wreathed in the blue wisps of smoke from his incense pot. He was a brown-skinned little man, dressed in black pajamas. He never acknowledged my presence but continued his ministrations with the studied purpose of a professional.

The district chief's back looked like the storage shelf for a bottle factory. There must have been ten or twelve of the glistening little flasks stuck there, and his skin was sucked tightly into the mouth of each one of them. The chief was lying with his eyes closed, but at a word from one of the other men he opened them and looked up at me in surprise. I tried to show no curiosity, surprise, or disapproval at the proceedings. Speaking softly, and I hoped with sufficient reverence for the occasion, I reminded the chief of our appointment and said that I could return later if he wished. I tried to act as if what I was seeing was as common as grits. The district chief said that another time would be better and he apologized for forgetting our scheduled meeting. Quickly, he began to explain why he had called in the medicine man instead of going to the province town for some "experimental" medicine. I knew he was afraid I would look down on this form of treatment and that he would lose face in my eyes for having indulged in it.

I felt very uncomfortable for the chief's sake and tried to reply in a supportive way and make comments that showed no disapproval of his form of medical care. All the while we were talking, the medicine man continued to remove the flasks from one place, heat them over what appeared to be an alcohol flame, and reseat them at another location. It was fascinating just to watch him at work, and I wondered what it would be like to take one of the treatments myself. I chuckled at the thought, because I would have been covered with the purplish circles for a couple of weeks and that would have been enough time to risk being seen by the people back in Cao Lanh. If I had gone to the rear in a polka-dotted skin-suit, the paper pushers would have had me put away for "going native." That was considered bad form, the sure sign of a man who had slipped beyond the bounds of propriety.

I continued to watch the medicine man at work for a while, then I slipped out the door without saying anything else to the chief. As I walked back to the team house, I had to admit once again that there was one thing I did like about my tour in Vietnam: I was able to witness another culture doing its own thing. That is something that most people don't get the chance to do, and I found that part of my work both interesting and challenging to my own preconceptions. I was supposed to be there to teach the Vietnamese, but I was learning a lot from them at the same time. I wasn't sure who was getting the better bargain.

Chapter 20

I looked up at the moonless night sky and for a moment I marveled that the stars always seemed to shine with such crystal clarity. It was tempting to just stare up there at the winking lights and let my mind wander off to some never-never land. I was halfway to Orion when Sergeant Abney kicked me in the shoulder and brought me back to earth. I looked to my left and saw that Abney had crawled up above me to the level of the earthen roadway. He peered over the edge and looked out into the darkness on the other side. After a few seconds he lowered his head and slid back down next to me. "Dark as a donkey's ass, *Trung úy*," he whispered with exasperation.

"Can you see anything at all?" I asked quietly.

"Not without moonlight. I can't tell anything beyond twenty or thirty meters. Gets all smeared together. You can't tell people from bushes."

"Well, if the Cong come through here tonight they'll have to kick us so we'll know they're here," I said with a forced smile. I didn't like being set up in a night ambush without being able to see anything at all. As a matter of fact I was uneasy about this whole operation. Sergeant Abney and I, along with our militia and three PBR's from the American navy, were in place on the banks of the Dong Tien canal. We had come on the basis of some information the navy boys had received through their own channels. They had heard that a Viet Cong Main Force battalion was going to be making a movement toward the Cambodian border. They were supposed to be coming tonight, and they were supposed to cross the canal in this area, which we now had set up for a company-size ambush.

The navy had sent three PBR's to help us out, and we had two RF platoons and one PF platoon strung out along the road embankment that paralleled the big canal. The roadbed formed the only high ground for miles around; in fact it was so high that it blocked the direct-fire guns of the PBR's. To make sure their guns would be in the fight, if one developed, each boat had off-loaded a .30 caliber machine gun and mounted it in the ambush position with the Vietnamese troops. I wondered how often it happened that an infantry officer used sailors to man an ambush two hundred miles from the ocean.

I had stationed one PBR on either flank of our position and one in the middle, right behind Abney and me. The middle boat was to be our commo link with the USS *Benewa*, which had two navy helicopter gunships on her deck, ready to give support if needed. In addition to their machine guns, all the PBR's had deck-mounted mortars, and they could be used effectively on the open ground out in front of us. By our usual standards we had a surplus of firepower. Still I was uneasy. We had no good estimate of the Main Force battalion's strength, we didn't know whether the entire unit was in on this particular move, and we didn't know why the battalion was headed toward the border. Was it to meet another unit? The NVA? Where were they? Somewhere out in the dark behind us? My stomach was in a knot and I could already feel the beads of sweat building on my upper lip.

I had a PRC-25 lying in the dirt beside me, and all the PBR's and both militia units were supposed to be with me on one frequency. Since I couldn't see in the dark, I had to depend on the commo link to tell me what was happening on each flank.

I was whispering with the PF platoon leader about our rear security when the radio suddenly transmitted softly, "Green Sleeves Bravo, Fieldhouse Zulu, over." One of the PBR's was calling in.

"Zulu, this is Bravo," I whispered into the hand mike. "Go ahead."

"This is Zulu. My man on the ground reports movement to his front, over."

"This is Bravo. Can he see anything definite?"

"This is Zulu. Negative."

"Tell him to sit tight until he can see what he's got. We don't want a herd of water bu—."

Suddenly the machine gun on the left flank opened up like a highspeed typewriter. Orange tracers raced out into the night, sprays deflecting off the ground and arcing crazily up into the night sky. Immediately behind the opening salvo, that entire side of the line opened up, firing out across the roadway into the flat rice fields beyond.

"Bravo, this is Zulu!" the voice practically yelled out at me from the hand mike. "We're in it now, they stepped right into us!" The radioman's voice was pitched high with excitement, and it was difficult to hear him over the roar of the weapons going off around him.

I turned to the PF platoon leader, whose troops were off to the right, and whispered urgently, "Go tell your men not to fire unless they see something!" I was afraid that everyone would start shooting now whether there was anything out there or not. The Vietnamese officer nodded and scurried off. I quickly looked back to our left flank, where the firing tempo had kept up. Now I could see occasional bursts of green and red tracer fire coming in to our position. We had somebody out there, but I didn't know who or how many.

"Zulu, this is Bravo." I spoke rapidly into the radio handset. "Can you put out illumination, over?"

"Roger illumination. Wait, out!"

Abney and I crawled up to the roadbed and tried to see what was happening on our left. We could see the tracers racing out from our fighters, and every now and then a return spray would come in from somewhere out there in the field. The nearest firing from our guys was only fifty yards or so away, but I could see nothing directly in front of us. Nobody on our right had started firing either, and I was glad the PF's weren't so green that they just opened up for the hell of it.

"Fieldhouse Golf, this is Green Sleeves Bravo, over." I called the PBR on our right flank.

"Bravo, this is Golf," came the whispered reply.

"This is Bravo. Can you give us illumination out in front

of your position, over?'' I figured that illumination rounds on both of our flanks would light up our whole front. I wanted to see what was going on.

I had hardly made the request to Golf when the first mortar-fired parachute flares popped over the left flank position. Damn! There they were, little shadow figures of men scurrying around in the flat field in front of us. Some of them froze when the flare popped; others went to ground and started firing back even more heavily than before. Some of the men around me started firing at the figures. That let the Cong know that we were there too, and it wasn't long before we began taking fire. I jerked my head in like a turtle when the first rounds started zipping by and cracking in the air.

As more flares went off over the right of our line, I stuck my head up and looked out. Christ, I thought, they're like ants! All across our front, the field was full of men. Some of them were no more than twenty yards away when the flares went off over them. The PF's on my right were ready, though, and they opened up like gangbusters. The RF's on my left got into it too. They were firing heavily. "Holy shit," I yelled to Abney, "here they come!"

When the Cong realized that they had been caught out in the open, they knew that their only option was to charge. Charge they did. Abney and I fired over the edge of the roadway at the figures in front of us. The muzzle blast of my M-16 blinded me immediately, and as always I had to suppress the panic that came from having to fight for my life without being able to see.

The two sailors firing the machine gun close by were just holding down the trigger, firing without letup. "Fire a burst of six! Fire a burst of six!" I yelled at them, never thinking that that was army lingo and the grounded squids probably didn't know what the hell I was talking about. I guessed they didn't because they continued to burn their ammunition until they ran out.

I saw one of the sailors run back to the PBR behind us and yell for some more ammo; but while he waited, the machine gun in the middle of our line was silent. With no machine gun firing it seemed awfully quiet around me. I turned and saw that Abney was also reloading his M-16. Suddenly afraid, I looked across the roadway. Three men dressed in black and strapped with ammo pouches were heading straight for us. The air seemed alive with green fire and lead; even the ground seemed to be jumping under the drum, drum of bullets. They were firing as they came. "Abney, watch out!" I yelled. I leaned forward on my knees and raised my rifle to fire. Abney hugged the dirt even closer as he worked feverishly to get a full magazine out of his ammo belt. I fired short bursts at the men in front of me, but again I went blind in my own muzzle blast. Suddenly Abney was up and firing too, and I vaguely saw a couple of Vietnamese militiamen running toward us, firing as they ran. Something hit me across the shoulders. I swung out wildly, only to realize that a dead man had collapsed on top of me. I never saw him until he hit. I still couldn't see very well and I didn't know if anyone was with him, so I swung my empty rifle in the air like a club.

"Hold it *Trung úy*, hold it!" I heard Abney shouting and felt him pulling at my leg. I dropped to the ground beside him and tried to blink away the rest of my night blindness. I started to reload my rifle as I asked frantically, "Is the line holding? I can't see shit!"

"Yeah, we're o.k.," he yelled back over the firing. "They turned back! Let's get some mortar fire out there before they get away!"

I hadn't even reached for the radio when we heard the mortar tube in the boat behind us start firing. I saw repeating muzzle blasts on the decks of the other two boats too, so I guessed they had all started on their own. "Shot out," I yelled to Abney. He nodded with a big grin on his face and made the thumbs-up sign.

I looked back over the edge of the road and saw a few figures out in the flare-lit field still jumping from one place to another. When the flares would get dim they would all jump up and run toward the rear. You could tell that they were just thinking about getting away. There were still a good many men out there, but they were only firing back sporadically as they tried to get beyond the range of the HE mortar rounds that had started falling on them. We continued to fire out into the field, but it was difficult to see any real point targets to shoot at. I sent Abney off to round up the platoon leaders so I could get their reports.

I heard the radio's hollow voice. "Bravo, this is Zulu, over."

I scrambled over to the radio and replied, "This is Bravo, go."

"This is Zulu, we have choppers en route, over."

"This is Bravo. Roger. Can you have them sweep deep and drop some flares out at two or three clicks? They might find some of these people still running, over."

"Roger, Bravo. I'll contact them now. Fieldhouse Zulu, out."

I wasn't off the horn but a few seconds before I heard the comforting pounding of the chopper rotors. They flew over our position at a fairly high altitude and continued out toward the retreating Viet Cong. We watched them drop large flares and saw them fire their miniguns a time or two, but they were soon back and hovering over our position, waiting for further instructions.

I worked things out with the sailors, the Vietnamese, and the pilots so that we could conduct a fast sweep of the field in front of us. The two choppers would go to either flank and each drop one of their big flares. The ground troops would all go over the top together and advance out into the field for one hundred meters. We were to count bodies, collect any weapons, supplies, or papers we could find, and return.

The choppers elevated and dropped their flares. Abney and I waved to the platoon leaders, who went off yelling to their troops, and everyone went over the top pretty much together. We ran across the roadway firing, just in case there was anybody out there who might want to rise up and shoot at us.

It was an eerie scene. I could see the two choppers hovering like giant black monsters. They were ugly specters in the blue-white light of the slowly falling parachute flares. The smoke from the previous flares and the mortar blasts still hung over the battlefield, like a gauzy shroud over a lighted stage. The line of advancing men was a study of black silhouettes. I watched them move into the field, and occasionally saw one black figure bend over a lump on the ground, pause, and move on. We made the sweep and returned within fifteen minutes.

We loaded into the three PBR's, said good-bye to the choppers, and started home. We had found eleven bodies, all dead, and thirteen weapons. I was told that some papers had been found on one of the dead men, but I didn't know anything else about them. We had had three men lightly wounded, one of them a sailor, and one Vietnamese killed. He had apparently been hit during the initial contact. I was relieved the operation was over. I could worry about the after-action reports tomorrow, I could worry about the captured papers tomorrow, I could worry about tomorrow tomorrow, but right now it was 0300 hours, the action was over, the tension was over, and all I wanted to do was crash on my bunk and get a couple of hours' shut-eye.

I was riding on the second PBR as we motored back to Tram Chim in the darkness. As I looked around me, I could feel that the sailors and the Vietnamese all exuded a sense of excitement and self-congratulation for a job well done. I had already told the navals and the militia platoon leaders what a great job everyone had done, but any residual excitement I felt was overwhelmed by exhaustion. I turned to Abney to see if he was feeling any more spry than I was. He was stretched out on the deck, face to the stars, fast asleep.

THE DAY HAD BEEN CLOUDLESS AND HOT. EVERY BITING BUG in Asia had been feeding off my carcass since early morning, and it had proved impossible to take more than five steps without having about ten pounds of mud build up on my boots and cling there like glue. We had tramped for miles regardless of the goop, and I was feeling pretty frazzled from the effort. Sergeant Abney and I were on yet another operation with a militia platoon from one of the villages in our district. This unit was one of those bedraggled outfits whose individual weapons ranged from pistols to M-16's, and whose leader was more concerned about being friendly than effective.

We were walking again because the flood season was over and the waters of the Mekong were receding into its banks. Most of the land in the district was now above water level, or at worst was covered with only a few inches of water; but even the "dry ground" was really just a viscous gray glue. The Mekong Delta muck would not resist a foot going into it, but pulling a foot out of it required working against the suction of the mud paste. Abney and I and the whole platoon were tired just from the effort of walking. We were covered with mud from the waist down and splattered with it everywhere else. Sweat salted my jungle fatigues and ran from under the brim of my camouflage bush hat. Sweat had darkened the Mike Force patch stitched on the front.

I was being extra careful these days because I was short: I didn't have much time to go before my tour in Vietnam would be over. I had been getting mentally prepared for, indeed anticipating, my "abdication" to the next DSA, but in the interim I wanted to stay busy and keep up the pressure on our local VC.

We had had a brief firefight earlier in the morning. Our group had surprised what appeared to be about a squad of Viet Cong as they worked around a small encampment. Two of the guerrillas had been killed outright, but the rest had fired a few shots and disappeared into the forest. We had spent a couple of hours trying to run them down, but had returned to their encampment without any luck. One of the dead guerrillas had been dragged into the camp clearing and a crude *Chết Cong* ("Kill communists") had been scratched into his chest with a knife. My reaction was both anger and surprise. I had never known a Vietnamese villager to mutilate a body; they usually had great respect for the dead. I didn't like it one bit, and I knew a lot of people in the local village weren't going to like it either when they saw a body that had been cut up like that. It was just going to cause me trouble.

I called the platoon leader over and gave him a rough time about it, saying I wanted him to find out who did it and I wanted him to take some action to ensure that such things would not happen again. It was against the Geneva rules to mutilate bodies, and that made me uneasy, but mostly I wanted to avoid any trouble with the villagers. I didn't want government troops to be identified with the bad habit of slicing up the dead. Once such things got started they could get worse rapidly, and the worst could be very bad indeed.

I stood over the slowly stiffening body of the dead Cong and glared as meanly as I could at the platoon of squatting militiamen. The platoon leader was yelling at them, demanding that the guilty party step forward. The men just stared blankly back at him. The only motion was the occasional flit of a palm frond as it was stirred by some accidental breath of humid air. I was hot, tired, and getting madder and madder. This cutting business was really going to cause me trouble, especially if the dead man belonged to one of the families in the village.

I was about to say something else to the platoon leader when Sergeant Abney came over and told me I was wanted on the radio. It was the familiar voice of Sergeant Robertson, calling from back at the team compound. He said a call had just come in from the province team stating that I should pack my gear and be prepared to leave the team immediately. Robertson said that the Red Cross had apparently contacted the province headquarters and requested that I be placed on emergency leave. The PSA had agreed and, in fact, had already sent a chopper to get me. Robertson said he didn't know what the leave was all about, but the chopper pilot had already contacted him and he had given the pilot our approximate coordinates in the field. He said the whirlybird should be at my location within a few minutes. I just stood there, staring at the radio, befuddled. Off in a jungle in Vietnam, I had been clothes-lined by a radio message that had its origins halfway round the world. Those days I could hardly think beyond distances of thirty or forty kilometers, let alone thousands of miles. I looked over at Abney, frowning in my confusion. I wondered what the hell was going on. Within a few minutes we heard the helicopter bearing in on us and I raised him on our PRC-25. We popped smoke and I directed him to a landing in a nearby rice paddy. I told the Vietnamese platoon leader that I had been summoned to an important meeting with the PSA and would have to leave immediately. I could tell that he was almost as bewildered as I was by the sudden appearance of the helicopter. I didn't know what else to say, though, so Abney and I got aboard the Huey and flew back to our team compound. I figured this was all some sort of a mistake and as soon as I got back to the team house I would straighten it out.

When we arrived at the compound, Sergeants Robertson and Fitz and Lieutenant Cantrell were waiting at the chopper pad. Abney and I jumped off the chopper and ran through the blowing dust and grit. Lieutenant Cantrell grabbed my arm and shouted in my ear, "You have to go with the chopper, *Trung úy*. Province called and told us to pack your bags. You're riding this slick back to Cao Lanh and then on into Can Tho. You're getting an emergency leave for Stateside." I saw my field gear and a stuffed duffle bag by Robertson's feet. I couldn't believe it. Just like that, I was going home!

"What's the rush?" I asked loudly, to be heard over the noise of the whirling chopper blades. "Do you know what the problem is?"

"No, we haven't heard anything for sure," said Cantrell in reply. "Seems like they said something about your father. Has he been sick?"

I just shrugged my shoulders. My father had had a heart problem for years, but I wasn't aware of any crisis. Cantrell looked at me and grinned. "Hell," he said, "just take your gear and be glad to get out of here." He picked up my duffle bag and walked off toward the waiting Huey.

Sergeant Robertson came over and said, "Province says you won't be coming back, *Trung úy*. You won't have any time left in-country on the other side of your leave. You'll have to turn in your basic load of ammo and your M-16. I put the six magazines of ammo in your duffle bag. Don't forget to turn them in."

I just stared at him. I couldn't keep up with what was going on. Everything was coming to an end so quickly. I didn't want to leave like this. There had been no last few days to swap lies and to reminisce about our exploits together. No time to make promises for the future. No time to curse the politicians, the military high command, the REMF's, and the government authorities. No final hours of camaraderie. No time to tell these men how much I respected them and how proud I was to have served with them. All I had was a few seconds to say good-bye.

Robertson squared himself front and center and saluted in his best parade-field manner, holding the fingers of his right hand just so at the edge of his eyebrow. "It's been a pleasure, sir," he said matter-of-factly. I was surprised for a moment, because we never saluted each other out on the teams. It could be fatal to telegraph to distant observers who was the man in charge. Also, our sense of brotherhood and sharing rendered such formalities superfluous. I just blinked at him for a second before I realized I had to get my arm to move and return his salute. As I dropped my salute Robertson broke into a grin and said, "Have a good trip home, *Trung úy*. Send us a letter from the States with a picture of the wife and kid."

I just reached out and grabbed his hand in mine. I couldn't think of anything to say. I could only think that I would probably never see the man again, and that I loved him like a brother. Hell, on more than one occasion we had almost died together. We were back-to-back, hold-'em-off-to-the-last-round, by-god jungle fighters. Now, in a few minutes I would leave and never see him again. Poof, just like that. I finally made some joking remark to Robertson as I shook his hand, and I think I said something about our getting together again back in the States.

Sergeant Abney was still covered with the sweat and mud of our last operation. He came over and snapped off his salute. We shook hands and exchanged good wishes. Sergeant Fitz, whom I had had such a hard time with initially, had become a good friend. We had even kidded each other privately about our fight that day in the compound. We exchanged good-natured salutes and a couple of final jibes as I turned to go back to the chopper.

Lieutenant Cantrell saluted as I approached. "Good-bye, *Trung úy*. Looks like I'll have to hold the fort until our replacement comes in. Remind the colonel that we're out here, will ya?"

"You bet," I said as I returned his salute. I couldn't think of anything else to say. I was in an emotional turmoil, elated at getting out of there alive and distressed at leaving my men behind to finish a job it seemed we had only started. I had figured I would have at least a few days to work out these emotions and to make my speeches, not just a few seconds.

"You can handle this team," I said, fishing for words. "You know the area and you know the chiefs. Just be careful with the men. Get 'em home in one piece." I know it wasn't exactly a call to the cannons, but it was all I could think of, and it took care of the main point. I climbed aboard the chopper and hauled my gear in beside me. As the Huey lifted off from the landing pad, I threw out a final salute to the four men standing there in the swirling dust and debris of the chopper's propwash. Trying for one last expression of goodwill and faith, I stuck out my fist and signaled "thumbs-up." The four just had time to wave back before they passed from my line of sight.

I sat there with a hollow feeling in my stomach. Where was

the elation I was supposed to feel at being free? I was going home—where was my joy? What was it that was nagging at me? It struck me that I had not had a chance to say good-bye to my good friend Tái, the district chief who had been in office when I first arrived. The old Hoa Hao called me his American son and was one of the most gracious human beings I have ever met. He too was now an invisible part of my past. I had not been able to say good-bye to Cô Ha or any of my Vietnamese friends in the village. I was feeling worse and worse about this whole thing. I felt I was running out on a commitment to my people. Yet at the same time a small, quiet spirit inside me was exuberant: "You made it! You made it! You got out alive!"

I SAT IN THE TAN SON NHUT AIRPORT, LOOKING LIKE A REject from some impoverished foreign legion. Having spent the early morning hours fighting the Viet Cong and the rest of the day checking out of IV Corps headquarters in Can Tho and MACV headquarters in Saigon, I had not had time to clean up or to put on a presentable uniform. My weathered boots and faded fatigues were stained with sweat and spattered with dried Delta mud. I was sporting a two-day beard, and the only military hat I had was a blue Vietnamese militia beret. It was not even a part of the uniform of the United States Army, but my team had packed my duffle bag for me and I couldn't find my standard American fatigue cap.

I felt conspicuous and out of place, sitting there with all the other GI's waiting for the late-night flight back to the States. Most of the men were dressed in their class-A uniforms, pressed and polished like real Stateside soldiers. My derelict appearance finally caught the attention of the MP's working at the final check-through point, and one of them was sent over to check me out. After reviewing my orders, he reminded me sharply that travel in the States required a class-A uniform. Did I have such a uniform? I assured him that I had a set of class A's in my duffle bag and that I would change before I attempted to board a domestic flight in the States. That seemed to satisfy the MP, so he went back to his desk where he huddled with two or three others who were standing there. They all kept giving me suspicious glances, and I was feeling more and more ill at ease. I was afraid they would pull me off the flight for some silly reason, so I sat there trying to look assured and unconcerned.

After a while I went and squatted against a wall, trying to make myself as inconspicuous as possible, and I thought back over the hectic day. I recalled looking back out of that helicopter's door and getting a final glimpse of the old mud fort at Tram Chim. I had looked out at the familiar pattern of canals, paddies, and tree lines for the last time, and had felt a strange melancholy when I realized that I would never see that land again. Like my teammates, I had become one with the surroundings. I had the pulse of the place, its sights and smells, its winds and rains, its droughts and floods, its bugs and beasts, its people and its beauty. I had been forced to absorb it all in order to survive. It was part of me, and now it was ripped away like a dried bandage off a raw wound.

I had sat there in the chopper seat, confused by my feelings. I couldn't resolve the competing anger, joy, resentment, and relief. I was a soldier honed for battle, reflexes tuned, adrenalin reserves waiting anxiously to be released. I was a person of importance, used to having my words listened to and my wishes respected. I had been procurator of my own little region. Now, very suddenly, I was a warrior without a battle, a king without a country.

As I sat against the wall of the air terminal and watched the people milling around inside, I thought wryly that the army had certainly brought me back to earth in a hurry. Within a matter of hours I had gone from being the most powerful man in Tram Chim to being questioned by an MP about whether I could even come up with a regulation uniform! "Quit bitching," I finally told myself. "You'd better be glad you're alive and going home standing up."

The boarding call for my flight finally came. As I got in line, I couldn't help but worry that the devil's last mortar round would fall right in the middle of my group and blow us all to hell. I think something like that was on many minds. There was a tenseness in the air despite our lighthearted conversation and sometimes forced jocularity. We boarded the plane without incident, though, taxied out, and began our takeoff. As the plane left the runway the pressure cap came off all our anxieties. When we felt the lift of the wheels we all shouted and cheered, tossed our hats in the air, and slapped one another on the back. We'd made it! We were going home!

I had flown to Vietnam from Oakland, California, and now I was flying back to the same terminal. My flight from Oakland had left at night, and the last sight I had had of the United States was the twinkling beauty of the Golden Gate Bridge as its span passed beneath us in the darkness. Craning to see the mainland behind us, I had seen the sparkling tendrils of the bridge stretching across the entrance to the bay, connecting vast galaxies of lights. Ahead had been only a stygian blackness. I had been practically numbed by feelings of emptiness and fear. Now everything was in reverse. I was coming home!

It was night as we approached the American mainland. The voice of the pilot came over the intercom and told us we were approaching the San Francisco Bay area, so we all stared out our windows, searching for that first sight of land. Suddenly, there it was again, that beautiful bridge glittering like a fairy's sculpture spanning the darkness. I remembered some lines from Sir Walter Scott that a teacher had long ago forced into my memory: "Breathes there the man with soul so dead,/Who never to himself hath said,/'This is my own, my native land!'/ Whose heart hath ne'er within him burn'd/As home his footsteps he hath turn'd/From wandering on a foreign strand!" Now I really knew what the poet meant. I had never seen a more beautiful sight. My heart within me burned.

The happiness and the expectation could be seen in every man's face. We were pumped up, we were smiling, we were ready for anything. Anything, that is, but what we got. We stepped off the plane to an empty tarmac. The only thing there to greet us was a tired ground crew and some guys from the Customs Service who wanted to shake us down as if we were prisoners coming in from Alcatraz rather than soldiers coming home from war. I wondered when we'd get our welcome home.

After getting through the Customs shed, we were quietly ushered onto buses for rides to our airfields or train terminals. When I got to the San Francisco airport, I had to go into a men's room and dig into my duffle bag for my khaki class-A uniform. The shirt and pants were a wrinkled mess, and the shoes were green with mildew. I found all my brass in the bottom of the bag too, but it was badly tarnished. I took some paper towels and cleaned things off as best I could and put on the uniform. I looked in the mirror and was embarrassed at having to go out looking like such a sad sack. I didn't know what else to do, though, so I stuffed my faded, dirty jungle fatigues and my blue beret into my duffle bag and went to catch my plane to Atlanta. I still wondered about the welcome home.

In the Atlanta airport I had a chance to get a shave and remove what was now a three-day growth of beard. I was still embarrassed to be seen in such a rumpled condition. Infantry tradition insisted that its officers and men appear in proper uniform with brass bright, shoes shined, and creases cracking. I looked like the foreman of a junkyard! I soon noticed, though, that the state of my uniform was not going to cause any comment. No one noticed if my uniform was correct or not. As a matter of fact, no one noticed me at all. I was either stared right through, or people would divert their eyes as I approached. I wondered if I smelled bad, or if the splotches on my skin from jungle rot were being mistaken for leprosy. It began to dawn on me that in this crowded airport I was somehow, in some subtle way, being shunned. I was home but yet I wasn't. I was among people, yet I was alone. I think it was there, in the Atlanta airport, that what was to become a permanent sense of dislocation first descended on me. I wondered if there was going to be a welcome home at all.

PART THREE

The Endings

Yt haps somtymes in saddnesse and pytie
that who faythful seryvs ys not faythful sene.

The Acts of King Arthur and
His Noble Knights
John Steinbeck (1902–1968)

Chapter 21

I crawled off the old prop-driven plane that had taken me to the small airfield outside my hometown. I was still in my short-sleeved khaki uniform, and the frigid winter air made my blood curdle. My wife, Susan, and my brother came to meet me at the airport, but worries about my father's condition took the edge off their welcome and dampened my impulse to laugh for joy. We went straight to the car and rode into town and to the old red-brick county hospital. I met my mother outside his room, and after a brief hug and a few tears we went inside to see my father.

Men of the Anglo-Saxon tradition do not greet each other with a hug, a kiss, or a Latin abrazo, even when they would love to give one. We have to make do with a firm handshake, an open smile, and a glad word. My father did his best to meet all three requirements. When I entered his room he looked up from his bed with a surprised expression. He smiled broadly and put out his hand. I took it, and we exchanged the words of greeting that custom required. I was shocked by his appearance and by the pallid skin color that I associated with death and had seen all too often on the other side of the world. I already knew that a handshake was not enough—I owed too much to this old man, this old farmer, this old philosopher. I leaned over and kissed him on the cheek, trying to say without words what I could never say with them.

My father died a few days later, never leaving the sterile room so different from the fields and forests he loved. I had gone to sit with him a while on that afternoon, and I could tell he knew the game was up. We reminisced about his college days and his exploits as a young man. We chuckled together once more over the tales that as children my brother and I had begged to hear again and again. When time came for me to leave, he cried. He held my hand for the last time and wept. He didn't cry over me, he didn't cry for the past, he cried for the future he knew he would never see. He said he knew he would never see "my little Heather" again. He was speaking of my daughter, whom he had really taken under his wing during the past year while I was in Vietnam and Susan was teaching school during the day. Heather had spent much of the year sitting on my father's knee, and she was the apple of his eye. He wanted so much to see her grow into a young lady, yet he knew the hope was futile.

I couldn't think of anything to say. I held his hand, and when he screwed a smile back on his face I told him not to worry, I would see him tomorrow. As I walked out of the hospital I tried to find some emotion, some sorrow, pity, regret, anger, anything, but I couldn't find it. I had burned out on death and tragedy. I had built up guards to deal with this sort of situation. I had a reflexive attitude of resignation that took what came without the intrusion of emotion. My reflexes were still in place; I couldn't just call them off instantaneously. I was emotionally sterile. I wondered if I was crazy.

When the call came that night that my father had died, I felt regret, but I couldn't summon up that sorrow, that pain that a son should feel at the passing of the man who had loved and raised him. At the funeral I saw his body lying there, but I had seen so many other bodies in such worse condition that seeing another one didn't evoke much response. This was my father, of course, but I don't think I let that fact penetrate. Psychologically I was pretending this dead man was no different from all the others I had seen. No need to be upset, it was just another corpse.

Despite my detachment I knew I should be feeling sadness and anguish. I felt guilty, as if I was cheating my father of something due him. Something inside was telling me that a son should be able to cry at his father's funeral! I have never resolved that sense of guilt. I feel that there is something still to come out, some duty still to be done. The voice within is still saying, "David, you should have cried at your father's grave. You owed him that, David, but you just stood there like a stone."

WHEN MY LEAVE WAS OVER, I DROVE TO FORT BENNING AND reported in at Building One. My tour of active duty was coming to an end, and all the paperwork of out-processing had to be done. I had decided not to remain in the army for a career. I had wrestled with the decision for quite a while, and I still had doubts about whether I was doing the right thing. It meant giving up my first choice of profession, and I still liked a lot of things about soldiering. I liked the challenges, I liked working with people, and I liked the camaraderie among men at arms; but I didn't like incompetence, and I didn't like ingratitude.

I felt that incompetence was an army problem. Poor leadership and poor judgment were problems enough when found in junior officers, but it seemed to me that those qualities were almost as prevalent in the higher ranks. A career of putting up with the system implied being indentured to mediocrity. To be sure, there were and are many very competent officers in the service, but the deadwood and the hangers-on make life miserable for subordinates who try to do their duty well.

The ingratitude wasn't a problem with the army, it was a problem with the country. I felt my country didn't give a damn about me or the sacrifice I and thousands of others were making in their name. I found I didn't like being shot at for low pay and less thanks. When men or women were in the army— or the air force, or the navy—they were in the *service*, that is, the service of their country. They performed that service at some sacrifice to themselves. They sacrificed their time, their efforts, their freedom, their families, and maybe even their lives. It was not unreasonable for a man to figure that his country owed him at least a little respect, a little thanks for the trouble, a little pat on the back for the effort. But thanks and respect were not available, not this time around. A Vietnam returnee had to go a long way to find anything like respect, and as for thanks, he could forget that altogether.

Instead, thousands of our countrymen were lauding the very enemy we had been sent to fight. College students and other naifs were waving the enemy flag in public parks and even visiting Hanoi, urging the North Vietnamese to kill us, their own compatriots. A clan of citizens within my own country was shouting encouragement to the Viet Cong and to the North Vietnamese as they practiced the art of murder, terror, and international outlawry. Complacent Middle America offered no protest, no counterpoint, only silence. Everyone just seemed to want the whole thing to go away. It had all become just too much trouble. There were too many loose ends, too many muddy political questions, too much blood on film.

When I was a teenager, the ringing words of John F. Kennedy's inaugural speech had fired my romantic dreams. He had proclaimed a shining society that would "pay any price, bear any burden, support any friend, face any foe" in the name of liberty, but it seems he was wrong. Our country had already found a price too high, a burden too heavy, a friend too incompetent, and a foe too intractable for us to continue to hold high the cause of liberty.

That was a bitter lesson for me to learn, for I had shared the dream of Camelot, and I suppose I always will. I have the sense from time to time that I am not alone, and I suspect that despite the limited understanding we have of events in distant places, there will always be those among us who have the gleam of the quest in their eyes. They are people of every sex and station and they yearn to be challenged to a cause. They will always be looking for that wrong to right, that ill to cure, that song to sing; and there will always be those who will go to arms in aid of the helpless and the downtrodden. Ignoring the political issues of the moment, these people will champion the weak and the poor in the face of evil and tyranny. And no matter what the outcome, in their romantic hearts they will keep the secret, if secret it must be, that they are better men for having held the lamp beside the golden door.

Chapter 22

IT was midsummer in south Georgia, and the humid heat would not relent even though the sun had dropped below the horizon. I sat on the steps of the apartment that Susan and I rented and watched the fading glow of sunset turn the western sky from a deep red to a purplish black. The low hum of our small window air-conditioning unit helped lull me into a depressed stupor. I felt hollowed out, empty, a carcass of nothing. Day after day for three months I had had nothing to do but watch my daughter, Heather, crawl around the apartment. I would feed her baby food for lunch and fry a hamburger for myself, but beyond these minimal demands, I had little to do but daydream and think morosely of Vietnam.

Susan was lucky—she had a job teaching. I had nothing to do until I began graduate school in the fall, so it was my reasonable assignment to sit home every day and play househusband. Though I loved my wife and daughter and was glad to be home alive, I was resentful of my daily chores, frustrated at the petty concerns that occupied my time. I felt that something was deeply wrong.

Like the ex-warrior chieftain who is forced to stay in the village and watch the tents, I was feeling useless and discarded. The crushing intensity of the Vietnam experience was gone. The insatiable demands, the incredible responsibilities, the impossible tasks were all left halfway around the world, unfinished, in the hands of others. I floundered in the vacuum of my new existence, and in the quiet of this early summer evening, I wept.

I sat there staring out at the fading sunset, tears rolling slowly down my face. As a child uses a security blanket, I wore a faded jungle fatigue shirt that had crawled with me through the sweat and the mud and the blood of Vietnam. It was an amulet, a souvenir to remind myself of the valuable and powerful person I once had been. In my heart I called after the departing sun. I yearned to go after it and to catch it, to see it rise again on the other side of the world. I thought about "my" people and wondered how they fared. Had the local Cong struck again? Had the bridge at Phu Tanh village been repaired? Was the rice crop going to be as good as expected? Was soap available in the villages? It hurt deeply to admit that there was really no reason to ask: there was nothing I could do. I sat there in the summer night and harbored a terrible sense of emptiness. I touched the fabric of the old fatigue shirt just to make sure it was real and to prove to myself that all my memories were not simply dreams.

I TOOK MY GI BILL BENEFITS AND RETURNED TO GRADUATE school in the fall of 1970. It was not the best of times for a Vietnam veteran to be on a college campus. The American invasion of the North Vietnamese and Viet Cong sanctuary areas along the Cambodian border had raised the hackles of the anti-war community. Student protests across the country were given even more impetus by the tragic incident at Kent State University, when a fumbling herd of National Guardsmen shot up what they thought was a threatening mob of protestors. The senseless deaths of four students and the oft-televised scenes of shooting and horror helped center the nation's consciousness on what was already a rapidly growing mood of doubt and anger about the war in Vietnam.

It was the fashion on college campuses to be outraged about the war, whether one really knew anything about it or not. Harsh polarization had set in, and intelligent discussion about American involvement in Vietnam had become virtually impossible. This was a bitter experience for me, and in seeking some rationalization I became convinced that most of my fellow students were victims of their narrow minds. I told myself that I shouldn't be bothered with trying to rectify the misguided attitudes of my peers; not only did the task appear impossible, but the constant justification of my own involvement to such a petulant audience seemed to be fawning and humiliating. Feeling like wounded Virtue on trial, I disdained any response to the prosecution.

Two years went by. I was keeping long hours, trying to do well in graduate school, yet every night Vietnam was still in my dreams. Every building corridor was a trail ripe for ambush, every loud noise was a jolt to my senses, every sudden movement was a cause to go on guard. I would often read or hear of myself, the veteran, being referred to as some common criminal, a fascist, or some sort of bloodthirsty baby killer. I was deeply offended, yet I remained silent. I walled up my thoughts and reactions and tried to go about what I thought was a normal life.

One day while I was working around the house, I looked idly through some old papers I had dragged out of a desk drawer and came across the address of Lieutenant Dick Davidson. Dick and I had been good friends in Vietnam. He had a MAT team in Kien Van, an adjacent district to mine, and we suffered through the same problems and fears. We saw each other only when we happened to be in the province town at the same time, but if we had to stay over for a night we would always bunk together and stay up late airing our gripes and congratulating each other on our minor successes. We got on well together and developed a strong friendship. Dick happened to be in Cao Lanh when I had passed through on my way out of country. He had scribbled his home address on a scrap of paper and asked me to write; he was due to come home about a month after me. With all the shuffling about, concerns at home after my father's death, and starting school again, I had misplaced the address and had never written. Now I dashed off a letter and waited eagerly for a reply.

A few days later a letter came in the mail. It was from Dick's mother. Dick was dead. Had been for two years. I couldn't believe it. Dick was dead! Dead! My mind froze shut. At first I refused to believe it. This couldn't be right! I simply refused to accept it. I was disoriented; something was wrong here. I thought if I very carefully reread the letter and the documents that came with it, I could figure out why I was being told this damnable tale. I read with agonized disbelief the story the letter told.

Two weeks after I had left Vietnam, Dick had been ordered to come back in to the province compound for his last two weeks of duty, a "safe" period awarded to those who made it that far. Ten days before he was to come home, his *liên đội*, a militia unit similar to a light infantry battalion, was to undertake a major operation in an area with which Dick was familiar. Since his replacement did not know the area or the Vietnamese troops, Dick volunteered to go out with his unit again. He didn't think it was fair to stick his green replacement with the difficult operation.

Dick's *liên đội* went out on the operation, but something went wrong. They walked into a Main Force Viet Cong battalion arrayed in ambush. The *liên đội* was pinned down. They either couldn't or wouldn't move. The Cong had them just where they wanted, and the slaughter began. Gunships sent in to give support were shot down; no artillery was available; finally the *liên đội* broke and the survivors began streaming to the rear.

It was late in the day before troop replacements arrived. Neither Dick nor Sergeant Franklin, his teammate, had come back in. Radio contact could not be established. When the fresh troops swept through the area in force, they found the gruesome results of a well-laid ambush: many victims, but no victors. Wise in the ways of war, the Cong had split. Among the victims were the two Americans.

Dick and Sergeant Franklin, a black noncom whom I remembered as a good soldier, were found side by side. They had been stripped of their weapons and personal belongings, but the piles of empty cartridge brass around them gave evidence that the two had held out to the last. Back to back and probably alone, they had apparently made every attempt to sell their lives dearly.

Hot, bitter tears flooded my eyes. I picked up the official report that Dick's mother had enclosed and quickly flipped through its pages. I kept denying what was clearly true, that Dick had been dead for nearly two years. While I was in school, living, learning, and for the most part having a good time, Dick had been lying cold under a government headstone. My shocked incredulity turned to deep sorrow, and then to frustrated rage. Dick was dead. Dead! And for what? I couldn't think of a single good reason. It certainly had not been for his family, for they had received only pain and loss. It had not been for the preservation of the Vietnamese people, for we had not preserved them. It had not been for a grateful nation, for it was clear that the nation was not at all grateful. Suddenly I was wracked with sobs and tears of protest. "No! No," I cried. And, "Why?" Over and over again, "Why?" I stood in our living room and shuddered as I moaned. I cursed the Cong, the army, the politicians, and the country as well. I cursed fate, luck, and maybe even God, I don't remember. I lurched around the living room like a drunken bull, kicking the walls and furniture in fury, shouting my rage to the ceiling. Susan was cooking dinner in the kitchen when I had first eagerly opened the letter. Now she just stood there and stared at me in open-mouthed shock. She must have thought I had gone crazy. I know she was frightened, and she had absolutely no idea what to do. She quickly gathered up little Heather and left the house in tears, frantically looking for a neighbor to get some help. I eventually made my way back to our bedroom and fell onto the bed. I lay there, pounding the mattress and crying, crying, crying.

I don't know how much time went by, but eventually Paul Burnam, a neighbor and fellow graduate student, came over and peeked hesitantly into the room. I was pulling myself back under control by then, and when he inquired if I was all right, I told him I was and that he needn't be concerned. Susan had sent him over, but Paul was clearly uncomfortable and had no idea what to do or say either, so after a few more minutes he left. Some time later Susan and Heather came back, and Susan picked up cooking where she had left off. I came out of our bedroom and read the evening newspaper. Calm was reimposed, and to this day it covers an ever-smoldering sense of terrible injustice.

TIME MOVED ON. IN 1974 I FINALLY FINISHED GRADUATE school. By then I had picked up two more university degrees, and Susan and I had added a son, Patrick, to our family. They were all ready for me to go out and get a "real job," and I was anxious to do it. After four years of hard labor and distraction I had made considerable progress in dealing with my demons, and I could usually manage most of them. For example I no longer leaped out of my skin at every loud pop or bang. Back in 1970 when I was interviewing for acceptance into graduate school, I had literally dived under the professor's desk when a dynamite explosion from a nearby excavation site had rocked the building. He sat there calmly and watched me crawl back out. I felt like a fool. In 1974 I no longer would do that, but I would still give quite a lurch before I could stop myself.

Pontifications and exhortations about the war in Vietnam no longer even entered my brain. They fell away like water off a duck's back. I had made my peace with the fact that as a people Americans really didn't know anything about poverty, deprivation, or suffering. In short, I could live with those around me and not constantly be at odds with the way they ran their lives and the way they thought about issues. That took a lot of deep inward adjustment for me, but basically my soul was quiet: live and let live.

I went on to become a university professor, mainly because I kept my eyes fixed on that goal. I refused to be pulled away by that tapping, tapping at my door. I have survived, and the years have marched by in their inevitable sequence. Heather, who went through her first year of life without me, appears none the worse for it. She is a teenager now, and I think her only awareness of my having been a soldier is that she has seen some old uniforms around and she knows I've been working on this book for years. She vaguely realizes that the story is about Vietnam. My son is old enough to have heard that I was in Vietnam, but young enough not to know or care what it all meant. Susan has had to live with me without being able to understand the stresses that sometimes drag at both of us. The blame is entirely mine because I have not yet been able to talk frankly and openly about the war with my family. It has only been through the help of these faceless pages that I have been able to put forth my tale. It has been a catharsis.

I KNOW I AM NOT ALONE IN MY RETICENCE. IT SEEMS THAT most of us who fought in Vietnam are now just silent observers. We are ex-soldiers-in-a-cause who have lost and lived to see the result, both in our own lives and in the far corners of Asia. For me personally, small quirks still remain a problem.

It is still difficult for me to ignore the threat of an ambush while driving down a shaded country lane. When the forest gets a little dark and green and the road gets a little too narrow, I feel the urge to stop and get out, to scout ahead lest I drive my family into a trap. I can get very nervous very quickly.

Along the corridors of the building where I work, I still find myself calculating the distance from doorway to doorway. I know I do it so I can leap for the closest one should some enemy jump from around a corner and spray the hall with a burst from his AK-47. I don't really think about it. I do it almost subconsciously as I walk along.

I still crush beer cans. Some people think I do it to be macho, but that's not the reason. I just remember that beer cans make excellent hand-grenade casings, and I feel uneasy leaving them around in perfect condition. I don't feel I have to crush everybody else's beer cans, just mine. If I don't, I get this funny feeling in my stomach and a cold breath runs down my spine.

I still can't bear to be around injured children. I am haunted by the memories of the bloodied and mangled bodies we used to make such frantic but primitive efforts to save. It still hurts to recall their frightened faces, their pain, and their lack of comprehension at what was happening to them. If I am around children now who have been the victims of some harsh physical or even mental trauma, I get this frantic urgency to *do* something! I want to stop the pain, stop the suffering, and I want to stop it *now*. I see in my mind's eye Vietnamese children practically digested by a well-placed land mine or a booby-trapped hand-grenade. Something inside me starts demanding that I stop the pain, stop the pain, stop the pain!

As for Southeast Asia, it seems to have suffered more than all the rest of us put together. We have seen the grafting of a new Indochinese empire by North Vietnam. We have seen Laos occupied by the Hanoi government. We have seen Cambodia pillaged and starved by Cambodian communists and then occupied by the North Vietnamese. South Vietnam has been occupied, colonized, and finally absorbed by North Vietnam. I think most veterans are pained at the obvious waste of our efforts and receive no comfort from the fact that every refuge around the South China Sea is littered with the evidence that we were right in the beginning.

I don't mean that the American methods were right—that is clearly not the case. I mean we were right to resist terror and war being inflicted on a poor and backward people; right to recognize that the turmoil in Vietnam was caused by the activities of a hostile government which had clear designs on a territory and people not hers by any law other than force of arms; right to be willing to stand for something, by God; and right to risk our own good fortune in a cause so remote to our own well-being. The South Vietnamese government had many faults, but Ho Chi Minh and his communist party have turned out to be the Specter haunting Southeast Asia, and that apparition has scattered before it a legacy of cruelty, famine, and tyranny which can only condemn it before a just and candid world.

Despite the nature of the enemy, many American veterans feel that they are the ones being blamed for the war in Vietnam. That is sheer calumny, and I maintain in the face of all accusers that we who served did so when our only thought was duty and our only cause was freedom. We were weighed in the balances and not found wanting.

SO FAR AS I CAN BE, I AM AT PEACE WITH MYSELF. I DO NOT accept any guilt about an "immoral" war in Vietnam. I do not believe it was an immoral war at all, rather a decent cause gone terribly wrong. I have few regrets about our collective, or my personal, experience in Vietnam. I do regret the misinformation and misguidance that were so often the hallmarks of the American and Vietnamese authorities. That disingenuousness, no matter its intent, was evil in its result. It dulled the ability of elected officials to deal effectively with a culturally foreign and physically remote situation which writhed in continuous metamorphosis.

I regret the suffering of the people of South Vietnam at the hands of their own kinsmen and at the hands of their American allies. While I had no sympathy for the government of South Vietnam, I hold the cause of the South Vietnamese people in my heart. I yearned for their freedom; I fought for it with them. Yet we failed. In striving to achieve our goal of helping a whole society, we Americans wrongly inconvenienced, injurea, and sometimes even killed our South Vietnamese friends. God forgive us.

I regret the absence of victory. It was an article of faith that American military actions inevitably resulted in success. Disengagement in the face of an aggressive and hostile enemy, while not quite defeat, leaves the same taste in the mouth. And I regret the callous heart of my country which did not shrink from calling her citizens to war, but once called, refused to sustain them with public support or sympathy. Rather than receive help and encouragement, members of the armed services, and especially of the army, became the targets of public scorn, distrust, and resentment. Those attitudes were as misdirected as they were inappropriate. Armies of the Western democracies follow, they do not make, public policy. The armed services, like it or not, follow the will of the people as expressed in the ballot box. If there was immorality in the war in Vietnam, it was that a democratic nation called her citizens to war, had them killed by the tens of thousands, and then, like a faithless lover, turned and scorned the survivors. Oh, perfidious nation!

Chapter 23

THIS final tale is an epilogue of sorts. It occurred relatively recently, yet I include it because I hope it indicates the opening of a new chapter in the history of the Vietnam war and its aftermath. In November 1982 I traveled to Washington, D.C., to take part in the Vietnam Veterans Memorial ceremonies. Thousands of other veterans were coming in from all across the country and I wanted to be there.

I wanted to go to the ceremonies for several reasons. I wanted to honor the dead, especially those I knew personally. I wanted to taste that old feeling of soldierly comradeship and sense of purpose that seemed so faint a memory. I wanted to see the memorial itself; I wanted to touch some of the names carved into its polished marble. And I wanted my damned parade.

On the first day of the activities I was one of many who participated at the National Cathedral in the reading of the names of all those who died in Vietnam. I was one of a long series of readers who would undertake a three-day candlelight vigil, continuously reading the names from the official casualty lists until all 57,937 had been read. I considered it an honor to participate in the ceremony and to speak the names of the dead into the quiet air of the vaulted cathedral.

We did our reading in pairs. My partner was an older man whose son had been killed in Vietnam. He and I read for half an hour and only went down the list from Bianconi to Blunkall. It was an emotional experience. Sometimes it was hard

to continue reading because I would look out into the audience
and see someone crying or wiping the tears from his eyes. A
lump would swell in my throat and tears would blur my own
vision. It brought home to me in a very stark way that I was
speaking the names of real men who had had real families,
real loves, and real aspirations. I was deeply moved by the
atmosphere of the cathedral, the solemnity of the proceedings,
and the deep expressions of sorrow. I was relieved that the
time to honor our dead had finally come.

IT WAS AN INTENSELY EMOTIONAL EXPERIENCE TO SEE ALL
those GI's again. Thousands of them came into town in their
old jungle fatigues or with some piece of an old uniform they
had dragged out of the attic or closet. There were veterans
there from every state in the Union. They came in by plane,
train, auto, and bus. Some hitchhiked and some just plain
hiked all the way from wherever. I didn't care what their
service, what their unit, what their rank—I loved seeing every
one of them. I think we all felt a strong sense of camaraderie.
Every handshake included the symbolic thumb-grip of the
brotherhood. Every man could feel like a hero.

Every veteran in town was looking for somebody he knew
from the old days. Men would just mill around in the crowd,
eyes darting from one face to the next. The emotions were
guarded, and the eyes rarely showed any expression except
the hope that the next face would draw that spark of recog-
nition. When two old friends would finally find each other,
the emotions would find release. There would be shouts, hugs,
and tears as men who had shared their own corner of hell
would meet again after more than a decade.

For those who couldn't find someone they actually knew,
just finding someone from the same brigade or even the same
division was enough. Men from the same unit, even if they
didn't know each other personally, knew they had shared a
common experience, a common terror, a common pain. It was
not unusual to see two men standing braced in each others
arms, sobbing out ten years' worth of anger, sorrow, and frustration.

I WENT DOWN TO THE VIETNAM VETERANS MEMORIAL ON
the first day I was in town. That was the Wednesday before

the official dedication on Saturday, November 13. Veterans were just beginning to trickle into town for the weekend ahead, and we had just begun the reading of the list of the dead at the National Cathedral. I was prepared not to like the monument. I had seen drawings of it and had not been impressed, and I was aware of the sometimes harsh controversy surrounding its design. So I was pensive as I walked up the small rise on the Mall near the Lincoln Memorial. I knew that at the crest of the rise I would be able to look down into a slight depression and see the black marble walls of a large "V" pressed into the hillside. I knew that each polished slab that made up the chevron would have inscribed on it the densely packed names of all the men killed in Vietnam. I had already heard the place described with displeasure as "The Valley of Death." I wondered what my own reaction would be.

I reached the top of the rise and looked down. The black granite slashed starkly across the new grass. I stopped and just stood there for a few minutes, allowing myself to take it all in from a distance. I knew immediately that at least I didn't dislike it. It was solemn, it was indeed unadorned, and it carried no message other than the names of the dead. Yet it did not strike me as inappropriate. It was longer than I had imagined, and reminded me of a large artillery revetment. I wondered if others saw that same facet of the design.

I walked on down to the polished stones of the monument. A small crowd of other veterans was already there, standing quietly by themselves or talking in hushed tones in groups of two or three. Many were standing close to the wall itself, peering at the endless list of the dead and trying to find the name of a friend lost so long ago. Finding the names somehow brought relief. Gruff-looking men in old uniforms stared with red eyes and quivering chins as they found the names of those who had once stood by their side. Those who had been at the monument for a while and had gotten over the initial emotions went up and put their arms around those who had just arrived and were freshly hurting.

I looked with dread for the names of my own dead. I was afraid that when my eyes fell upon them, they would leap off the black wall and strike me like a hammer. I was afraid of the pain. I was right. When I found their names I cried. It hurt so deeply to see those good names of long ago written so freshly on the wall of stone. I touched each name, trying to reach back to them across time and mortality. It was a way to shake their hands again, to hear their voices, to see their smiles, and to tell them that David Donovan remembered.

I must have stayed there for a couple of hours, just walking around, looking at faces, staring at the monument, going back to the special names I had found, letting it all soak in. The atmosphere was one of quiet, peace, and dignified respect for the dead. I sat alone for a long time on the grassy slope in front of the monument, thinking my own thoughts and analyzing my own emotions. I wanted to know if I should like this thing or dislike it.

Finally, I settled it. I walked away with a feeling of satisfaction; I liked it. There for all the world to see was a list of nearly fifty-eight thousand men who had died for a cause from which they could expect no benefit. The wall says one thing very clearly: If blood be the price of honor, then the veterans of Vietnam have surely paid enough.

AND I FINALLY GOT MY PARADE. FOR ONE DAY IT WAS LIKE being in the army again. It was Veterans Day, November 13. The word got around in crisp military terms: parade assembly time was 0845 hours. Old soldiers tried to remember how to fall in, dress right, and keep in step. Everyone was feeling so good that the fine points of parade technique didn't really matter. We were getting our parade! That was enough in itself.

The uniform of the day was old combat boots worn white with age, faded jungle fatigue shirts over old blue jeans, and service headgear of every description. On November 13, 1982, after more than ten years of waiting, the American Army of Vietnam moved out for its splendidly ragtag parade down Constitution Avenue.

As we made the sweeping left turn from the Mall onto Constitution Avenue, I could see clearly down the broad street. The sidewalks were crammed with cheering people. Since I was on the outside of the front rank, people reached out to shake my hand and pound my back. I wasn't special, I was just accessible. Men, women, and children were cheering and waving flags. The most common cheer was "Welcome home! Welcome home!" Our formation was more like a rambling cattle herd than soldiers on parade. It was so bad it was good and added to the joy of the occasion. Nobody was worried about anything, everybody was having a good time.

The swelling was in my chest again, the tears kept filling my eyes, but this time not from sadness—it was from pleasure and immense relief. A parade! For me. A great weight was lifted from my shoulders. Cheering crowds, smiling women, waving children—simple things really, but things soldiers have always yearned for and always will.

THERE IS A LARGE VIETNAMESE COMMUNITY AROUND THE Washington, D.C. area. I had wondered what their reaction would be to all this attention to the Vietnam veterans. Would they be interested and come out to the ceremonies and parade, or would they all stay home, uncertain what the reaction might be to their presence? I worried they might prefer to stay away out of fear of some embarrassing incident. They did. It was rare to see a Vietnamese in the crowd of onlookers. I thought it was sad that they were not there to at least see the parade and perhaps feel some of the relief I experienced.

The parade ended down by the Vietnam Veterans Memorial. All the units broke up to go to the official dedication. Thousands and thousands of veterans filled the valley, spilled over the hill in front, and clogged the Mall all the way over to the Lincoln Memorial. Toward the end of the ceremonies I made my way through the crowd, shook hands with some recently made friends for a last time, and began the slow walk back to my car. It was over for me, I was going home.

Far beyond the edge of the crowd, where there were only a smattering of curious onlookers, I moved toward a small clump of trees. I was almost upon them before I saw the Vietnamese family, a mother and father and two children. The man and woman were looking at me intently and I realized it was because I had chosen to wear my blue Vietnamese beret, and my jungle fatigue jacket still had on it the Vietnamese rank insignia that marked me as a *cô vàn*. They looked at me as if they could tell I had been one of the Americans close to their people. They didn't say anything, either one of them. Their message was in their eyes and on their faces. It was a message of pain, of sorrow, and of great loss.

As I approached, the man gazed sadly into my eyes. I hope he saw there a responsive look of understanding and of deep regret at his pain. I felt a spark of friendship as he silently stuck out his hand to grab mine. A smile never came to his lips, a cheer never came from his throat, yet I saw the flicker in his eyes and the tears on his wife's face. I wanted to say something to them, I wanted to hug them all just as I had done so many of my comrades these last few days. Instead I simply grasped his hand, shook it, and tried to say everything through my own eyes. I paused for a second, but then I kept on walking. I didn't stop. I didn't know what to do or what to say. We Americans might have lost a war, but that family had lost a country.

As I walked on away through the trees, I looked back over my shoulder at the Vietnamese family. They seemed so lost and helpless against the backdrop of the Lincoln Memorial and the huge crowd of Americans milling around down in the valley. I wanted to go back and talk with them, to tell them how deeply I felt their loss. I wanted to tell them that I and my kind had never called them "slopes" and had never thought of them as less than ourselves. I wanted so badly to let them know that I was David Donovan, that I had fought the Terror, that no one may know me now but I was once a warrior king!

Glossary

AK-47 Kalashnikov Assault Rifle. A fully automatic rifle of Soviet design. The basic individual weapon of the communist forces.

An Long A village of Tram Chim district which sits on the banks of the Mekong River and has a large stone fortress left there from the French colonial era.

Ao días A traditional Vietnamese woman's dress, which is always worn with pants because the long skirt is slit all the way to the hip on either side.

Arc-Lite The code name for B-52 bombing missions along the Cambodian-Vietnamese border.

A-team The basic ten-man team of the United States Special Forces. The A-teams often led irregular military units which were not responsible to the Vietnamese military command.

Bà Married woman. Used as a title, like Mrs.

Bác-sĩ Doctor. Also used to refer to American army medics.

Ba Mười Ba A brand name of a Vietnamese beer.

Ba si dê Home-brewed rice whiskey.

Beaten zone The area where the majority of bullets will strike when a machine gun is laid-in to cover a part of a defensive perimeter or part of an ambush zone.

Brown Water Navy A term applied to the U.S. Navy units assigned to the inland boat patrols of the Mekong River delta.

Can Tho A large city in the Mekong delta which served as the headquarters of the IV Corps military region.

Cao Lanh The provincial capital of Kien Phong province.

Chào Hello or goodby—depending on the context.

Chiêu hồi Open arms. The name applied to the program of persuading the enemy to turn themselves in to the American or Vietnamese forces. The name was also used to refer to those enemy who did turn themselves in.

Chinook A large, twin-rotor helicopter used primarily for carrying cargo or large numbers of soldiers on nontactical movements.

CIDG Civilian Irregular Defense Group.

CINCPAC Commander-in-Chief Pacific. The military headquarters in Hawaii to which the American military officials in Vietnam reported.

Civilian Irregular Defense Group American-financed irregular military units which were led by members of Special Forces A-teams. Members of these units were Vietnamese nationals, but were usually members of ethnic minorities in the country.

Claymore mine An American anti-personnel mine which was set up above ground and was aimed so that detonation would send out a blast of hundreds of steel balls in the desired direction. The name was taken from the name of the huge Scottish broadsword which was also used to cut a swath through enemy ranks.

Cô Unmarried woman. Used as a title, like Miss.

Commo bunker A bunker containing vital communications equipment and which was usually included in the last redoubt of established defensive positions.

CORDS Civil Operations and Revolutionary Development Support. An American program using both civil and military advisors which stressed development programs for the civilian populations in the rural areas.

COSVN Central Office for South Vietnam. The main headquarters of the National Liberation Front. A headquarters often sought but never found by the American and South Vietnamese forces.

Country team The staff and personnel of an American embassy assigned to a particular country.

Cô vàn Advisor. An American assigned to Vietnamese military units or to political divisions within the country to help direct and train Vietnamese military and civilian officials.

C-ration The combat ration issued to American soldiers. Each ration consisted of a can of some basic course, a can of fruit, a packet of some type of dessert, a packet of powdered cocoa, a small pack of cigarettes, and two pieces of chewing gum.

Dại úy   Captain.

Đi   Go.

Đi đi mau!   Get the hell outta here! Literally, "Go go quickly."

Dong Tien   A district within Kien Phong province in the Mekong River delta. It began on the banks of the Mekong and extended westward across the Plain of Reeds. The main location of the present story.

District team   The American personnel assigned to act as advisors to Vietnamese military and civilian officials at the district level.

District Mobile Company   The major Viet Cong fighting unit organized within each district in Vietnam. The District Mobile Company was assigned to carry out various assignments from direct offensive operations to sabotage and terrorism.

Dust-off   An emergency medical evacuation by helicopter.

Em   Brother, good friend. Also used as a familiar reference to a servant or helper.

Flack vest   An armored vest issued to American soldiers. They were hot, heavy, and often not worn despite the protection they offered.

Free-fire Zone   An area cleared of civilians within which artillery and aircraft could fire without having to obtain clearance. Any persons found within a free-fire zone were presumed to be enemy.

"Fu gas"   From *fou gasse*, a French vernacular military expression for a type of land mine. In American usage it referred to a home-made anti-personnel mine which consisted of a buried 50-gallon drum filled with jellied gas. A Claymore mine was placed at the bottom of the barrel and was used to detonate the "fu gas."

Ghe   A medium-sized Vietnamese boat with a small hutch or cabin amidships.

Gunship   A combat helicopter, commonly a UH-1 "Huey" armed with multiple machine guns, rockets, and automatic grenade launchers. Primarily used in support of infantry operations.

HE   High Explosive. A term used to describe a type of artillery, mortar, or rocket round. HE rounds were designed as destructive explosives as opposed to those designed to give illumination or to provide smoke marking.

HES   Hamlet Evaluation System. An evaluation system devised and run by Americans in Saigon which required monthly computerized reports from all the DSA's in the country.

Hoa Hao A sect of the Buddhist religion which originated in the Mekong Delta in the early 1900's. The sect was often at odds with the central government in Saigon, but was also staunchly anticommunist.

Hong Ngu The northernmost Mekong River town in Kien Phong province. The town was only a few kilometers from the Cambodian border and carried out a busy contraband trade.

Kien Phong A large province of South Vietnam which was bordered on the east by the Mekong River and which included vast expanses of the Plain of Reeds. The province wherein a large portion of the present story occurred.

Kien Van A district in Kien Phong province immediately to the south of Tram Chim district.

Kill zone The radius of a circle around an explosive device within which it is predicted that 95% of all occupants will be killed should the device explode.

Kilometer 1,000 meters, or 0.62 miles.

Klick Kilometer.

Không xấu Don't worry about it. Literally, not bad.

Landing zone A designated area for the landing of helicopters and the off-loading of men and cargo.

liên đội Company group. A Vietnamese military unit consisting of three militia infantry companies.

Lima Zulu International phonetic alphabet for LZ, or Landing Zone.

LZ Landing Zone.

M-16 The standard issue, fully automatic assault rifle used by the South Vietnamese and American forces.

M-79 A grenade launcher. The shoulder-fired weapon resembled a sawed-off, hugely bored shotgun, and could lob its projectiles more than a hundred meters.

MACV Military Assistance Command Vietnam. American army units and teams assigned to advise the Vietnamese military and civilian government, and the support elements for those advisory units.

Main Force Battalion The primary Viet Cong fighting force within each province of South Vietnam. These units were often large enough and well enough equipped to participate in direct attacks on large Vietnamese and American installations and units.

MAT Mobile Advisory Team. The five-man teams of American advisors who were assigned to live and work out in the Vietnamese villages.

Máy bay Airplane. Sometimes the words *whop whop* were added, making reference to a helicopter.

Medevac Medical evacuation by helicopter.

Meter 39.37 inches, or 1.09 yards.

Minigun An electronically controlled, extremely rapidly firing machine gun. These were most often mounted on aircraft to be used against targets on the ground.

National Liberation Front The communist organization in South Vietnam which led the fight against the Saigon government and their American allies. The Front was putatively an independent organization in the south, but in fact, it followed the dictates of the North Vietnamese government.

NCO Noncommissioned officer. A person bearing one of the sergeant ranks in the armed services.

NLF National Liberation Front.

Nước mắm A Vietnamese sauce made by percolating water through large vats of salted fish. The sauce is an inherent part of Vietnamese meals since each bite of food is first dipped in the sauce before being eaten.

OCS Officer Candidate School. Schools run within each service to train men and women from the enlisted ranks to become officers.

PBR Patrol Boat, River. The U.S. Navy designation for the fast, heavily armed boats used for helping safeguard the major canals and rivers and their tributaries in South Vietnam.

PF Popular Forces units or individuals belonging to those units.

Phải Must. Also used to accentuate a verb.

Plain of Reeds A large area of the Mekong River delta which begins on the north bank of the Mekong and extends northwestward almost to Saigon. The area is flat tableland with a mean altitude only a few feet above sea level. It is typified by large expanses of grasses and reeds broken by strands of thick forest.

Popular Forces Militia units organized within each village. The primary duty of these units was to provide village security and to undertake offensive operations against guerrilla units in the local area. PF units were supposed to be used only within their local village area, and were the most poorly paid and equipped of Vietnamese military units.

PRC-25 Portable Radio Communications, Model 25. A back-packed FM receiver-transmitter used for short-distance communications. The range of the radio was 5–10 kilometers, depending on the weather, unless attached to a special, nonportable antenna which could extend the range to 20–30 kilometers. Pronounced "Prick-25."

Province team The American civilian and military advisors assigned duties at the provincial capitol.

PRU Province Reconnaissance Unit. Pronounced as a word, "Proo." An irregular unit organized within each province for the official purpose of reconnoitering guerrilla sanctuaries and collecting intelligence on guerrilla activities. These units were operated under the auspices of the CIA and were also the operating arm of the Phoenix program.

PSA Province Senior Advisor. The senior American advisor in each province in Vietnam and the commander of the province team. While the PSA was usually an American army colonel, the post was sometimes filled by a State Department official.

PX Post Exchange. Department or grocery stores on military posts where soldiers and their families can purchase a wide variety of personal-use items at a lower cost than available in civilian stores.

Regional Forces Militia units organized within each district in South Vietnam to engage in offensive operations against local Viet Cong forces, RF units were better paid and equipped than PF units and could be assigned duties anywhere within the home district.

REMF Rear Echelon Mother Fucker. An unnecessarily harsh pejorative referring to those assigned to duties in the rear, such as it was. More particularly, a reference to those from any higher headquarters who were perceived not to understand the difficulties of one's duties.

RF Regional Forces units or individual soldiers belonging to those units.

RTO Radio-telephone operator. Most commonly, the man assigned to carry the PRC-25 radio while out on an operation.

Shĩ quan Mỹ American officer.

Slick A UH-1 helicopter used as a troop carrier in tactical air assault operations, or as a light cargo carrier in logistical support operations. The helicopter did not have protruding armaments and was therefore "slick."

Spec-4 Specialist Fourth Class. An enlisted rank immediately above Private First Class. Most enlisted men who had completed their individual training and had been on duty for a few months were Spec-4's. Probably the most common rank in the Vietnam-era army.

SP Pack Special Purpose Package. A box containing a standard assortment of candies, cigarettes, toilet articles, writing papers and pens, and other sundries. The packs were issued free of charge to all combat units, and each MAT team received one pack per month.

Syrette A collapsible tube of morphine attached to a hypodermic needle. The contents of the tube were injected by squeezing it like a toothpaste tube.

TA-50 An individual soldier's standard issue of combat clothing and equipment.

Tanglefoot Single-strand barbed wire strung in a meshwork pattern at about ankle height. A barrier designed to make it difficult to cross the obstructed area by foot. Usually placed around permanent defensive positions.

Tango boat U.S. Navy designation of a type of landing boat modified for waterborne operations in the Mekong River delta.

Tan Son Nhut The large airbase on the outskirts of Saigon. The airfield was used by civil and military aviation, making it one of the busiest airfields in the world. Hundreds of thousands of American soldiers arrived and departed Vietnam through the Tan Son Nhut terminal.

Tên yi? What is your name?

TFES Territorial Forces Evaluation System. The companion report of the HES. A computerized military evaluation system devised by American authorities in Saigon and used by them to assess the readiness of the militia forces. Each month advisors at the district level had to fill out the long computer print-out sheets and report on many different aspects of quantity and quality in the militia forces.

Thiêu úy Second Lieutenant.

Tôi I, me, my.

Tram Chim The village which served as the district headquarters for Dong Tien district. The village where Lieutenant Donovan and MAT-32 were stationed.

Trung sĩ Sergeant.

Trung úy First Lieutenant.

Two-niner-two The RC-292 ground plane antenna which was used to extend the range of the MAT and district team's PRC-25 radios.

VC Viet Cong.

VCI Viet Cong Infrastructure. It was the aim of the Viet Cong to have a complete government in place when their victory was finally won. Thus, where manpower allowed, communist cadres were secretly assigned positions as village chiefs, police officers, postmen, District-level officers, Province-level officers, and National-level officers. The VCI were the "shadow government" of the National Liberation Front and were awaiting the day they could step forward and claim their offices.

Viet Cong Common name for the National Liberation Front. The term means "Vietnamese Communist," and was originally used only in the pejorative sense. The name was also used to refer to individual members of the NLF, whether they were guerrilla soldiers, messengers, spies, or political officers.

Water Taxi A small, engine-powered boat with a sheltered passenger compartment. These native craft plied the major canals and rivers of Vietnam and provided a means of transportation from one village to the next.

White Mice The National Police of South Vietnam. Known for their corruption and their willingness to be used for political purposes. So-called because of the white hats and shirts of their uniforms.

White Phosphorus A type of explosive round from artillery, mortars, or rockets. Also a type of aerial bomb. The rounds exploded with a huge puff of white smoke from the hotly burning phosphorus, and were used as marking rounds or incendiary rounds.

Willie Peter White Phosphorus.

WP White Phosphorus.

About the Author

DAVID Donovan—a pseudonym—was formerly a first lieutenant in the United States Army. He is now a university professor of biological science.

The confusion...
the horror...
the truth...
=VIETNAM=